THE MEANING OF MECCA

M.E. McMillan

The Meaning of Mecca

The Politics of Pilgrimage in Early Islam

SAQI

ISBN 978-0-86356-437-6

First published by Saqi Books, London, 2011

A full CIP record for this book is available from the British Library.
A full CIP record for this book is available from the Library of Congress.

Printed and bound by Thomson Press (India)

SAQI
26 Westbourne Grove, London W2 5RH
www.saqibooks.com

For my parents

And proclaim the Pilgrimage to mankind
And they will come to you...

Qur'ān 22: 27

Contents

Acknowledgements

Many people have helped me in the course of producing this book and I am delighted to have the opportunity to thank them here.

First: my parents – for reasons too numerous to list – and my late Granda, William Milford, for his uncanny knack of always knowing what to say and when to say it.

Everyone at Al Saqi bookshop, particularly Salwa Gaspard and Safa Mabgar, for all their help in finding books; and to Lynn Gaspard at Saqi Books for making this process so painless. And thanks to Will Brady for doing such a terrific job on the layout.

My deepest gratitude goes to Professor Hugh Kennedy, without whom this project would never have started, and Professor Robert Hoyland, without whom it would never have ended. And for invaluable assistance at various points along the way: Mr Norman Penney, Professor Alan Jones, Professor Donald S. Richards, Dr Richard Kimber and Dr Angus Stewart.

I would also like to thank Dr Julian and Alison Johansen for the Zamzam water (look at the effect it had!); Professor Jeremy Johns for changing the way I look at the world; Professor Richard W. Bulliet for the inspiration of his work and for being so generous with his time and knowledge; Werner Daum for his helpful comments, and Professor Gerald Hawting whose help made all the difference when it mattered.

And my friends Yaron Peretz, Nasr Abu Al-Rub, Ingrid Alvarez, and a special thank you to Rosie Cleary for her words of wisdom.

Finally, I would like to thank my friend-mentor-fairy godmother, the late and very-much-missed Dr Elizabeth A.M. Warburton whose inspiration made this book possible and who has been with me every step of the way. All errors are my own.

NOTE ON CONVENTIONS

References: Abbreviated forms are given throughout the text. Full references for all sources are found in Appendix B and the Bibliography. Arabic sources are fully transliterated in the footnotes and Bibliography. Footnotes in the text are cited in chronological order.

Translations: Translations are my own with the exception of those from SUNY's al-Ṭabarī series. References to these translations are given in the footnotes; full details are in the Bibliography.

Transliterations: Where Arabic place names have well-known English equivalents of their names – Mecca (instead of Makkah); Medina (instead of al-Madīnah); Iraq (instead of al-ʿIrāq) – the English version has been used here. Other place names, all proper names and all Arabic words have been transliterated throughout the text including those characters which require diacritical marks and long vowels. The symbol ʿ is used to denote *ʿayn*; ʾ to denote *hamzah*; and *h* to denote *tāʾ marbūṭah*.

Dates: Both sets of dates – Muslim and Christian/Common Era – are given throughout the text with the exception of chapter or sub-title headings which refer to a specific *ḥajj*. In these cases, only the Muslim date is given but throughout the text of the chapter or sub-section, both dates are cited.

INTRODUCTION

The Politics of Pilgrimage

In 68/688, pilgrims gathered in the Holy City of Mecca during the holy month of *Dhū al-Ḥijjah* to perform one of their faith's most solemn and most important rituals: the *ḥajj*.

The *ḥajj*, the fifth and final of Islam's pillars, is an obligation on all Muslims who are fit and able and who can afford it. Once in a lifetime, they are required to present themselves in Mecca to show their submission to God's will by participating in a series of rituals which, according to Muslim tradition, the Prophet Muḥammad set out during his Farewell *Ḥajj* in 10/632.

As the Islamic year is lunar and not tied to the seasons, the *ḥajj* can fall at any time of the year. A pilgrimage in the baking heat of an Arabian summer when temperatures can easily pass 40 degrees Celsius is a real test of faith. In the medieval period, the supply of water was often a problem and chroniclers record numerous incidents of pilgrims running out of it en route to the Holy City.

Mecca's geographical position did little to make the pilgrimage any easier: situated in a rocky ravine, the Holy City was often prone to devastating flash floods which swept away all before them.

For a believer, however, the rewards far outweigh the risks. A successful pilgrimage means nothing less than the remission of sins and the chance to begin life anew.

The spiritual high point of the *ḥajj* in this regard is the "standing" on the Mount of Mercy at 'Arafāt, 20 km south east of Mecca. Here, pilgrims gather en masse to ask God for His forgiveness. Here, the midday and afternoon prayers are combined to allow the maximum amount of time to be spent in supplication to God. And it was here that the Prophet Muḥammad preached his famous sermon during the Farewell *Ḥajj* in 10/632.

But when the pilgrims gathered on the Mount of Mercy in 68/688, they found all was not as it should be. Instead of seeing the caliph's banner on display as a symbol of his authority, they saw four different banners: one for each of the rival groups competing for control of the caliphate.

One banner belonged to 'Abd Allāh bin al-Zubayr, a member of the early Islamic elite and a resident of the Prophet's City of Medina. He was acknowledged as caliph in the Holy Cities and throughout much of the Islamic world. He believed political power belonged in Arabia and in the hands of those who had known the Prophet best and sacrificed the most for the faith during the early days of Islam.

Another banner belonged to Muḥammad bin al-Ḥanafiyyah, a member of the Prophet's family, though not a direct descendant of the Prophet himself. He too believed power belonged in the hands of those who had known the Prophet best. But to Ibn al-Ḥanafiyyah and those who supported him, that meant the Prophet's family.

Another banner belonged to 'Abd al-Malik of the Umayyad family. This family, late converts to Islam, took control of the caliphate following the first civil war and moved the seat of power to Syria. They believed the caliphate was rightfully theirs after the murder of their kinsman, the third caliph 'Uthmān. By 68/688, they were fighting to reclaim territories they had lost in recent years to Ibn al-Zubayr.

The fourth banner belonged to the rebel group, the *Khawārij*, whose rallying cry was "Judgement belongs to God" and who believed anyone had the right to be caliph so long as he was sufficiently pious.

These four groups held radically different views as to who should be caliph and why. Yet, in spite of these differences, they turned up at the same place at the same time with the same objective.

Events at the pilgrimage in 68/688 thus pose two key questions relevant to our understanding of the political culture of early Islam: was leadership of the *ḥajj* understood to equate to leadership of the community? And did the *Ḥaram*, as well as being the religious centre of Islam, have the potential to become its political centre too?

The Muslim sources for this period – Ibn Khayyāṭ, al-Ya'qūbī, al-Ṭabarī, al-Mas'ūdī *et al* – record who led the *ḥajj* each year and these records show that events on the *ḥajj* in 68/688 were no isolated occurrence. There were several pilgrimage seasons in the early Islamic period which witnessed power struggles played out against the backdrop of the *Ḥaram* at the time of the *ḥajj*: in 35/656 (at the end of 'Uthmān's caliphate); in 39/660 (at the end of 'Alī's); and in 129/747 (near the end of the Umayyad era). What these *ḥajj* seasons have in common is that they occurred in times of political upheaval when power was being realigned.

The Muslim sources also show that successive caliphs, regardless of their political persuasion, were keen to lead the *ḥajj* in person. Of the four *Rāshidūn* caliphs, three – Abū Bakr, 'Umar and 'Uthmān – led the pilgrimage. Only 'Alī failed to do so but the unsettled political circumstances of his caliphate largely explain why.[1]

A number of Umayyad caliphs were also seen in Mecca. Several of them went further than leading the *ḥajj* themselves and used it to project their power into the future by appointing their successor sons to lead it.[2]

The Umayyad period in power was interrupted in the 60s/680s when 'Abd Allāh bin al-Zubayr took control of large parts of the Islamic world. He too was keen to lead the pilgrimage and, based as he was in Medina, he followed the example of previous caliphs resident there and led every *ḥajj* he could.[3]

This pattern of caliphal involvement with the *ḥajj*, combined with events at the pilgrimages of 35/656, 39/660, 68/688 and 129/747 when political rivals used the *Ḥaram* as the place to stake their claim for power and the *ḥajj* as the means to do it, point to a political subtext for the pilgrimage which has often been obscured by its more obvious spiritual significance. It is that subtext which we seek to explore here. Each chapter therefore begins with a list of *ḥajj* leaders for the period under discussion. When taken as a whole, these lists show that members of certain groups in society were appointed to lead the *ḥajj* – and were repeatedly invited to do so regardless of who was caliph – while other groups were conspicuous by their absence from leadership of the ritual. The consistency in these patterns of leadership implies there was nothing random about who led the *ḥajj* each year but that successive caliphs devised and implemented carefully thought out policies for the pilgrimage. By doing so, they infused the Holy City of Mecca with a meaning far beyond religion.

This convergence of religion and ritual, power and politics, did not however begin with the caliphs: it began with the Prophet when he led his Farewell *Ḥajj* in 10/632 and set the precedents every subsequent visitor to Mecca, whether politician or pilgrim, would seek to follow.

It is therefore with the Prophet's pilgrimage in 10/632 that we begin.

---

1 See Chapter 2 below for a full examination of the circumstances of his caliphate and their impact on his ability to lead the pilgrimage.

2 See Chapters 3 to 9 below for the pilgrimage seasons of the Umayyad caliphate.

3 See Chapters 4 and 5 below for an examination of Ibn al-Zubayr's pilgrimage seasons.

ONE

The Prophet's Precedent: The Farewell *Ḥajj* of 10/632

THE PROPHET AND THE PILGRIMAGE

In 10/632, the Prophet Muḥammad left Medina to return to Mecca to perform what Islamic tradition would remember as the Farewell Pilgrimage, the *Ḥijjat al-Wadāʿ*.

Only ten years earlier, Muḥammad had been forced to flee his home city in the dead of night, his life in danger because of the prophetic mission he refused to give up. But the intervening decade had brought him a level of success that allowed him – almost uniquely in history – to be recognized as a Prophet in his own country.

Muḥammad's goal in Mecca was to perform the *ḥajj*. The city was an ancient cultic centre and the Kaʿbah had long been home to a pantheon of pagan idols revered by Arab tribes throughout the peninsula.[1] Four months of the year were set aside for pilgrimage: the spring month of *Rajab* for the lesser pilgrimage known as the *ʿumrah* and the last two months of the year and the first of the new year for the main pilgrimage or *ḥajj*.[2] Raiding amongst tribes ceased during these months and many of them took advantage of their time in Mecca to engage in trade.[3] Over the years, the city's economy had become so closely linked with this commercial activity that

1 Peters, *Hajj*, 21-30.

2 Peters, *Mecca*, 29, & *Hajj*, 57-58; Goitein, "Ramadan, The Month of Fasting", in Hawting, *Development*, 153-154.

3 Peters, *Hajj*, 33-35; Goitein, "Ramadan, The Month of Fasting", in Hawting, *Development*, 153-154.

fear of losing it lay behind much of the opposition to Muḥammad and his new religion.

The Farewell Pilgrimage saw Muḥammad reinforce the centrality of Mecca as a cultic centre but shift the spiritual focus away from the multitude of pagan gods towards the One God – Allāh. He also set about returning the *ḥajj* to what he believed were its true origins.[4] According to Muslim sacred history, it was Ibrāhīm (Abraham) and his son Ismā'īl (Ishmael) by the bondswoman Hajar who originally built the Ka'bah.[5] When they finished, Ibrāhīm received divine instructions not to associate any gods with God and to proclaim pilgrimage to the Sacred House.[6]

Muḥammad saw himself as the restorer of this message and in Mecca in 10/632 he, too, proclaimed pilgrimage to the Sacred House.[7] At 'Arafāt, just outside the Holy City, he delivered a sermon in which he explained the rituals of the pilgrimage and where they were to be done.[8]

He joined the lesser pilgrimage, the *'umrah*, with the main pilgrimage and abolished the intercalary month to make the Islamic year lunar.[9] As the lunar year is eleven days shorter than the solar year, the *ḥajj* falls earlier each year and, over a thirty-year cycle, rotates through all four seasons. The abolition of the intercalary month thus placed the Islamic pilgrimage outside the cycle of the seasons. This break with the past left no room for ambiguity about the meaning of the new *ḥajj*: it was an act of worship directed to God, and only God, not a celebration of nature or a god of nature.[10]

Rather ominously during his sermon, the Prophet warned his listeners to pay careful attention to what he was saying because he did not know if he would ever be with them again in Mecca.[11] Days later, on his way home to Medina, he fell ill and died soon afterwards.

The Farewell Pilgrimage is an important part of Islamic sacred history. Western scholarship has, however, questioned whether the rituals of the pilgrimage were finalized at that time or whether this process occurred over a much longer period.[12] Attempts to understand the historical

4 This sacralization of Mecca did not occur in a vacuum: the direction of prayer, the *qiblah*, had already been changed from Jerusalem to Mecca; Guillaume, *Muḥammad*, 289. This took place eighteen months after the Prophet left Mecca.

5 Peters, *Mecca*, 19-21, & *Hajj*, 3, 5-6.

6 Qur'ān 2: 125-127 & 22: 26-30.

7 Hawting, *Development*, xix.

8 Guillaume, *Muḥammad*, 649 & 650-651; Ibn Hishām, *Sīrah*, II 601 & 603.

9 Peters, *Hajj*, 57-58.

10 Graham, "Islam in the Mirror of Ritual", in Hawting, *Development*, 365-366.

11 Guillaume, *Muḥammad*, 649 & 650-651; Ibn Hishām, *Sīrah*, II 601 & 603.

12 Peters, *Hajj*, 58.

development of the *ḥajj* are further complicated because the accounts we have of Muḥammad's life and religious mission were written over a century after his death; a time delay which has provoked considerable – and often impassioned – debate over their likely reliability.[13]

As well as tracing the development of the pilgrimage, scholars have also sought to find a historical context for the rites performed during it. Some see traces of stone worship, pre-Islamic pagan practices, or the influence of Judaism in the rituals of the *ḥajj*.[14] Others have interpreted them as independent developments originating within Arab-Islamic culture.[15]

The origins of the rituals may never become fully clear. And perhaps the last word on the subject should go to the great philosopher al-Ghazālī who declared that, for Muslims, the *ḥajj* stands beyond explanation. Like Islam itself, it is a willing act of submission to God. God commands it, therefore it is done.[16]

THE RITUALS OF THE *ḤAJJ*[17]

Day 1: *Dhū al-Ḥijjah* 8

The *ḥajj* takes place in *Dhū al-Ḥijjah*, the twelfth – and final – month of the Islamic year and lasts for six days: from the 8th to the 13th.[18]

The first day is known as *Yawm al-Tarwiyah*, the day of quenching.[19] On this day pilgrims enter the state of ritual purity, *iḥrām*, and declare their intention, *niyyah*, to perform the *ḥajj*.

The state of *iḥrām* places a number of obligations on pilgrims which are aimed at focusing their attention on the internal and the spiritual rather than the external and the secular. Pilgrims must therefore abandon everyday activities such as shaving, cutting hair and wearing scents or perfumes. They must also abstain from sex.

---

13 Hawting, *First Dynasty*, 1, 5 & 6-7, & "The *Hajj* in the Second Civil War", in Netton, *Golden Roads*, 36-37; Peters, *Hajj*, 54 & 368; Hawting, *Development*, xvi & xxv-xxvii. This point ties in with the debate over the sources: see Appendix A.

14 The essays in Hawting, *Development*, provide a comprehensive overview of this subject.

15 See Hawting, *Development*, xxxiii; Graham, "Islam in the Mirror of Ritual", in Hawting, *Development*, 364-366.

16 Lazarus-Yafeh, "The Religious Dialectics of the Hadjdj", in Hawting, *Development*, 281-282; Graham, "Islam in the Mirror of Ritual", in Hawting, *Development*, 352 & 364.

17 The rituals are set out here as they are understood by Muslims.

18 Gaudefroy-Demombynes, *Pèlerinage*, 235; Kamal, *Guide*, 6-10; Mohamed, *Hajj & 'Umrah*, 88-89; Davids, *Hajj*, 332-338.

19 Kamal, *Guide*, 6; Mohamed, *Hajj & 'Umrah*, 85; Davids, *Hajj*, 332.

For the state of *iḥrām* to be complete, pilgrims have to adopt specific clothing.

For men, this consists of two pieces of white fabric; one wrapped around the waist, the other draped over the right shoulder.[20] The adoption of these garments by all male pilgrims creates a powerful visual image of unity, reinforcing the spiritual harmony among pilgrims as members of the same community of the faithful. Women are required to dress modestly and leave their hands and face uncovered.

The *iḥrām*, along with the *niyyah*, is one of the four pillars, *arkān*, of the *ḥajj*. These four pillars are obligatory and failure to complete any one of them renders the entire *ḥajj* invalid.[21]

The pilgrims now enter the Holy Mosque and circle the Kaʿbah seven times counter-clockwise. This circumambulation is the *ṭawāf al-qudūm*, the *ṭawāf* of arrival or welcome.[22]

Upon completion, pilgrims proceed to Minā reciting what is known as the *talbiyah* as they go. *Talbiyah* comes from the verb *labbā* which means to follow or obey. It begins with the words "Here I am O Lord, here I am..." and, in this context, has the meaning of answering God's call to come to Mecca and perform the *ḥajj*.

The pilgrims stay in Minā until they have prayed the dawn, *fajr*, prayer the following day.[23]

Day 2: *Dhū al-Ḥijjah* 9

The second day of the *ḥajj* is the spiritual high point of the pilgrimage.[24]

After sunrise, the pilgrims leave Minā for the Mount of Mercy, the *Jabal al-Raḥmah*, in ʿArafāt. Of such importance is this day for the pilgrims that the Prophet is reported to have said there is no *ḥajj* without ʿArafāt.[25]

Here, pilgrims perform the *wuqūf*, the "standing"; the second of the four pillars of the *ḥajj* which must be completed for the ritual to be considered valid.[26]

---

20 For the *niyyah*, see Davids, *Hajj*, 332; for the *iḥrām*, Ruthven, *Islam*, 31; Mohamed, *Hajj & ʿUmrah*, 40-41; Davids, *Hajj*, 131-142 (particularly 133).

21 Kamal, *Guide*, 48-51; Davids, *Hajj*, 285.

22 This is for pilgrims who are performing a combined *ʿumrah* and *ḥajj* or a *ḥajj* alone. They may also perform the *saʿy*, the running between the two hills, at this point but it may be left until the third day of the pilgrimage. If performing *ʿumrah* and *ḥajj* separately – but within the same year – it is possible to skip the *ṭawāf* and *saʿy* here and perform it on the third day of the pilgrimage.

23 Gaudefroy-Demombynes, *Pèlerinage*, 236; Bushnak, A.A., "The Hajj Transportation System" in Sardar and Zaki Badawi, *Hajj Studies Volume 1*, 100; Mohamed, *Hajj & ʿUmrah*, 42; Davids, *Hajj*, 332.

24 Kamal, *Guide*, 8 & 52-53; Mohamed, *Hajj & ʿUmrah*, 44; Peters, *Hajj*, 31; Davids, *Hajj*, 332.

25 Al-Māwardī, *Aḥkām*, 111; Gaudefroy-Demombynes, *Pèlerinage*, 251; Davids, *Hajj*, 325, 332 & 389.

26 Al-Māwardī, *Aḥkām*, 109; Gaudefroy-Demombynes, *Pèlerinage*, 241-246; Kamal, *Guide*, 48 & 51-54; Davids, *Hajj*, 285.

During their *wuqūf*, the pilgrims seek God's forgiveness and mercy. On this day, the gates of Heaven are said to be open wide and in order for pilgrims to take advantage of this and maximize the amount of time spent in supplication to God, the noon and afternoon prayers are shortened and combined at midday.[27]

After midday, a sermon is preached in the place where the Prophet delivered his famous sermon during the Farewell *Ḥajj*.[28]

The pilgrims leave for Muzdalifah after sunset and spend the night there.[29]

Day 3: *Dhū al-Ḥijjah* 10

The third day of the *ḥajj* is the *Yawm al-Naḥr*, the day of sacrifice. Muslims around the world join symbolically with the pilgrims in Mecca by celebrating the *'Īd al-Aḍḥā*, the festival of sacrifice.[30]

This particular day is one of the busiest in terms of the number of rituals to be performed. Pilgrims begin the day by travelling to Minā after the dawn prayer. Their goal is the largest of the three pillars there, the one known as the *Jamrah al-'Aqabah*.[31]

In an act charged with spiritual significance, each pilgrim throws seven stones at this pillar to cast out the devil.[32]

By doing so, they tap into the roots of their faith as one of the three great monotheisms: the stoning ritual recalls the actions of Ibrāhīm, a figure of central importance to Jews and Christians as well as Muslims.

Three times, the devil was said to have tried to tempt Ibrāhīm to disobey God's command to sacrifice his son, Ismā'īl. Ibrāhīm's response each time was to throw seven stones at the devil.[33]

When the pilgrims finish the stoning ritual, they undertake the rite which gives this day its name: *al-hady*, the sacrifice. Another deeply symbolic act, the sacrifice represents Ibrāhīm's willingness to give his son to

---

27 Qur'ān 2:198-199. See also Ruthven, *Islam*, 45; Davids, *Hajj*, 333.

28 Gaudefroy-Demombynes, *Pèlerinage*, 249-250; Ruthven, *Islam*, 44-45; Davids, *Hajj*, 332.

29 Al-Māwardī, *Aḥkām*, 111; Gaudefroy-Demombynes, *Pèlerinage*, 256; Kamal, *Guide*, 9; Bushnak, "The Hajj Transportation System", 100; Mohamed, *Hajj & 'Umrah*, 44-46; Davids, *Hajj*, 333.

30 Davids, *Hajj*, 334.

31 Al-Māwardī, *Aḥkām*, 111; Kamal, *Guide*, 9; Bushnak, "The Hajj Transportation System", 100; Mohamed, *Hajj & 'Umrah*, 46-48; Davids, *Hajj*, 334.

32 Ruthven, *Islam*, 46; Davids, *Hajj*, 301, 334 & 388.

33 Davids, *Hajj*, 301 & 388. For the connections with Ibrāhīm, see Qur'ān 2:125-127; al-Azraqī, *Akhbār Makkah*, I 21-51; al-Nahrawālī, *Akhbār Makkah*, III 29-42; von Grunebaum, *Medieval Islam*, 78, & *Muhammadan Festivals*, 19; Hitti, *Capital Cities of Arab Islam*, 6; Cook, *Muhammad*, 37-38; Ruthven, *Islam*, 35 & 37-38; Peters, *Mecca*, 4, & *Hajj*, 31.

God. God rewarded Ibrāhīm's obedience by substituting a ram for Ismāʿīl. After the sacrifice, pilgrims end their state of *iḥrām* by cutting their hair or shaving before they leave Minā for Mecca.[34]

In the Holy City, they carry out the *ṭawāf al-ifāḍah*, the circumambulation around the Kaʿbah, during which they make seven circuits of it.[35] This *ṭawāf* is another of the four obligatory rites necessary for a successful completion of the *ḥajj*.[36]

The pilgrims then proceed to the hills of Ṣafā and Marwah to perform the *saʿy*, the rushing, which is the last of the four obligatory rituals.[37]

Starting at Ṣafā, they go back and forth seven times between the two hills in remembrance of Hajar's actions as she ran back and forth between them frantically searching for water for her young son Ismāʿīl.[38]

The completion of the *saʿy* signals the lifting of all the restrictions of the state of *iḥrām*.[39]

The pilgrims now return to Minā to spend the next two to three days there.[40]

Day 4: *Dhū al-Ḥijjah* 11

The fourth day of the *ḥajj* is the first of three known as *al-Tashrīq*, the drying of the meat from the sacrifice.[41]

The pilgrims resume their symbolic stoning of the devil in Minā but this time, they do so with a greater intensity for they now stone not one but all three pillars.[42]

After midday, they stone the smallest of the three pillars with seven stones before moving on to do the same at the middle and largest pillars.[43]

---

34 Al-Māwardī, *Aḥkām*, 111; Bushnak, "The Hajj Transportation System", 100; Mohamed, *Hajj & ʿUmrah*, 52-53. All restrictions of the state of *iḥrām*, with the exception of sex, are now lifted.

35 Al-Māwardī, *Aḥkām*, 111; Gaudefroy-Demombynes, *Pèlerinage*, 297; Kamal, *Guide*, 9; Bushnak, "The Hajj Transportation System", 100; Mohamed, *Hajj & ʿUmrah*, 54-55; Davids, *Hajj*, 335.

36 Kamal, *Guide*, 9, 48 & 55-61; Davids, *Hajj*, 285.

37 Davids, *Hajj*, 285.

38 For the ritual, see al-Māwardī, *Aḥkām*, 111; Mohamed, *Hajj & ʿUmrah*, 56-57; Davids, *Hajj*, 335. For the connection to Hajar, see Ruthven, *Islam*, 35, 38 & 43-44; Davids, *Hajj*, 383.

39 Davids, *Hajj*, 335.

40 Kamal, *Guide*, 10; Bushnak, "The Hajj Transportation System", 100; Mohamed, *Hajj & ʿUmrah*, 58-69; Davids, *Hajj*, 335.

41 Mohamed, *Hajj & ʿUmrah*, 85; Davids, *Hajj*, 336. The words *tashrīq* and *aḍḥā* both have meanings related to sunrise. I am grateful to Werner Daum for drawing this to my attention. This has led to speculation about the pre-Islamic origins of some of these rituals.

42 Al-Māwardī, *Aḥkām*, 111; Gaudefroy-Demombynes, *Pèlerinage*, 273; Kamal, *Guide*, 10; Mohamed, *Hajj & ʿUmrah*, 60-61; Davids, *Hajj*, 336.

43 Mohamed, *Hajj & ʿUmrah*, 60; Davids, *Hajj*, 336.

If, for some reason, the pilgrims were unable to perform the *ṭawāf al-ifāḍah* the previous day, they may go to Mecca to do so on this day.[44]

Day 5: *Dhū al-Ḥijjah* 12

The fifth day of the *ḥajj* sees pilgrims repeating their actions of the previous day and stoning the three pillars which symbolize the devil.[45]

They may then leave Minā to return to Mecca but they must do so before the *maghrib*, the evening prayer.[46]

Day 6: *Dhū al-Ḥijjah* 13

The sixth and final day of the *ḥajj* involves the performance of the same rituals as the previous day if they were not performed then.[47]

Upon completion, the pilgrims leave Minā for Mecca where they undertake the *ṭawāf al-wadāʿ*. During this farewell *ṭawāf*, the pilgrims again circumambulate the Kaʿbah seven times.[48]

With the completion of the last circuit of the Kaʿbah, the pilgrims have reached the end of their *ḥajj*. They now have the spiritual satisfaction of knowing they have fulfilled their obligation to God by performing the fifth pillar of their faith.

Many pilgrims now take advantage of their proximity to the Prophet's City of Medina to make a visit, *ziyārah*, there. Such a visit is not part of the pilgrimage rituals but most Muslims wish to see the place their Prophet made his home.

THE MEANING OF MECCA FOR THE MUSLIM COMMUNITY

These rituals of the *ḥajj* to Mecca, the City of God, and the *ziyārah* to Medina, the City of His Prophet, anchor the Islamic faith in its Arabian origins and preserve the sense of historical continuity with Muḥammad and the earliest community of Muslims.[49] The *ḥajj* gives Muslims the chance to

44 Mohamed, *Hajj & 'Umrah*, 62; Davids, *Hajj*, 336.

45 Al-Māwardī, *Aḥkām*, 111-112; Gaudefroy-Demombynes, *Pèlerinage*, 273; Kamal, *Guide*, 10; Mohamed, *Hajj & 'Umrah*, 64; Davids, *Hajj*, 336.

46 Davids, *Hajj*, 336.

47 Gaudefroy-Demombynes, *Pèlerinage*, 273; Kamal, *Guide*, 10; Mohamed, *Hajj & 'Umrah*, 68-69; Davids, *Hajj*, 336.

48 Bushnak, "The Hajj Transportation System", 100; Mohamed, *Hajj & 'Umrah*, 70-71; Davids, *Hajj*, 337.

49 Tschanz, D.W., "Journeys of Faith, Roads of Civilization", *Saudi Aramco World*, volume 55 number

follow their Prophet's precedent, to walk where he walked, and to enact the rituals he laid down in the Farewell *Ḥajj*.

Yet, with its emphasis on Ibrāhīm, the *ḥajj* delves even deeper into history than the era of the Prophet and the beginnings of Islam. By ritualizing the experiences of Ibrāhīm and his family within the rites of the *ḥajj*, Islam places itself in direct religious descent from the monotheistic traditions of Judaism and Christianity and lays claim to a universalism not confined to time or place. The *ḥajj* effectively becomes the *shahādah*, the statement of faith, in action, validating not only monotheism in general (There is no god but God) but Islamic monotheism in particular (and Muḥammad is the Messenger of God).

For the pilgrims themselves, performing the *ḥajj* does more than bring them closer to God; it brings them closer to one another as members of the same community.[50] Of the five pillars of the faith, the *ḥajj* is the most public demonstration of the faith and the faithful as a social entity. By performing the *ḥajj*, Muslims reinvigorate their spiritual bonds with one another, forging their community anew and demonstrating the enduring power of the message delivered by the Prophet Muḥammad.

As a result, the *ḥajj* transforms individual pilgrims into a society within a society: the *ummah* in microcosm, a mass migration of people from all corners of the Islamic world, along with whatever goods, knowledge and ideas they choose to bring with them.[51]

This community on the *ḥajj* does not, however, become detached from the rest of the Muslim community during the days of the ritual, as there are aspects of the rituals which act as points of contact to draw in every member of the faith.

To begin with, the very location of the *ḥajj*, Mecca, is the centre of every Muslim's spiritual life.[52] It is the *qiblah*, the direction of the daily prayer. Five times a day, Muslims interrupt their activities and turn towards Mecca to affirm their faith. Prayer, or *ṣalāh*, is the second of Islam's five pillars and

---

1 2004, 2-11 (in particular 2); Endress, *Islam*, 31.

50 Angawi in *Hajj Studies*, 11; Turner & Turner, *Image and Pilgrimage*, 188 & 192; Michon, "Religious Institutions" in *The Islamic City*, ed. Serjeant, 29; Hourani, *Arab Peoples*, 150; Ruthven, *Islam*, 261; Black, *A History of Islamic Political Thought*, 12; Hitti, *History*, 136; Lapidus, *A History of Islamic Societies*, 828.

51 Kamal, *Guide*, 2; Ahsan, *Social Life*, 282; Gellens, "The search for knowledge in medieval Muslim societies: a comparative approach" in Eickelman & Piscatori, *Muslim Travellers: Pilgrimage, migration and the religious imagination*, 51; Hourani, *Arab Peoples*, 151; Bulliet, *The Case for Islamo-Christian Civilization*, 145.

52 Qur'ān 2:144 & 149-150, 5:97, & 42:7. Von Grunebaum, *Muhammadan Festivals*, 20 & 40; Watt, *Muhammad: Prophet and Statesman*, 183-184; Bashear, *Arabs and Others in Early Islam*, 45; Asad, *The Road to Mecca*, 88.

with its focus on Mecca it functions almost as a precursor for the *ḥajj*: the daily prayer is a spiritual migration towards Mecca; the *ḥajj* the physical realization of that internal journey.

Secondly, the *iḥrām*, the ritually prescribed clothing worn by men during the *ḥajj*, is the burial clothing for all male believers. And just as death is the end of one life and the beginning of another, the *ḥajj* also symbolizes the end of one life to facilitate a spiritual re-birth.[53]

And third, the 10th of *Dhū al-Ḥijjah* is known as the *Yawm al-Naḥr*, the day of sacrifice. On this day, the pilgrims make their sacrifice in remembrance of Ibrāhīm's readiness to sacrifice his son as an act of submission to God. Muslims in the wider community join with those on the *ḥajj* by marking the *'Īd al-Aḍḥā*, the feast of the sacrifice, one of the major rites in the Islamic calendar. In this way, they express their spiritual solidarity with the pilgrims and reinforce the social bonds which unite them as a community.[54]

With Muslims on the *ḥajj* linked so strongly to their fellow Muslims in the wider community, and vice versa, leadership of the pilgrimage has the capacity to assume a significance beyond that of overseeing the correct performance of a religious ritual. In the period after the Prophet's death, it provided his successors with an opportunity to demonstrate their leadership of the community he founded and, in the process, to enhance their political legitimacy. It proved to be an opportunity they were only to willing to take.

---

53 Hitti, *Capital Cities*, 11; Nassef, A., in *Hajj Studies*, 9; Zaki Badawi, M.A., in *Hajj Studies*, 18; Michon, "Religious Institutions", 30.

54 Ahsan, *Social Life*, 282; Michon, "Religious Institutions", 31; Kertzer, *Ritual, Politics, and Power*, 62; Hourani, *Arab Peoples*, 151; Bulliet, *Islamo-Christian Civilization*, 43.

TWO

Following in the Prophet's Footsteps: The Era of the Rightly Guided Caliphs

Table 1 shows who led the *ḥajj* during the caliphates of the four Rightly Guided caliphs, the *Rāshidūn*: Abū Bakr, 'Umar b. al-Khaṭṭāb, 'Uthmān b. 'Affān and 'Alī b. Abī Ṭālib.

Table 1

Year	*Ḥajj leader*	*Relationship to caliph*	*Governor of a Holy City?*
Abū Bakr			
11/633	'Abd al-Raḥmān b. 'Awf[1] *or*	x	x
	'Attāb b. Asīd[2] *or*	x	Mecca
	'Umar[3]	x	x
12/634	Abū Bakr[4] *or*	CALIPH	-
	'Umar[5] *or*	x	x
	'Abd al-Raḥmān[6]	x	x

1 Ibn Khayyāṭ, *Ta'rīkh*, I 84; al-Ṭabarī, *Ta'rīkh*, I 2015.

2 Ibn Khayyāṭ, *Ta'rīkh*, I 84; al-Ṭabarī, *Ta'rīkh*, I 2015.

3 Ibn Khayyāṭ, *Ta'rīkh*, I 84-85; al-Mas'ūdī, *Murūj al-Dhahab*, 3631 (references are to paragraphs in Pellat's edition).

4 Ibn Khayyāṭ, *Ta'rīkh*, I 86 & 91; al-Ya'qūbī, *Ta'rīkh*, II 26; al-Ṭabarī, *Ta'rīkh*, I 2077 & 2078; al-Mas'ūdī, *Murūj*, 3631.

5 Ibn Khayyāṭ, *Ta'rīkh*, I 91; al-Ṭabarī, *Ta'rīkh*, I 2078.

6 Ibn Khayyāṭ, *Ta'rīkh*, I 91; al-Ṭabarī, *Ta'rīkh*, I 2078.

'Umar			
13/635	'Abd al-Raḥmān b. 'Awf[7] *or* 'Umar[8]	x CALIPH	x -
14/636	'Umar[9]	CALIPH	-
15/637	'Umar[10]	CALIPH	-
16/637-638	'Umar[11]	CALIPH	-
17/638	'Umar[12]	CALIPH	-
18/639	'Umar[13]	CALIPH	-
19/640	'Umar[14]	CALIPH	-
20/641	'Umar[15]	CALIPH	-
21/642	'Umar[16]	CALIPH	-
22/643	'Umar[17]	CALIPH	-
23/644	'Umar[18]	CALIPH	-

7 Ibn Khayyāṭ, *Ta'rīkh*, I 88; al-Ya'qūbī, *Ta'rīkh*, II 52; al-Ṭabarī, *Ta'rīkh*, I 2211-12; al-Mas'ūdī, *Murūj*, 3631.
8 Al-Ṭabarī, *Ta'rīkh*, I 2211.
9 Ibn Khayyāṭ, *Ta'rīkh*, I 88 & 99; al-Ya'qūbī, *Ta'rīkh*, II 52; al-Ṭabarī, *Ta'rīkh*, I 2212 & 2388; al-Mas'ūdī, *Murūj*, 3631.
10 Ibn Khayyāṭ, *Ta'rīkh*, I 88 & 99; al-Ya'qūbī, *Ta'rīkh*, II 52; al-Ṭabarī, *Ta'rīkh*, I 2212 & 2425; al-Mas'ūdī, *Murūj*, 3631.
11 Ibn Khayyāṭ, *Ta'rīkh*, I 88 & 99; al-Ya'qūbī, *Ta'rīkh*, II 52; al-Ṭabarī, *Ta'rīkh*, I 2212 & 2480; al-Mas'ūdī, *Murūj*, 3631.
12 Ibn Khayyāṭ, *Ta'rīkh*, I 88 & 99; al-Ya'qūbī, *Ta'rīkh*, II 52; al-Ṭabarī, *Ta'rīkh*, I 2212 & 2569; al-Mas'ūdī, *Murūj*, 3631.
13 Ibn Khayyāṭ, *Ta'rīkh*, I 88 & 99; al-Ya'qūbī, *Ta'rīkh*, II 52; al-Ṭabarī, *Ta'rīkh*, I 2212 & 2578; al-Mas'ūdī, *Murūj*, 3631.
14 Ibn Khayyāṭ, *Ta'rīkh*, I 88 & 99; al-Ya'qūbī, *Ta'rīkh*, II 52; al-Ṭabarī, *Ta'rīkh*, I 2212 & 2579; al-Mas'ūdī, *Murūj*, 3631.
15 Ibn Khayyāṭ, *Ta'rīkh*, I 88 & 99; al-Ya'qūbī, *Ta'rīkh*, II 52; al-Ṭabarī, *Ta'rīkh*, I 2212 & 2595; al-Mas'ūdī, *Murūj*, 3631.
16 Ibn Khayyāṭ, *Ta'rīkh*, I 88 & 99; al-Ya'qūbī, *Ta'rīkh*, II 52; al-Ṭabarī, *Ta'rīkh*, I 2212 & 2646; al-Mas'ūdī, *Murūj*, 3631.
17 Ibn Khayyāṭ, *Ta'rīkh*, I 88 & 99; al-Ya'qūbī, *Ta'rīkh*, II 52; al-Ṭabarī, *Ta'rīkh*, I 2212 & 2693; al-Mas'ūdī, *Murūj*, 3631.
18 Ibn Khayyāṭ, *Ta'rīkh*, I 88 & 99; al-Ya'qūbī, *Ta'rīkh*, II 52; al-Ṭabarī, *Ta'rīkh*, I 2212 & 2721; al-Mas'ūdī, *Murūj*, 3631.

'Uthmān			
24/645	'Abd al-Raḥmān b. 'Awf[19] *or* 'Uthmān[20]	x CALIPH	x -
25/646	'Uthmān[21]	CALIPH	-
26/647	'Uthmān[22]	CALIPH	-
27/648	'Uthmān[23]	CALIPH	-
28/649	'Uthmān[24]	CALIPH	-
29/650	'Uthmān[25]	CALIPH	-
30/651	'Uthmān[26]	CALIPH	-
31/652	'Uthmān[27]	CALIPH	-
32/653	'Uthmān[28]	CALIPH	-
33/654	'Uthmān[29]	CALIPH	-
34/655	'Uthmān[30]	CALIPH	-
35/656	'Abd Allāh b. al-'Abbās[31]	x	x

19 Ibn Khayyāṭ, *Ta'rīkh*, I 132; al-Ya'qūbī, *Ta'rīkh*, II 73; al-Ṭabarī, *Ta'rīkh*, I 2809; al-Mas'ūdī, *Murūj*, 3631.
20 Al-Ṭabarī, *Ta'rīkh*, I 2809.
21 Ibn Khayyāṭ, *Ta'rīkh*, I 133; al-Ya'qūbī, *Ta'rīkh*, II 73; al-Ṭabarī, *Ta'rīkh*, I 2810; al-Mas'ūdī, *Murūj*, 3631.
22 Ibn Khayyāṭ, *Ta'rīkh*, I 134; al-Ya'qūbī, *Ta'rīkh*, II 73; al-Ṭabarī, *Ta'rīkh*, I 2811; al-Mas'ūdī, *Murūj*, 3631.
23 Ibn Khayyāṭ, *Ta'rīkh*, I 134; al-Ya'qūbī, *Ta'rīkh*, II 73; al-Ṭabarī, *Ta'rīkh*, I 2819; al-Mas'ūdī, *Murūj*, 3631.
24 Ibn Khayyāṭ, *Ta'rīkh*, I 134; al-Ya'qūbī, *Ta'rīkh*, II 73; al-Ṭabarī, *Ta'rīkh*, I 2828; al-Mas'ūdī, *Murūj*, 3631.
25 Ibn Khayyāṭ, *Ta'rīkh*, I 134; al-Ya'qūbī, *Ta'rīkh*, II 73; al-Ṭabarī, *Ta'rīkh*, I 2833; al-Mas'ūdī, *Murūj*, 3631.
26 Ibn Khayyāṭ, *Ta'rīkh*, I 134; al-Ya'qūbī, *Ta'rīkh*, II 73; al-Ṭabarī, *Ta'rīkh*, I 2864; al-Mas'ūdī, *Murūj*, 3631.
27 Ibn Khayyāṭ, *Ta'rīkh*, I 134; al-Ya'qūbī, *Ta'rīkh*, II 73; al-Ṭabarī, *Ta'rīkh*, I 2888; al-Mas'ūdī, *Murūj*, 3631.
28 Ibn Khayyāṭ, *Ta'rīkh*, I 134; al-Ya'qūbī, *Ta'rīkh*, II 73; al-Mas'ūdī, *Murūj*, 3631.
29 Ibn Khayyāṭ, *Ta'rīkh*, I 134; al-Ya'qūbī, *Ta'rīkh*, II 73; al-Ṭabarī, *Ta'rīkh*, I 2926; al-Mas'ūdī, *Murūj*, 3631.
30 Ibn Khayyāṭ, *Ta'rīkh*, I 134; al-Ya'qūbī, *Ta'rīkh*, II 73; al-Ṭabarī, *Ta'rīkh*, I 2941; al-Mas'ūdī, *Murūj*, 3631.
31 Ibn Khayyāṭ, *Ta'rīkh*, I 154; al-Ya'qūbī, *Ta'rīkh*, II 73-74; al-Ṭabarī, *Ta'rīkh*, I 3011 & 3039; al-Mas'ūdī, *Murūj*, 3631.

'Alī			
36/657	'Abd Allāh b. al-'Abbās[32] *or* 'Ubayd Allāh b. al-'Abbās[33]	cousin cousin	x x
37/658	'Abd Allāh[34] *or* 'Ubayd Allāh[35] *or* Qutham b. al-'Abbās[36]	cousin cousin cousin	x x Mecca
38/659	Qutham[37] *or* 'Ubayd Allāh[38]	cousin cousin	Mecca x
39/660	Shaybah b. 'Uthmān b. Abī Ṭalḥah[39]	x	*Ḥājib* (Keeper) of the Ka'bah

ABŪ BAKR: LEADERSHIP OF THE *ḤAJJ* AND THE NATURE OF AUTHORITY IN ISLAM

In Table 1, Ibn Khayyāṭ, al-Ya'qūbī, al-Ṭabarī and al-Mas'ūdī cite Abū Bakr as leader of the *ḥajj* in 12/634. But Ibn Khayyāṭ and al-Ṭabarī also cite the early convert 'Abd al-Raḥmān b. 'Awf and the future caliph 'Umar as alternative leaders for that year's *ḥajj*.

Al-Ṭabarī, for one, drew his information for leadership of the *ḥajj* from different sources – Abū Ma'shar and al-Wāqidī – who did not always agree. His response to that dilemma was the same as that of the sources in general: to present all the information available rather than make a definitive judgement on it. The discussion below will therefore consider the possibility that any one of these three men may have led the pilgrimage in that particular year.

32 Ibn Khayyāṭ, *Ta'rīkh*, I 173; al-Ya'qūbī, *Ta'rīkh*, II 120; al-Ṭabarī, *Ta'rīkh*, I 3273; al-Mas'ūdī, *Murūj*, 3631.
33 Al-Zubayrī, *Nasab Quraish*, 27; Ibn Khayyāṭ, *Ta'rīkh*, I 173.
34 Ibn Khayyāṭ, *Ta'rīkh*, I 174; al-Ya'qūbī, *Ta'rīkh*, II 120.
35 Al-Zubayrī, *Nasab Quraish*, 27; al-Ṭabarī, *Ta'rīkh*, I 3390.
36 Al-Ya'qūbī, *Ta'rīkh*, II 120.
37 Ibn Khayyāṭ, *Ta'rīkh*, I 181; al-Ṭabarī, *Ta'rīkh*, I 3443; al-Mas'ūdī, *Murūj*, 3632.
38 Al-Ya'qūbī, *Ta'rīkh*, II 120.
39 Ibn Khayyāṭ, *Ta'rīkh*, I 182; al-Ya'qūbī, *Ta'rīkh*, II 120; al-Ṭabarī, *Ta'rīkh*, I 3448; al-Mas'ūdī, *Murūj*, 3632 (see also the record for the year 37/658: 3632).

For Muslims, Muḥammad was a unique leader: a Prophet who wielded political power.[40] For Muslims therefore, religious acts, such as prayer and pilgrimage, were not simply acts of spiritual devotion but demonstrations of political allegiance.[41] To pray with Muḥammad meant not only to accept his religious message; it was an acknowledgement of his political authority. To follow where he led on the battlefield or on the pilgrimage was not only an act of devotion to God but also a show of loyalty to the Prophet He had chosen. That Abū Bakr was the Prophet's deputy, *khalīfah*, over prayer was often cited as one of the reasons he was considered most suitable to succeed the Prophet.[42]

Leading the *ḥajj* gave Abū Bakr the chance to create a sense of political and personal continuity with the Prophet: Muḥammad led it in 10/632[43] and had appointed Abū Bakr to lead it the year before.[44] It also gave him a platform to underscore his religious credentials and as a successor to a prophet, this was of paramount importance. A caliph could never hope to emulate the Prophet's religious authority: Muḥammad's legitimacy was beyond question in the eyes of those who belonged to the community he founded.[45] Leading a ritual like the *ḥajj*, however, allowed Abū Bakr to achieve the seemingly impossible goal of exercising a political authority that was firmly rooted in religion while not encroaching upon the sacred territory of Muḥammad's prophecy.

As well as the caliph, a number of men are cited by the sources as leading the *ḥajj* during Abū Bakr's caliphate. All of them –'Abd al-Raḥmān,[46] 'Attāb b. Asīd,[47] 'Umar b. al-Khaṭṭāb,[48] and the caliph himself[49] – hailed

40 Von Grunebaum, *Medieval Islam*, 108; Burckhardt, "Fez" in *The Islamic City*, 167; Michon, "Religious Institutions" in *The Islamic City*, 13, 14 & 17; Nashabi, "Educational Institutions" in *The Islamic City*, 71 & 76; Schacht, *An Introduction to Islamic Law*, 1, 11 & 74; Black, *A History of Islamic Political Thought*, 9 & 10; Lapidus, *Islamic Societies*, 30 & 184; Robinson, *Islamic Historiography*, 133 & 138.

41 Watt, *Prophet & Statesman*, 30; Goitein, *Studies in Islamic History and Institutions*, 122; Endress, *Islam*, 3. Al-Ṭabarī, *Ta'rīkh*, II 228, shows that participation in prayer functioned as political allegiance. In the political circumstances following the death of the first Umayyad caliph Mu'āwiyah, Kūfan supporters of al-Ḥusayn b. 'Alī urged him to come and take control of their city, telling him that they did not attend Friday prayer – during which they would have been obliged to show their loyalty to the caliph – because of their support for him.

42 Al-Ṭabarī, *Ta'rīkh*, I 1842; Afsaruddin, *Excellence & Precedence*, 185.

43 Ibn Khayyāṭ, *Ta'rīkh*, I 58; al-Ya'qūbī, *Ta'rīkh*, I 438-443; al-Ṭabarī, *Ta'rīkh*, I 1751-56; al-Māwardī, *Aḥkām*, 111; Watt, *Prophet & Statesman*, 227; Ruthven, *Islam*, 44-45; Peters, *Hajj*, 50.

44 Ibn Khayyāṭ, *Ta'rīkh*, I 57; al-Ṭabarī, *Ta'rīkh*, I 1721; al-Mas'ūdī, *Murūj*, 3630.

45 Sharon, M., *Black Banners*, 33.

46 Al-Zubayrī, *Nasab Quraish*, 265.

47 Al-Zubayrī, *Nasab Quraish*, 187.

48 Al-Zubayrī, *Nasab Quraish*, 347.

49 Al-Zubayrī, *Nasab Quraish*, 278.

from the Prophet's tribe of Quraysh and all but 'Attāb were Companions of the Prophet and early converts to Islam. While 'Attāb may have lacked the precedence of an early conversion,[50] he could nevertheless claim a connection with the Prophet: Muḥammad made him governor of Mecca,[51] an appointment Abū Bakr later confirmed.[52] If 'Attāb did lead the *ḥajj* in 11/633, his appointment may have owed much to practicality because, as governor of the Holy City, he was already *in situ* and could carry out the task with relative ease.

As the sources cite a range of possible leaders for the *ḥajj* seasons of Abū Bakr's caliphate, it is difficult to determine if these men were appointed to the task because of their personal merit; their relationship with the Prophet; their membership of the tribe of Quraysh; or a combination of all three.

The Quraysh were certainly important to Abū Bakr – Madelung refers to his time in power as "the caliphate of Quraysh"[53] – and this importance is evident in Abū Bakr's military campaigns. He repeatedly appointed members of the pre-Islamic Meccan aristocracy (all Qurashī) to lead armies in the *riddah* campaigns and the early raids outside Arabia: members of two of the main clans in Quraysh, 'Abd Shams and Makhzūm, led most of these armies.[54] By contrast, only one of the early Muslims who sacrificed so much in the early days of the faith was given a prestigious military command during the *riddah* campaigns – Shuraḥbīl b. Ḥasanah – and not one of the Prophet's early allies in Medina, the *Anṣār*, was given the chance to lead a Muslim army.[55]

But, important though the Quraysh were to Abū Bakr, when it came to leadership of a ritual like the *ḥajj*, Qurashī descent by itself may not have been enough, for the pre-Islamic Meccan aristocrats who led the armies of the faith they were so slow to embrace were not seen leading the faithful on their pilgrimage. To have the privilege of following in the Prophet's footsteps in Mecca, early conversion and/or a personal connection to the Prophet may also have been needed.

50 Al-Ṭabarī, *Ta'rīkh*, I 1841; Afsaruddin, *Excellence & Precedence*, 36-79.
51 Al-Zubayrī, *Nasab Quraish*, 187; Ibn Khayyāṭ, *Ta'rīkh*, I 50 & 61; al-Balādhurī, *Futūḥ*, 40.
52 Ibn Khayyāṭ, *Ta'rīkh*, I 91; al-Ya'qūbī, *Ta'rīkh*, II 26.
53 Madelung, *Succession*, 28.
54 Ibn Khayyāṭ, *Ta'rīkh*, I 66; al-Ya'qūbī, *Ta'rīkh*, II 17 & 20; Madelung, *Succession*, 45.
55 Madelung, *Succession*, 45.

'UMAR AND 'UTHMĀN: THE *ḤAJJ* AS A CHANNEL OF COMMUNICATION

Once caliph, 'Umar followed the Prophet's example of leading the *ḥajj* and led at least ten (14/636 to 23/644) of his eleven pilgrimage seasons.

There was no religious requirement compelling him to lead the *ḥajj* on such a regular basis. The *ḥajj* is a duty to be performed once in a lifetime and there is no obligation upon a Muslim, even one resident in one of the Holy Cities, to perform it so often. Prior to 'Umar, no one had dominated the performance of the pilgrimage to such a degree but, prior to his caliphate, no one had needed to: there had been no empire to sustain.[56]

To survive politically, empires usually require elaborate ceremonials and an equally elaborate court to support them: the former providing the means by which the emperor receives obedience; the latter, the physical setting where he receives it.[57] But Islam, as a religion based on the submission of the individual's will to the will of God, makes no provision for the sort of ostentatious display of power often associated with empire.[58]

What Islam does provide is a number of ritual acts such as prayer and pilgrimage where the caliph could show *his* obedience to God while simultaneously showing himself as leader of the Muslim community.[59] And the *ḥajj*, based as it is in the birth place of the faith, is one of the most high profile of these acts.

One of the consequences of the massive territorial expansion of the Islamic polity during 'Umar's caliphate was that the *ḥajj* became more than a religious ritual; it became part of the politics of empire. Every year, 'Umar would summon his governors from every province in the empire to come to Mecca during the *ḥajj* so he could check how effectively they were carrying out their gubernatorial duties.[60]

This yearly recall of governors to Mecca was advantageous for other reasons. In an age when information travelled slowly, the arrival in Mecca of people from the newly conquered territories made the success of the

56 Ibn Khayyāṭ, *Ta'rīkh*, I 92-93, 94, 95-98, 99-100, 101, 101-103, 103-104, 105, 107-108, 109, 110-112, 113, 114-116, 120-123, 124 & 125; al-Ya'qūbī, *Ta'rīkh*, II 28, 29, 30, 31-34, 38-39, 40, 41, 42, 46, 47, 48 & 49.

57 Kertzer, *Ritual*, 2, 3, 13, 29 & 62; al-Azmeh, *Muslim Kingship*, 3-34 (particularly 31); Stetkevych, *Poetics*, 34.

58 Crone, *Medieval Islamic Political Thought*, 41.

59 Heilman, *Popular Protest*, 110. Crone, *Medieval Islamic Political Thought*, 45, makes the point that the Prophet identified God as king. In such circumstances, the caliph was no emperor, merely one subject amongst many.

60 Al-Ṭabarī, *Ta'rīkh*, I 2662.

conquests, the *futūḥ*, real to residents of the Holy City in the most tangible way. The governors of these provinces would not have travelled alone: Arab troops stationed in their areas would have taken advantage of the *ḥajj* season to visit home, and new converts eager to make their *ḥajj* and see the Holy Places for the first time may also have accompanied them. Aside from creating an impressive spectacle, the influx of so many people to the Holy City would have had a considerable impact on the local economy as pilgrims from the provinces often financed their trip by bringing goods and merchandise to sell or exchange in Mecca.

In an ever-expanding empire, the *ḥajj* thus proved an invaluable way of absorbing the provincial periphery into the caliphal centre.[61] It facilitated communications and enabled the flow of information, as well as people, around the enormous territories of the Islamic empire. Furthermore, the *ḥajj*, with its capacity to reinforce the idea of a geographical centre and provide a route to that centre, helped bind the caliphate as a unified political entity together.

When ʻUthmān became caliph, he followed ʻUmar's example and led at least ten (25/646 to 34/655) of his twelve *ḥajj* seasons. His motivation for doing so was the same as ʻUmar's: ʻUthmān required his governors to appear before him at the *ḥajj* every year.[62]

This use of the *ḥajj*, a religious ritual, as the backdrop for what were essentially political meetings showed how ʻUthmān, and ʻUmar before him, understood the dual nature of the authority they exercised. There was, after all, no reason these meetings had to take place in Mecca at the time of the *ḥajj*. ʻUmar and ʻUthmān, as caliphs, could just as easily have ordered the governors to come to Medina, where they were resident, and the governors would have been obliged to present themselves or risk losing their positions. But the fact that ʻUmar – and later ʻUthmān – chose the *ḥajj* as the setting for this annual get-together of provincial governors indicated their understanding of the pilgrimage as a place where religious ritual and political power came together. For them, leadership of the ritual was thus as inherently political as it was religious.

This point is further demonstrated by who ʻUmar and ʻUthmān appointed to lead the *ḥajj* in their absence. As Table 1 shows, ʻUmar may have appointed ʻAbd al-Raḥmān b. ʻAwf, an early convert, Companion

61 Ibn Khayyāṭ, *Ta'rīkh*, I 131, 132, 133, 134, 135, 137-138, 139, 139-141, 141-142 & 144; al-Yaʻqūbī, *Ta'rīkh*, II 59-60, 61-62, 63 & 64-65.

62 Al-Ṭabarī, *Ta'rīkh*, I 2944 & 3027.

of the Prophet, and member of the Quraysh, to lead his inaugural *ḥajj* in 13/635. The same man is also believed to have led 'Uthmān's inaugural *ḥajj* in 24/645. 'Abd al-Raḥmān may thus have led the first *ḥajj* of Abū Bakr's caliphate, the first of 'Umar's and the first of 'Uthmān's.[63] In 'Uthmān's case, this may have been more than coincidence: 'Uthmān became caliph because he promised the members of the *shūrā* he would govern in accordance with the Qur'ān, the example of the Prophet *and* the policies of his caliphal predecessors.[64] By appointing 'Abd al-Raḥmān to lead his inaugural pilgrimage, 'Uthmān may have used this *ḥajj* to demonstrate he was, quite literally, following in his predecessors' footsteps.

The birth of the Islamic empire had a major impact not only on the *ḥajj* but also on the Holy Cities. Medina was now much more than the city sanctified by its association with the Prophet: it was the political and administrative centre of an emerging trans-national empire. Mecca was now much more than the Holy City of the Muslims of Arabia; it was the religious centre of Muslims scattered throughout the conquered territories.

Many inhabitants of the newly conquered territories, particularly the Arabs, embraced the faith and their conversion to Islam swelled the numbers of the Muslim community. 'Umar and 'Uthmān, as the men responsible for the smooth running of the *ḥajj*, had to make sure the Holy Mosques in the Holy Cities were able to accommodate the increase in the number of pilgrims. 'Umar was the first to begin work and in 17/638, renovations were made to the *Ḥarām* in Mecca.[65] He also ensured access to the Holy Cities was improved and routes to them were constructed and maintained.[66]

But this access to the Ḥijāz was to have its limits: the religious, political and administrative centre of an empire rapidly becoming a global force was to be the exclusive preserve of Muslims alone.[67] Citing the Prophet's words that "There can be no two religions in Arabia"[68] 'Umar expelled some of the Jewish and Christian communities from the peninsula, thus making a

63 The sources are far from united about who led these pilgrimages and this particular point comes with that qualification.

64 Al-Ṭabarī, *Ta'rīkh*, I 2794-95.

65 Al-Ya'qūbī, *Ta'rīkh*, II 39; al-Ṭabarī, *Ta'rīkh*, I 2528.

66 Al-Ṭabarī, *Ta'rīkh*, I 2523 & 2529.

67 Madelung, *Succession*, 74-75.

68 Al-Balādhurī, *Futūḥ*, 28; al-Ya'qūbī, *Ta'rīkh*, II 47. This, however, was never realized: the Holy Cities became the preserve of Muslims but the same does not apply to the rest of the peninsula and to cite one example: to this day, there remains a sizeable Jewish community in Yemen. I am grateful to Werner Daum for drawing this point to my attention.

distinction between the birth place of the faith and the rest of the territories governed in its name.[69]

During 'Uthmān's caliphate, the number of Muslims continued to increase and he too had to extend the mosques in the Holy Cities. The Sacred Mosque in Mecca was the first to benefit and in 26/646-647, enlargements were made to it.[70] Three years later, it was the turn of the Mosque of the Prophet in Medina: it too was enlarged and widened.[71]

Through the building projects they sponsored in Mecca and Medina, 'Umar and 'Uthmān laid the framework for a policy of caliphal patronage towards the Holy Cities which subsequent caliphs, particularly the Umayyads, were eager to follow.

'Umar and 'Uthmān were undoubtedly successful in using the *ḥajj* as a channel of communication through the lands they administered. But this idea of the *ḥajj* as a conduit of information was not without risks, as 'Uthmān discovered to his cost at the *ḥajj* of 35/656. He was the first caliph, but not the last, to discover that the flow of information through the *ḥajj* was not a one-way process: it could just as easily be manipulated by rebels as it was by rulers.

That year, rebels from the provinces of al-Baṣrah, al-Kūfah and Egypt used the *ḥajj* as cover for their true intentions. Posing as pious pilgrims, they travelled the highways and byways of Islam before reaching Medina where they planned to bring their political grievances to 'Uthmān in person.[72]

And therein lay the problem not only for 'Uthmān but for every ruling caliph: how to ensure that the pilgrims who arrived in the Holy Cities intended to do nothing more than pray? The rebels against 'Uthmān were by no means united in their aims. In fact, at times, each group seemed to aspire to entirely different objectives.[73] Yet, in spite of their lack of unity, their presence in the Ḥijāz signalled that the caliph had lost control of the provinces.

The most immediate casualty of this changing state of affairs was 'Uthmān himself but he was not the only one: the idea of a unitary caliphate, led by one man based in Medina, was also under threat from the centrifugal forces coming from the provinces. The rebels' demands that the governors of their provinces be dismissed, presumably to be replaced by men of their choosing, was further

69 Al-Balādhurī, *Futūḥ*, 25-26, 28, 29, 32, 34 & 66-67; al-Ṭabarī, *Ta'rīkh*, I 2594-95.

70 Ibn Khayyāṭ, *Ta'rīkh*, I 134; al-Balādhurī, *Futūḥ*, 46; al-Ya'qūbī, *Ta'rīkh*, II 58-59.

71 Ibn Khayyāṭ, *Ta'rīkh*, I 139; al-Balādhurī, *Futūḥ*, 6; al-Ya'qūbī, *Ta'rīkh*, II 60-61.

72 Ibn Khayyāṭ, *Ta'rīkh*, I 145; al-Ṭabarī, *Ta'rīkh*, I 2950-51 & 2954; Hinds, "The Murder of the Caliph 'Uthmān", 450-469; Madelung, *Succession*, 121. According to Abū Mikhnaf, they had planned their actions during the pilgrimage the previous year: al-Balādhurī, *Ansāb*, V 59.

73 Al-Ṭabarī, *Ta'rīkh*, I 2955 & 2956-57.

evidence of this desire to gain autonomy from the caliphal centre.[74] That the rebels made use of the *ḥajj*, a process which had thus far served to reinforce the centripetal character of the caliphate, showed how easily the politics of pilgrimage could be manipulated by ruler and rebel alike.

The rebels' attack against 'Uthmān meant that in 35/656 he could not lead the pilgrimage in person. Instead, he called upon 'Abd Allāh b. al-'Abbās, a son of the Prophet's uncle, to go to Mecca and ask Khālid b. al-'Āṣ, of the Makhzūm clan of Quraysh, to lead the *ḥajj* on his behalf.[75] If Khālid should, for whatever reason, refuse to do so, then 'Abd Allāh was to lead it himself.[76] Khālid did refuse and in 35/656 the *ḥajj* was led for the first time by a relative of the Prophet. It would not be the last.

'ALĪ B. ABĪ ṬĀLIB: ALL ROADS DO NOT LEAD TO MECCA

Following 'Uthmān's murder, the Prophet's cousin and son-in-law 'Alī b. Abī Ṭālib became caliph. His caliphate included four *ḥajj* seasons, 36/657 to 39/660, not one of which he led in person.

A caliph's leadership of the pilgrimage was a demonstration of his authority: the tangible enactment of an intangible concept. However, before such a demonstration could take place, a caliph had first to enjoy the political authority necessary to facilitate it. 'Alī, whose caliphate was in trouble from the start, arguably never did.

The problem he faced throughout his caliphate was that he did not receive the unanimous support of the community. The observation made by his cousin, 'Abd Allāh b. al-'Abbās, that whoever received the oath of allegiance after 'Uthmān's death would be suspected of his blood turned out to be true.[77] 'Alī played no part in 'Uthmān's murder but his detractors cast him as the person who gained the most from it and who should be made to pay for it.[78] 'Alī was therefore obliged to fight for his authority and this fight took him away from the Ḥijāz. He initially went to al-Kūfah to gather support to fight an army led by Ṭalḥah and al-Zubayr, two members of the *shūrā* which elected 'Uthmān caliph.[79]

74 Al-Ṭabarī, *Ta'rīkh*, I 2956.

75 Al-Ṭabarī, *Ta'rīkh*, I 3039-40; Madelung, *Succession*, 97-98. For Khālid's descent, see Madelung, *Succession*, 97; for 'Abd Allāh's, see al-Zubayrī, *Nasab Quraish*, 25-26.

76 Al-Ṭabarī, *Ta'rīkh*, I 3039-40; Madelung, *Succession*, 97-98.

77 Al-Ṭabarī, *Ta'rīkh*, I 3039-40.

78 Al-Ṭabarī, *Ta'rīkh*, I 3090-91 & 3255.

79 The *shūrā* had six members - the two mentioned here and 'Alī, 'Uthmān, Sa'd b. Abī Waqqāṣ and

Victory, however, brought no let-up in the challenges against him. The next one came from the governor of Syria, Muʿāwiyah, who sought revenge for the murder of his Umayyad kinsman ʿUthmān.

The outcome of the battle they fought at Ṣiffīn was inconclusive but resulted in yet another challenge to ʿAlī's authority: from a group of his own supporters who disapproved of his decision to agree to arbitration in the aftermath of the battle.

Against such a backdrop of political instability, it is perhaps not surprising ʿAlī did not lead the pilgrimage. In some cases, it was sheer practicality which prevented him from doing so. The first *ḥajj* of his caliphate, 36/657,[80] saw him on the battlefields near Ṣiffīn and according to at least one report he was also engaged in combat during his second *ḥajj* season in 37/658.[81]

For much the same reason that he did not lead the pilgrimage, ʿAlī did not adopt a policy of patronage for the Holy Cities. Patronage is an expression of "soft" power, the power to provide rather than pressure, and ʿAlī's authority never had the opportunity to take root and develop the capacity required for displays of caliphal largesse.

In his absence from the Ḥijāz, ʿAlī relied on his family to deputize for him in Mecca. While the sources disagree over who he appointed to lead the *ḥajj*, they do agree that all the contenders were his cousins, making him the first caliph to appoint a member of his family to lead the *ḥajj*.[82] ʿUthmān, for all the patronage he had so controversially bestowed upon his family, did not honour any of them with leadership of the *ḥajj*.[83] ʿAlī's appointees, however, were not merely his relatives; they were relatives of the Prophet and his decision to appoint them to lead the *ḥajj* may have been an attempt to demonstrate his legitimacy in the most tangible form: he could claim a propinquity to the Prophet none of his predecessors could.

That ʿAlī understood the political importance of this relationship, particularly in Mecca, was shown by his decision to appoint a member of the Banū Hāshim, Qutham b. al-ʿAbbās, governor of that city. This decision stood in marked contrast with his usual practice of appointing the *Anṣār* to governorships. When he became caliph, he made a virtual clean

ʿAbd al-Raḥmān b. ʿAwf: al-Yaʿqūbī, *Taʾrīkh*, II 53; al-Ṭabarī, *Taʾrīkh*, I 2724 & 2778.

80 Al-Ṭabarī, *Taʾrīkh*, I 3272 & 3273.

81 Madelung, *Succession*, 261.

82 Al-Zubayrī, *Nasab Quraish*, 17 & 18, for the relationships between the fathers of these men, the caliph's father, and the Prophet's.

83 Ibn Khayyāṭ, *Taʾrīkh*, I 157; al-Yaʿqūbī, *Taʾrīkh*, II 64, 70 & 71; al-Ṭabarī, *Taʾrīkh*, I 2952-54; al-Jahshiyārī, *Kitāb al-wuzarāʾ*, 21; Madelung, *Succession*, 90.

sweep of his predecessor's governors in favour of the *Anṣār*.[84] Yet, when it came to leading the *ḥajj* and governing the Holy City of Mecca, it was not the Prophet's helpers 'Alī relied upon to enforce his authority but the Prophet's family. In the politically charged atmosphere of the time – one of the main challenges to his rule came from Mecca in the form of Ṭalḥah and al-Zubayr – the appointment of a Meccan, who was a relative of the Prophet, to this governorship may have been less contentious than that of an *Anṣārī* from Medina.

'Alī's absence from the *ḥajj* was symptomatic of a broader structural change taking place within the caliphate at this time. 'Umar and 'Uthmān had used the *ḥajj* as a centralizing dynamic to reinforce the political primacy of the Ḥijāz over the rest of the Islamic territories. With 'Alī, that began to change. When he left Medina for al-Kūfah to fight Ṭalḥah and al-Zubayr, no one could have known the political epicentre of the caliphate was leaving with him, never to return.

The idea of a unified caliphate run from the Ḥijāz came under more pressure when, post-Ṣiffīn, the people of Syria acknowledged their governor, Mu'āwiyah, as caliph and the province seceded. With two caliphs, both based outside the Ḥijāz, competing for control of the caliphate, the *ḥajj* could no longer be utilized to express a centripetal view of the caliphate; at that particular time, a centralized caliphate, run by a caliph based in Medina, simply did not exist.

THE *ḤAJJ* AS A PLATFORM FOR REBELLION

Muslims are deeply aware that the *ḥajj* is a duty they owe Allāh.[85] Four of its rites – the *arkān* or pillars – are time-sensitive and must be performed in a certain place at a certain time or the entire pilgrimage is rendered null and void. The stakes for Muslims could not be higher. Nothing short of salvation is at risk.

For a caliph, the stakes were also high but the consequences of failure were political rather than religious. His legitimacy as Commander of the Faithful rested on his ability to ensure the rites of Islam could be performed safely.[86] The Holy Cities and the *ḥajj* therefore offered a stage like no other

84 Ibn Khayyāṭ, *Ta'rīkh*, I 185-186; al-Ya'qūbī, *Ta'rīkh*, II 77; al-Ṭabarī, *Ta'rīkh*, I 3087; Madelung, *Succession*, 151.

85 Qur'ān 3:97.

86 Al-Ya'qūbī, *Ta'rīkh*, II 188, refers to comments that whoever controls the *Ḥaramayn* and leads the

where rebels could question a ruler's authority. If a rebel could succeed in upstaging the caliph, or his appointed representative, in the very heart of Islam at the time of the *ḥajj*, the caliph's credibility could be seriously, perhaps fatally, undermined.

To add to a rebel's justification for doing so, a precedent existed for making use of the Holy City to change the established political order: a precedent set by none other than the Prophet himself when he and his supporters captured Mecca in 8/630.[87] By reclaiming the city from the pagan Meccans, the Prophet reclaimed the Ka'bah for God and ensured that the *ḥajj*, from then on, would be in the hands of the Muslims.

Muḥammad's conquest of Mecca was more than a religious victory; it was also a political one. The Meccan opposition, which had so long stood against him, finally gave in and acknowledged him as the dominant political force in the region.[88]

As a result, the Prophet became the rebel-turned-ruler *par excellence* and rulers and rebels alike could claim him as inspiration for their actions. His leadership of the Farewell *Ḥajj* in 10/632 allowed rulers to cite him as their example for leading the ritual while his seizure of Mecca two years earlier allowed rebels to do likewise. Both groups sought to draw on his example and manipulate the religious legitimacy unique to the Holy Cities and the *ḥajj* to proclaim their political agendas; the former to promote and project their power, the latter to try and take it away from them.

This dynamic of competing political agendas came fully into play at the *ḥajj* of 39/660. That year, the governor of Syria, Mu'āwiyah b. Abī Sufyān made his claim for the caliphate. He had been vying with 'Alī since the Battle of Ṣiffīn but the *ḥajj* of 39/660 saw him change tactics. He set out to undermine his rival's credibility in the Holiest City at the holiest time of the year by sending his representative, Yazīd b. Shajarah al-Rahāwī, to seek leadership of the ritual on his behalf.[89]

ḥajj is the rightful caliph. Al-Māwardī, *Aḥkām*, 108-112, devotes a chapter to leadership of the pilgrimage. For the political potential of pilgrimage, see Kertzer, *Ritual, Politics, and Power,* 104; Bianchi, *Guests of God*, 37 & 40-41. For its revolutionary potential, see Turner & Turner, *Image and Pilgrimage*, 193; Kertzer, *Ritual, Politics, and Power,* 1-2, 14, 29 & 112.

87 Ibn Hishām, *Sīrah,* II 389-428; Ibn Khayyāṭ, *Ta'rīkh*, I 50; al-Ya'qūbī, *Ta'rīkh*, I 376-380; al-Ṭabarī, *Ta'rīkh*, I 1618-1649; Guillaume, *Muḥammad*, 540-561; Cook, *Muhammad*, 24; Peters, *Mecca*, 81-83. Hawting puts forward an alternative interpretation of the conquest of Mecca: "Al-Hudaybiyya and the Conquest of Mecca: A Reconsideration of the tradition about the Muslim takeover of the sanctuary".

88 Kennedy, *Prophet*, 42-43.

89 Ibn Khayyāṭ, *Ta'rīkh*, I 182.

Muʿāwiyah's actions were a clear indication that he sought to unite political control of the caliphate, currently fragmented between Iraq and Syria, under his centralized control. His message to ʿAlī was clear: he regarded himself as rightful leader of the *ummah* and, therefore, of the community's rituals.

The pilgrims were worried about the consequences of this dispute for their *ḥajj*. They knew that if they failed to perform any of the four obligatory *arkān*, their pilgrimage would be rendered invalid.

Mediation therefore ensued between the rival groups to ensure the ritual could proceed. In the end, it was neither ʿAlī nor Muʿāwiyah who chose the leader of the *ḥajj* but the pilgrims themselves. They agreed upon Shaybah b. ʿUthmān b. Abī Ṭalḥah, the keeper or *ḥājib* of the Kaʿbah, as a compromise candidate.

Shaybah's nomination meant that Muʿāwiyah failed in his objective to have the *ḥajj* led in his name. He had, nevertheless, every reason to feel satisfied with the outcome. The propaganda victory was his: he had manoeuvred ʿAlī's *ḥajj* leader, Qutham b. al-ʿAbbās, into the dubious position of having to negotiate for what should have been his by right and he had then succeeded in preventing him from leading the *ḥajj*.

By questioning ʿAlī's legitimacy in this way, Muʿāwiyah had again forced ʿAlī to deal with him as an equal – just as he had done in the aftermath of Ṣiffīn – and had succeeded, yet again, in undermining his religious and political authority: this time, in front of the masses of pilgrims.

CONSPICUOUS BY THEIR ABSENCE: WHO DID NOT LEAD THE *ḤAJJ*

The *ḥajj* of 39/660 demonstrated the complex nature of authority in Islam. The struggle between ʿAlī and Muʿāwiyah was political but, in this instance, it was played out against the backdrop of a religious ritual.

This complex nature of authority is also borne out by who did *not* lead the *ḥajj* during this period. Abū Bakr, who believed that the caliphate belonged to the Prophet's tribe but not to the Prophet's family, did not appoint anyone other than a Qurashī to lead the *ḥajj* during his caliphate. No one from the *Anṣār* was invited to do so. Nor was anyone from the Prophet's family. ʿUmar, who held the same view, followed suit. ʿUthmān also sidelined the *Anṣār* but was compelled by circumstances to rely on a member of the Prophet's family, ʿAbd Allāh b. al-ʿAbbās, to lead the *ḥajj* for him in 35/656.

'Alī, as a member of the Prophet's family, held a different view from his predecessors over who was – and who was not – eligible for the caliphate. He was seen as the candidate of the *Anṣār* and of the Prophet's family and it was to the latter he gave leadership of his *ḥajj* seasons – perhaps believing that they, as Qurashī Meccans *and* relatives of Muḥammad, were the most suitable representatives of his authority in the Holy City during the turbulent times of the late 30s/650s.

There was, however, one area of *ḥajj* policy where these caliphs were as one: all four kept leadership of the ritual in their own hands or in the hands of their political allies.

That Abū Bakr, 'Umar, 'Uthmān, and 'Alī would choose to appoint a political ally to lead the *ḥajj* might seem a statement of the overwhelmingly obvious, as no caliph would consider appointing someone other than a political ally to lead such a high-profile event.

If viewed from another perspective, however, this question provides an insight into how the *Rāshidūn* caliphs understood the nature of the power on display in Mecca. The *ḥajj* is first and foremost a religious ritual. Yet no religious figure, such as a Qur'ān reciter or someone renowned for his piety or religious knowledge, was appointed to lead the *ḥajj* during this period. Abū Bakr, 'Umar, 'Uthmān and 'Alī all seemed united in the view that the *ḥajj* was a religious ritual which required political leadership.

THREE

Muʿāwiyah b. Abī Sufyān: A New Regime and a New *Ḥajj* Policy

Muʿāwiyah b. Abī Sufyān became caliph in 40/661; a position he held until his death in 60/680.[1] His caliphate covered twenty *ḥajj* seasons: 40/661 to 59/679 inclusive. Table 2 shows his choice of leaders for the *ḥajj* during the two decades of his caliphate.

Table 2

Year	***Ḥajj leader***	***Relationship to caliph***	***Governor of Medina?***
40/661	al-Mughīrah b. Shuʿbah[2]	x	x
41/662	ʿUtbah b. Abī Sufyān[3] *or* ʿAnbasah b. Abī Sufyān[4]	brother brother	x x
42/663	ʿUtbah[5] *or* ʿAnbasah[6]	brother brother	x x

1 *EI* 2nd edition, s.v. Muʿawiya.
2 Ibn Khayyāṭ, *Taʾrīkh*, I 187; al-Ṭabarī, *Taʾrīkh*, II 4; al-Masʿūdī, *Murūj*, 3632; Ibn ʿAsākir, *TMD*, Vol. 60, 42.
3 Ibn Khayyāṭ, *Taʾrīkh*, I 189; al-Yaʿqūbī, *Taʾrīkh*, II 151; al-Ṭabarī, *Taʾrīkh*, II 16; al-Masʿūdī, *Murūj*, 3632; Ibn ʿAsākir, *TMD*, Vol. 38, 266 & 267.
4 Al-Ṭabarī, *Taʾrīkh*, II 16.
5 Ibn Khayyāṭ, *Taʾrīkh*, I 190; al-Yaʿqūbī, *Taʾrīkh*, II 151; Ibn ʿAsākir, *TMD*, Vol. 38, 266 & 267.
6 Al-Ṭabarī, *Taʾrīkh*, II 27; al-Masʿūdī, *Murūj*, 3632.

43/664	Marwān b. al-Ḥakam[7]	cousin	yes
44/665	CALIPH[8]	-	-
45/666	Marwān[9]	cousin	yes
46/667	ʻUtbah[10] *or* ʻAnbasah[11]	brother brother	x x
47/668	ʻUtbah[12] *or* ʻAnbasah[13]	brother brother	x x
48/669	Marwān[14] *or* Saʻīd b. al-ʻĀṣ[15]	cousin cousin	yes x
49/670	Saʻīd[16]	cousin	yes
50/670-671	CALIPH[17] *or* Yazīd[18]	- son	- -
51/671	CALIPH[19] *or* Yazīd[20]	- son	- -
52/672	Saʻīd[21]	cousin	yes

7 Ibn Khayyāṭ, *Taʾrīkh*, I 190; al-Yaʻqūbī, *Taʾrīkh*, II 151; al-Ṭabarī, *Taʾrīkh*, II 67; al-Masʻūdī, *Murūj*, 3632; Ibn ʻAsākir, *TMD*, Vol. 57, 241 & 242.

8 Ibn Khayyāṭ, *Taʾrīkh*, I 191; al-Yaʻqūbī, *Taʾrīkh*, II 150 & 151; al-Ṭabarī, *Taʾrīkh*, II 70; al-Masʻūdī, *Murūj*, 3632.

9 Ibn Khayyāṭ, *Taʾrīkh*, I 192; al-Yaʻqūbī, *Taʾrīkh*, II 151; al-Ṭabarī, *Taʾrīkh*, II 81; al-Masʻūdī, *Murūj*, 3632; Ibn ʻAsākir, *TMD*, Vol. 38, 267 & Vol. 57, 241 & 242.

10 Ibn Khayyāṭ, *Taʾrīkh*, I 193; al-Yaʻqūbī, *Taʾrīkh*, II 151; al-Ṭabarī, *Taʾrīkh*, II 84; al-Masʻūdī, *Murūj*, 3632; Ibn ʻAsākir, *TMD*, Vol. 38, 266 & 267.

11 Ibn ʻAsākir, *TMD*, Vol. 47, 21.

12 Al-Yaʻqūbī, *Taʾrīkh*, II 151; al-Ṭabarī, *Taʾrīkh*, II 85; al-Masʻūdī, *Murūj*, 3632; Ibn ʻAsākir, *TMD*, Vol. 38, 267.

13 Ibn Khayyāṭ, *Taʾrīkh*, I 193; al-Ṭabarī, *Taʾrīkh*, II 85; Ibn ʻAsākir, *TMD*, Vol. 47, 21.

14 Al-Yaʻqūbī, *Taʾrīkh*, II 151; al-Ṭabarī, *Taʾrīkh*, II 85; al-Masʻūdī, *Murūj*, 3632; Ibn ʻAsākir, *TMD*, Vol. 57, 243.

15 Ibn Khayyāṭ, *Taʾrīkh*, I 194.

16 Ibn Khayyāṭ, *Taʾrīkh*, I 194; al-Yaʻqūbī, *Taʾrīkh*, II 151; al-Ṭabarī, *Taʾrīkh*, II 87; al-Masʻūdī, *Murūj*, 3632; Ibn ʻAsākir, *TMD*, Vol. 21, 125 & 126.

17 Ibn Khayyāṭ, *Taʾrīkh*, I 198; al-Yaʻqūbī, *Taʾrīkh*, II 150 & 151; al-Ṭabarī, *Taʾrīkh*, II 94; al-Masʻūdī, *Murūj*, 1823; Ibn ʻAsākir, *TMD*, Vol. 21, 125 & 126.

18 Al-Ṭabarī, *Taʾrīkh*, II 94; al-Masʻūdī, *Murūj*, 3632; Ibn ʻAsākir, *TMD*, Vol. 65, 406.

19 Ibn Khayyāṭ, *Taʾrīkh*, I 199 & 205; al-Masʻūdī, *Murūj*, 3634; Ibn ʻAsākir, *TMD*, Vol. 21, 125; al-Dhahabī, *Taʾrīkh*, II 258.

20 Al-Yaʻqūbī, *Taʾrīkh*, II 151; al-Ṭabarī, *Taʾrīkh*, II 156; Ibn ʻAsākir, *TMD*, Vol. 21, 126, & Vol. 65, 406.

21 Ibn Khayyāṭ, *Taʾrīkh*, I 205; al-Yaʻqūbī, *Taʾrīkh*, II 151; al-Ṭabarī, *Taʾrīkh*, II 157; al-Masʻūdī, *Murūj*, 3634; Ibn ʻAsākir, *TMD*, Vol. 21, 125 & 126.

53/673	Saʿīd[22]	cousin	yes
54/674	Marwān[23]	cousin	yes
55/675	Marwān[24]	cousin	yes
56/676	al-Walīd b. ʿUtbah[25] *or* ʿUtbah[26]	nephew brother	x x
57/677	al-Walīd[27] *or* ʿUthmān b. Muḥammad b. Abī Sufyān[28]	nephew nephew	yes x
58/678	al-Walīd[29]	nephew	yes
59/679	ʿUthmān[30] *or* al-Walīd[31] *or* Muḥammad b. Abī Sufyān[32]	nephew nephew brother	x yes x

MUʿĀWIYAH AND LEADERSHIP OF THE *ḤAJJ*

Muʿāwiyah's elevation to the caliphate in 40/661 brought an end to the *fitnah*, the time of trial, and the *ummah* once again saw their communal identity reflected in one caliph.[33]

22 Ibn Khayyāṭ, *Taʾrīkh*, I 210; al-Yaʿqūbī, *Taʾrīkh*, II 151-152; al-Ṭabarī, *Taʾrīkh*, II 163; al-Masʿūdī, *Murūj*, 3634; Ibn ʿAsākir, *TMD*, Vol. 21, 125 & 126.

23 Ibn Khayyāṭ, *Taʾrīkh*, I 211; al-Yaʿqūbī, *Taʾrīkh*, II 152; al-Ṭabarī, *Taʾrīkh*, II 170; al-Masʿūdī, *Murūj*, 3634; Ibn ʿAsākir, *TMD*, Vol. 21, 126, & Vol. 57, 242 & 243.

24 Ibn Khayyāṭ, *Taʾrīkh*, I 212; al-Yaʿqūbī, *Taʾrīkh*, II 152; al-Ṭabarī, *Taʾrīkh*, II 172; al-Masʿūdī, *Murūj*, 3634; Ibn ʿAsākir, *TMD*, Vol. 21, 126, & Vol. 57, 242 & 243.

25 Ibn Khayyāṭ, *Taʾrīkh*, I 212; al-Yaʿqūbī, *Taʾrīkh*, II 152; al-Ṭabarī, *Taʾrīkh*, II 173; Ibn ʿAsākir, *TMD*, Vol. 63, 207 & 208.

26 Al-Masʿūdī, *Murūj*, 3634; Ibn ʿAsākir, *TMD*, Vol. 38, 266.

27 Ibn Khayyāṭ, *Taʾrīkh*, I 213; al-Yaʿqūbī, *Taʾrīkh*, II 152; al-Masʿūdī, *Murūj*, 3634; Ibn ʿAsākir, *TMD*, Vol. 63, 207 & 208; Ibn al-Athīr, *al-Kāmil*, III 514; Ibn Kathīr, *Bidāyah*, VIII 81.

28 Ibn ʿAsākir, *TMD*, Vol. 40, 22 & 23.

29 Ibn Khayyāṭ, *Taʾrīkh*, I 214; al-Yaʿqūbī, *Taʾrīkh*, II 152; al-Ṭabarī, *Taʾrīkh*, II 181 & 188; al-Masʿūdī, *Murūj*, 3634; Ibn ʿAsākir, *TMD*, Vol. 63, 207 & 208.

30 Al-Yaʿqūbī, *Taʾrīkh*, II 152; al-Ṭabarī, *Taʾrīkh*, II 195; al-Masʿūdī, *Murūj*, 3634; Ibn ʿAsākir, *TMD*, Vol. 40, 23.

31 Ibn ʿAsākir, *TMD*, Vol. 63, 208; al-Dhahabī, *Taʾrīkh*, II 266.

32 Ibn Khayyāṭ, *Taʾrīkh*, I 216.

33 Lapidus, "The Separation of State and Religion in the Development of Early Islamic Society", 364.

The new caliph introduced a number of far-reaching changes: he was the first of the Prophet's successors to receive the oath of allegiance, the *bay'ah*, outside the Ḥijāz;[34] he relied for support on the pre-Islamic Meccan aristocracy rather than the Islamocracy of Medina;[35] and he made Syria the seat of political power.[36]

Yet there was also a degree of continuity with the practices of his predecessors as Mu'āwiyah re-instated the practice of caliphal leadership of the *ḥajj*. His caliphate covered twenty *ḥajj* seasons, two of which he led in person: 44/665 and 50/670-671 or 51/671. He also performed the *'umrah* once. By doing so, he achieved two goals at once: he satisfied his religious obligation as a Muslim to perform the fifth pillar of the faith and he succeeded in placing himself firmly in the footsteps of the Prophet.

This latter point is worth examining because Mu'āwiyah is often depicted negatively in Muslim tradition, seen as less Muslim than some of his contemporaries because of his late conversion, but such a view often obscures the relationship which later developed between Muḥammad and Mu'āwiyah.[37] The Prophet appointed him his secretary,[38] a position of considerable trust, and Mu'āwiyah requested that when he died, he be buried along with the relics of the Prophet (a shirt and nail clippings) he had gathered during the time he worked with him.[39] It may not, therefore, be unreasonable to suggest that Mu'āwiyah, once caliph, was no different from his *Rāshidūn* counterparts in wishing to create a sense of continuity with the Prophet by emulating his leadership of the pilgrimage.

Leading the *ḥajj* also linked Mu'āwiyah to those of his *Rāshidūn* predecessors with whom he wished to be associated politically. Of these caliphs only Mu'āwiyah's rival 'Alī, preoccupied as he was by the fight to enforce his authority, did not lead the ritual. Mu'āwiyah's leadership of the pilgrimage in emulation of what the Prophet, Abū Bakr, 'Umar, and 'Uthmān had done, implied that 'Alī – rather than Mu'āwiyah – was the political interloper.

Mu'āwiyah reinstated another caliphal practice for the *ḥajj*: he, like 'Umar and 'Uthmān before him, adopted a policy of patronage for the Holy

34 Al-Ṭabarī, *Ta'rīkh*, II 4-5; Hoyland, *Seeing Islam*, 136 & 138; Hitti, *History*, 189.

35 Wellhausen, *Arab Kingdom*, 61-62; Hawting, *First Dynasty*, 31-32.

36 Blankinship, *Jihad*, 24; Hoyland, *Seeing Islam*, 136.

37 Al-Balādhurī, *Ansāb*, IV A 1; Ibn Kathīr, *Bidāyah*, VIII 20-21 & 117; Hawting, *First Dynasty*, 23; Kennedy, *Prophet*, 82; Blankinship, *Jihad*, 24.

38 Kennedy, *Prophet*, 82 & 84; Robinson, *'Abd al-Malik*, 64-65.

39 Al-Ṭabarī, *Ta'rīkh*, II 201; Hawting, *First Dynasty*, 44.

Places.[40] He had the Kaʿbah draped in silk brocade[41] – a practice future caliphs would also endorse – and provided slaves to guard it.[42]

Thus Muʿāwiyah's caliphate, in spite of the new political centre of gravity in Syria, did not see an abandonment of the rituals which required the Ḥijāz as their backdrop.

Where, however, Muʿāwiyah's *ḥajj* policy differed from that of his predecessors was the number of times he led the pilgrimage. On average, he did so once a decade. Based as he was outside the Ḥijāz, a significantly greater effort was required for him to travel to Mecca than for caliphs resident in Medina. In addition to the six days of the rituals themselves, as well as the time needed to make a visit, *ziyārah*, to Medina, Muʿāwiyah would have needed up to thirty days to reach the Ḥijāz and the same for the return journey. Once there, his stay would most likely have been extended beyond the days allocated for the religious rites so he could meet members of the local elite. Up to three months may therefore have been required for him to perform the *ḥajj*, a significant amount of time for a ruling caliph to be absent from his geographical power base. Within this context, the relevant question may not be why Muʿāwiyah led the *ḥajj* less often than his Ḥijāz-based predecessors but why this caliph chose to base himself outside the Ḥijāz.

The answer was a simple one of power and politics. Muʿāwiyah had governed Syria since ʿUmar's caliphate and built up a considerable power base in the province during that time.[43] He may therefore have judged it politically expedient to rule from, and receive provincial governors on, "home" territory rather than in Mecca as ʿUmar and ʿUthmān had done.

More importantly, perhaps, for someone who lacked the *sābiqah* which many in Mecca and Medina possessed in abundance, Syria was a province that was predominantly non-Muslim: there, Muslims were the ruling elite who governed the non-Muslim masses. In such a place, Muʿāwiyah was not as likely to face so many uncomfortable questions about his late conversion and his legitimacy to rule as he would have done in the Ḥijāz, the home of the original Islamocracy and, thus, of the caliph's political opponents. Medina was, after all, unique amongst the cities of Islam: its people alone had been conquered by the Qur'ān.[44] But the new leader of the Muslim

---

40 Peters, *Mecca*, 96-97.

41 Al-Yaʿqūbī, *Taʾrīkh*, II 150.

42 Al-Yaʿqūbī, *Taʾrīkh*, II 150.

43 Al-Balādhurī, *Futūḥ*, 141, & *Ansāb*, IV A 11 & 127; Hawting, *First Dynasty*, 23-24 & 28; Kennedy, *Prophet*, 82.

44 Al-Balādhurī, *Futūḥ*, 7.

community had not been one of them; a fact he was reminded of during his first *ḥajj* as caliph in 44/665 when he was said to have spoken rudely to the *Anṣār* (*aghlaẓa lahum fi'l-qawl*) who responded by reminding him of their role at the Battle of Badr when they fought on the Prophet's side and he had not.[45]

Mu'āwiyah's political legitimacy was a recurrent theme during his first caliphal *ḥajj* and he seemed keen to use his display of piety in the birth place of the faith to reinforce his political authority. He did not limit his attention to the sacred sites but found the time to pay homage to the Umayyad family's political martyr, 'Uthmān, by visiting his house.[46] This visit was a more overtly political act than it may first appear as 'Uthmān's house was one of the criticisms levelled against him by his opponents. Mu'āwiyah's decision to visit it during his *ḥajj* was therefore a display of allegiance to the murdered caliph.[47]

Such veneration of 'Uthmān would continue throughout Mu'āwiyah's caliphate and become a recurring theme of Umayyad political discourse. It was more than respect for a deceased relative; it was a way to demonstrate publicly the moral legitimacy which formed the basis of his family's authority.[48]

The memory of 'Uthmān would again feature prominently when Mu'āwiyah made his second *ḥajj* several years later. It was during this *ḥajj* that Mu'āwiyah ordered the removal of the Prophet's pulpit to Syria. He was reported as saying he did not think the Prophet's *minbar* and staff, *'aṣā*, should remain in the city whose people were responsible for murdering 'Uthmān.[49]

These words, if accurately reported, are significant for two reasons. First, they again demonstrate the caliph's connection with 'Uthmān and his personal feelings about the inhabitants of the city which witnessed his kinsman's murder. They also show those feelings had not changed from the time of his first *ḥajj* when he met the Banū Hāshim and curtly informed them: "You killed 'Uthmān."[50]

Secondly, the caliph's words indicate his understanding of the power to be derived from objects associated with the Prophet. By delivering the *khuṭbah* from the Prophet's pulpit, Mu'āwiyah could project a powerful visual image of himself as the legitimate heir to the Prophet's authority.

45 Al-Ya'qūbī, *Ta'rīkh*, II 132.
46 Ibn Kathīr, *Bidāyah*, VIII 132.
47 Al-Ya'qūbī, *Ta'rīkh*, II 70.
48 Wellhausen, *Arab Kingdom*, 135; Crone, *Medieval Islamic Political Thought*, 34.
49 Al-Ṭabari, *Ta'rīkh*, II 92. Al-Ya'qūbī, *Ta'rīkh*, II 150; al-Mas'ūdī, *Murūj*, 1823.
50 Al-Ya'qūbī, *Ta'rīkh*, II 131.

And there were the politics of prayer to consider: cursing ʿAlī during public prayers was a key plank of Umayyad political strategy and Muʿāwiyah often took advantage of the *khuṭbah* to condemn him.[51] If he moved the Prophet's pulpit to Syria, he could undermine his arch rival and reinforce his own authority by railing against him from the very pulpit used by the founder of the faith. In the end, the plan proved too sensitive for the residents of the Prophet's City and the caliph was obliged to change his mind.[52]

What, perhaps, was most significant about Muʿāwiyah's second *ḥajj* was its timing. It took place the year before – or the year after – a *ḥajj* led by his son Yazīd. The motivation for this sequencing of pilgrimages was, as will be shown below, entirely political.

POLITICAL CHOREOGRAPHY: THE *ḤAJJ* OF THE CALIPH'S SUCCESSOR SON

Muʿāwiyah's appointment of his son Yazīd to lead the *ḥajj* was the first time a caliph had asked such a close member of his family to lead the pilgrimage.[53] Yazīd's leadership of the ritual was a pretext for Muʿāwiyah to set another new precedent: the nomination of this same son to be his heir.[54] The concept of a caliph designating his own successor was not, in itself, new. Abū Bakr had done so when he appointed ʿUmar b. al-Khaṭṭāb to be caliph after him.[55] Muʿāwiyah's innovation lay in the nature of his choice. By selecting his son to be the next Commander of the Faithful, Muʿāwiyah left himself open to the charge that he had turned the caliphate into a *mulk*, monarchy.[56] In the words of one of his detractors, ʿAbd Allāh b. ʿUmar: "There were caliphs before you who had sons ... and they did not see in their sons what you see in yours."[57]

Muʿāwiyah's determination to nominate his son was a double blow to those Muslims who had never been particularly enthusiastic about his

51 Al-Ṭabarī, *Taʾrīkh*, II 111-112, where the caliph instructs his governor of al-Kūfah to curse ʿAlī and praise ʿUthmān.

52 Al-Ṭabarī, *Taʾrīkh*, II 92.

53 *EI* 2nd edition, s.v. Yazīd b. Muʿāwiya.

54 Al-Zubayrī, *Nasab Quraish*, 127; Ibn Khayyāṭ, *Taʾrīkh*, I 196 & 199-205; al-Ṭabarī, *Taʾrīkh*, II 173-177 & 196; al-Masʿūdī, *Murūj*, 1829; Ibn Khaldūn, *Muqaddimah*, 206 & 210; Wellhausen, *Arab Kingdom*, 133; Hodgson, *Venture of Islam*, Vol. 1 219; Hitti, *History*, 196; Robinson, *ʿAbd al-Malik*, 19.

55 Al-Zubayrī, *Nasab Quraish*, 104; al-Yaʿqūbī, *Taʾrīkh*, II 24; al-Māwardī, *Aḥkām*, 10; Ibn Khaldūn, *Muqaddimah*, 210; Madelung, *Succession*, 55-56.

56 Ibn Kathīr, *Bidāyah*, VIII 19; Hawting, *First Dynasty*, 43; Kennedy, *Prophet*, 88; Madelung, *Succession*, 326; Hitti, *History*, 197-198.

57 Ibn Khayyāṭ, *Taʾrīkh*, I 199.

assumption of the caliphate. For, not only did he seem intent on restricting power to his direct descendants, he also seemed intent on restricting how that decision was to be reached. The process of *shūrā*, consultation, the method considered by many early Muslims as the most suitable for choosing a leader, was to be cast aside in favour of the personal choice of one man.[58]

From the caliph's point of view, opposition to his plans came from the usual suspects: members of the Ḥijāz-based early Islamic elite whose influence had been eclipsed by Mu'āwiyah's rise to power. But because of their standing in the community – they were members of the Prophet's family (Ibn 'Abbās), descendants of early converts ('Abd Allāh b. al-Zubayr), and the sons of former caliphs ('Abd al-Raḥmān b. Abī Bakr, 'Abd Allāh b. 'Umar and al-Ḥusayn b. 'Alī) – their views could not be easily cast aside.[59] Mu'āwiyah had to bring them on board or secure Yazīd's nomination amongst the wider community and leave them isolated in their opposition.

To prepare the groundwork for Yazīd's nomination as his heir, Mu'āwiyah needed to raise his son's political profile.[60] The *ḥajj*, as a high-profile public religious ceremony and a mobile representation of caliphal power deployed in the worship of God, was an ideal way for the caliph's chosen successor to appear in a position of leadership. Mu'āwiyah appointed Yazīd to lead it in 50/670-671 or 51/671. The *ṣā'ifah*, the summer campaign against the Byzantines, was another representation of caliphal power and Yazīd was appointed to lead it around this time.[61]

Yazīd's rising political profile did not occur in a vacuum: the timing of his leadership of the *ḥajj* and *ṣā'ifah* appears related to the death – some say political assassination[62] – of one of the caliph's former rivals, al-Ḥasan b. 'Alī, a year or two previously: in 49/669-670 or 50/670-671.[63]

The significance of this chronology lies in what Mu'āwiyah may or may not have promised al-Ḥasan back in 41/661 when he was eager to have him depart the political stage. One of al-Ḥasan's conditions for doing so had

---

58 Al-Māwardī, *Aḥkām*, 6-8 & 10-11; Kennedy, *Prophet*, 88-89.

59 Ibn Khayyāṭ, *Ta'rīkh*, I 199-200; al-Balādhurī, *Ansāb*, IV A 122-123; al-Ya'qūbī, *Ta'rīkh*, II 138; al-Ṭabarī, *Ta'rīkh*, II 175-177; Wellhausen, *Arab Kingdom*, 141-142 & 164-165; Chejne, *Succession*, 43-44; Crone, *Medieval Islamic Political Thought*, 71-72.

60 Elad, *Medieval Jerusalem*, 149.

61 Ibn Khayyāṭ, *Ta'rīkh*, I 196; al-Ya'qūbī, *Ta'rīkh*, II 138; al-Ṭabarī, *Ta'rīkh*, II 86; al-Mas'ūdī, *Murūj*, 1819; Hoyland, *Seeing Islam*, 136; Hitti, *History*, 201.

62 Ibn al-Athīr, *al-Kāmil*, III 460; al-Dhahabī, *Ta'rīkh*, II 218; Madelung, *Succession*, 331.

63 It is not clear when al-Ḥasan died and many of the sources hedge by citing both years: Ibn Khayyāṭ, *Ta'rīkh*, I 194; al-Ya'qūbī, *Ta'rīkh*, II 133; al-Ṭabarī, *Ta'rīkh*, III 2323-24; Ibn al-Athīr, *al-Kāmil*, III 460; al-Dhahabī, *Ta'rīkh*, II 211-212 & 220; Ibn Kathīr, *Bidāyah*, VIII 33, 44-45. Al-Dīnawarī, *Akhbār*, 168, perhaps wisely, does not give a date.

reportedly been an assurance from Muʿāwiyah that the next caliph would be chosen by means of a *shūrā*.[64] With al-Ḥasan no longer around to confirm or deny the speculation over the *shūrā*, the caliph was free to prepare the way for his son's nomination as his heir.[65]

Muʿāwiyah's decision to appoint his son to lead the *ḥajj* and the *ṣā'ifah*, and in such close timing to one another, suggests an attempt to communicate a particular message to the political elite and to the wider Muslim community. This message was underlined by the caliph's decision to sequence Yazīd's leadership of the *ḥajj* with his own. Muʿāwiyah's caliphate included twenty *ḥajj* seasons, two of which he led in person and one of which he invited his son Yazīd to lead. In a caliphate which lasted so long, it was unlikely to be coincidence that Yazīd's leadership of the *ḥajj* happened within a year of his father's. For Muʿāwiyah, the idea would have been to link his son – and soon to be appointed successor – to his own authority. If leadership of the community involved leading the community in the performance of their religious rituals, the combination of the caliph and his son leading successive *ḥajj* seasons would have presented them as an indivisible political unit.[66]

Ibn Aʿtham records that Yazīd was appointed to lead the *ḥajj* the same year his father wrote to the governors of the provinces informing them of his wish to have the *bayʿah* given to his son. As a result, Yazīd's *ḥajj* became something of a public relations exercise:

> ... he (Yazīd) distributed a great deal of money (*amwāl kathīrah*) in the Holy Cities to buy (*yashtarī*) people's hearts. Then he left and people were pleased (*rāḍūna*) with him.[67]

---

64 See Ibn Aʿtham, *Futūḥ*, IV 151, 152-153, 157, 158-161 for the circumstances of his stepping aside and of the *shūrā*. Ibn Khayyāṭ, *Ta'rīkh*, I 187, gives no details of any conditions and al-Ṭabarī, *Ta'rīkh*, II 3-7, make no mention of a *shūrā*. See Madelung, *Succession*, 329-333, for an examination of how al-Ḥasan is portrayed in the sources.

65 Al-Yaʿqūbī, *Ta'rīkh*, II 138. See also Ibn Aʿtham, *Futūḥ*, IV 224, where the *bayʿah* to Yazīd comes after al-Ḥasan's death (IV 205-206), & Ibn Kathīr, *Bidāyah*, VIII 80.

66 Some sources suggest the caliph took advantage of his pilgrimage or his *ʿumrah* to have the oath of allegiance given to his son as his heir: Ibn Khayyāṭ, *Ta'rīkh*, I 199-205; Ibn Aʿtham, *Futūḥ*, IV 235-249; al-Ṭabarī, *Ta'rīkh*, II 173-177. As these sources indicate, the need to link the oath of allegiance and the pilgrimage (greater or lesser) was due to so many of the caliph's political enemies being resident in the Holy Cities and going on the pilgrimage was therefore a way to summon them to show their obedience. Al-Masʿūdī, *Murūj*, 1827-28, however, places the caliph's attempts to have his son acknowledged as his heir in 59/678-679. According to his version, the events took place in Syria rather than Arabia and involved dignitaries visiting the caliph from Iraq. A subsequent paragraph, 1830, refers to Marwān b. al-Ḥakam, the governor of Medina, and his place in the succession after Yazīd.

67 Ibn Aʿtham, *Futūḥ*, IV 224-225.

Muʿāwiyah had other sons but none of them was in the running for the succession and none of them was given leadership of the *ḥajj* or the *ṣāʾifah*.[68]

Yazīd's position in the succession was consolidated by his father's decision to concentrate leadership of the *ḥajj* during the early part of his reign within the Sufyānid branch of the ruling family. By doing so, he made sure that no potential rival to Yazīd was allowed to use the occasion of the *ḥajj* as a means of self-promotion.

THE RULING FAMILY AND LEADERSHIP OF THE *ḤAJJ*

In the early years of his caliphate, Muʿāwiyah relied on his brothers, ʿUtbah and ʿAnbasah, to lead the *ḥajj* for him.[69] Between them, they led half of the *ḥajj* seasons during Muʿāwiyah's first decade in power.

The caliph's decision to honour two of his brothers with repeated leadership of the ritual might, at first glance, seem nothing more than nepotism but placed within the context of dynastic politics, Muʿāwiyah's actions require a different interpretation. This caliph was faced with the dilemma of all political dynasties: how to build up the authority of the ruling family vis-à-vis external enemies, without allowing any part of that family to become more powerful than the ruler's own branch of it.

Such a balancing act was particularly difficult to address if the sons of the ruler in question were not yet of an age where they could reasonably participate in the process of governance. Muʿāwiyah's son and eventual successor, Yazīd, was in his mid-teens when his father became caliph.[70] At this age, Yazīd would have been considered a legal adult but the idea of sending someone so young to the Ḥijāz to lead the *ḥajj* was not feasible. Islam's old guard would have seen it as yet another insult to their position by the usurping Umayyad.

Muʿāwiyah, therefore, looked to his brothers for help. By appointing them to lead the *ḥajj*, he was able to entrench his position within the ruling family until such times as his own family – and the next generation of power holders – came of political age. By 50/670-671 or 51/671, Yazīd had reached his mid-twenties; an age when it was acceptable for him to lead the *ḥajj*. And he duly did so.

68 Al-Zubayrī, *Nasab Quraish*, 127-128; al-Yaʿqūbī, *Taʾrīkh*, II 151; al-Balādhurī, *Ansāb*, IV A 247; al-Ṭabarī, *Taʾrīkh*, II 204; Ibn al-Athīr, *al-Kāmil*, IV 10; Ibn Kathīr, *Bidāyah*, VIII 144. Ibn al-Athīr in the reference above states that one of the caliph's sons, ʿAbd Allāh, was not suitable for the caliphate; and another, ʿAbd al-Raḥmān, died young.

69 Al-Zubayrī, *Nasab Quraish*, 125 & 126.

70 According to al-Ṭabarī, he was born in 25/645-646: *Taʾrīkh*, I 2810.

This generational shift was also seen in the caliph's appointment of his nephews to lead the *ḥajj* during the second decade of his caliphate. One of ʿUtbah's sons, al-Walīd, is recorded as possibly leading all four pilgrimages from 56/676 to 59/679, while some sources cite another of the caliph's nephews, ʿUthmān b. Muḥammad b. Abī Sufyān, as leader of the *ḥajj* in 57/677 and 59/679.

In total, Muʿāwiyah appointed his immediate family (including himself) to lead eleven of his twenty *ḥajj* seasons (55 per cent); a figure which rises to twelve (60 per cent) if the caliph's intentions for the first *ḥajj* of his reign, 40/661, are taken into consideration.

That Muʿāwiyah saw leadership of the *ḥajj* as the prerogative of the Umayyad family, and especially his Sufyānid branch of it, thus seems clear from his choice of leaders for the ritual. It emerges even more clearly as a matter of policy when Ziyād b. Abīhi's request to go on the *ḥajj* – and, by implication, to lead it – is taken into consideration. For, in spite of Ziyād's loyalty to the caliph and his achievements on behalf of the Umayyads as governor of Iraq, his apparent wish to lead the *ḥajj* went unfulfilled.[71] The caliph's decision not to invite him to do so suggested that their dubious fraternal relationship had its limits.

Another event demonstrates the importance of the Umayyad family to Muʿāwiyah's *ḥajj* policy and the politics behind it: this time not by their involvement in a particular *ḥajj* but, paradoxically, by their complete lack of involvement in it.

Muʿāwiyah, as we have seen, challenged for leadership of the *ḥajj* in 39/660. That year, he sent Yazīd b. Shajarah al-Rahāwī, who was not an Umayyad, to seek leadership of the *ḥajj* on his behalf. Yazīd ultimately failed in his aim but perhaps it did not matter whether he succeeded or not; it was enough of a political victory for Muʿāwiyah that Yazīd managed to prevent his rival, ʿAlī, from having the pilgrimage led in his name.

That particular pilgrimage would be the one and only time Muʿāwiyah looked beyond the Umayyad family for a leader of the *ḥajj*. Once he was acknowledged by the *ummah* as their caliph, his political needs changed and he wanted his family to be seen in positions of leadership. But in

71 Al-Masʿūdī, *Murūj*, 1824, notes the reaction of the people of Medina to Ziyād's (proposed) governorship of the Holy City. See also al-Yaʿqūbī, *Taʾrīkh*, II 139. Ibn al-Athīr, *al-Kāmil*, III 445 & 493, also notes his wish to govern the Holy Cities and lead the pilgrimage. The language used by Ibn al-Athīr is not that specifically associated with leadership of the ritual but that of performing it. It may, however, have been understood that if a senior political figure – and also a "relative" of the caliph – asked to go on the pilgrimage, he would have been appointed to lead it.

39/660, when he was still in the process of securing the caliphate, it was more expedient to have someone else take the political risks in public. That way, in the event of failure, the blame would not fall within Mu'āwiyah's immediate circle.

LEADING THE *ḤAJJ* BY PROXY: THE GOVERNORSHIP OF MEDINA AND THE POLITICS OF MARTYRDOM

All of Mu'āwiyah's governors of the City of the Prophet were Umayyads. By making this governorship the exclusive preserve of the ruling clan, he hoped to ensure that Umayyad interests were defended in a city which did not always see its interests reflected in those of the ruling elite. He increased the prestige of the position by asking the city's governor to lead the *ḥajj* on a regular basis: around half the *ḥajj* seasons in Mu'āwiyah's reign were led by his governors of Medina.[72]

In this way, he managed to preserve a sense of historical continuity with the Prophet and the first three caliphs, all of whom had set out from this city to lead the pilgrimage.

Two men would become synonymous with the governorship of Medina during Mu'āwiyah's caliphate, his cousins Marwān b. al-Ḥakam and Sa'īd b. al-'Āṣ.[73] They occupied the position on an alternate basis for nearly the whole of Mu'āwiyah's caliphate; their combined governorships running from 42/662-663 to 57/677.[74]

Marwān became governor in 42/662-663,[75] remained in the position until 48/668[76] or 49/669,[77] and led the *ḥajj* three times during his governorship. He was sacked to make way for Sa'īd b. al-'Āṣ who held the post until 54/674. Sa'īd also led the *ḥajj* on three occasions during his governorship.[78] His dismissal signalled the reinstatement of Marwān whose second stint as governor turned out to be shorter than his first.[79] It did, nevertheless, see him lead the *ḥajj* on two more occasions. But in 57/677, he was sacked by

72 Peters, *Mecca*, 96.

73 *EI*, s.v. Marwān b. al-Ḥakam & s.v. Sa'īd b. al-'Āṣ.

74 Al-Balādhurī, *Ansāb*, IV A 135.

75 Al-Ṭabarī, *Ta'rīkh*, II 16. Ibn Khayyāṭ, *Ta'rīkh*, I 189, & al-Dhahabī, *Ta'rīkh*, II 209 & III 72, place his appointment in the previous year.

76 Ibn Khayyāṭ, *Ta'rīkh*, I 193 & 217; Ibn 'Asākir, *TMD*, Vol. 21, 125, & Vol. 57, 242; al-Dhahabī, *Ta'rīkh*, II 211 & III 72.

77 Al-Ṭabarī, *Ta'rīkh*, II 87. He was out of the governorship by the time of the pilgrimage in 49/670.

78 Al-Balādhurī, *Ansāb*, IV B 130.

79 Ibn Khayyāṭ, *Ta'rīkh*, I 210 & 217; al-Ṭabarī, *Ta'rīkh*, II 164; Ibn 'Asākir, *TMD*, Vol. 21, 125.

the caliph for the second time.[80] His replacement on this occasion was not, as history might have suggested, Sa'īd b. al-'Āṣ (he died around this time),[81] but the caliph's nephew, al-Walīd b. 'Utbah b. Abī Sufyān.[82] He, too, would lead the *ḥajj* on a number of occasions.

Why Mu'āwiyah chose these men to govern Medina, and Marwān and Sa'īd in particular, owed much to the political circumstances of the time. Marwān and Sa'īd had something in common which Mu'āwiyah recognized as politically useful: they were both related to the murdered caliph 'Uthmān. Marwān was 'Uthmān's cousin;[83] had served as his *kātib*, secretary;[84] was married to one of 'Uthmān's daughters;[85] and his father al-Ḥakam had been brought back from exile by 'Uthmān.[86] Perhaps most importantly of all, Marwān was one of the few to stay with 'Uthmān on the *Yawm al-Dār*, the day the caliph was killed.[87] Sa'īd's relationship with 'Uthmān also went beyond descent:[88] he had served as his governor of al-Kūfah.[89] And he, like Marwān, had been with 'Uthmān on the *Yawm al-Dār*.[90]

Vengeance for 'Uthmān was Mu'āwiyah's rallying cry in his quest to win the caliphate. Once he secured it, the memory of the Umayyads' political martyr provided him with the ideology to underpin his power and 'Uthmān was transformed into the Umayyads' legitimizing device *par excellence* as Mu'āwiyah sought to justify his authority in the name of his murdered kinsman.

For this to retain its potency as a propaganda tool, it had to be repeatedly demonstrated. One strategy Mu'āwiyah adopted was to curse 'Uthmān's rival, 'Alī, on a regular basis during the *khuṭbah*.[91] Another was his choice

80 Ibn Khayyāṭ, *Ta'rīkh*, I 213 & 217; al-Ṭabarī, *Ta'rīkh*, II 180; Ibn 'Asākir, *TMD*, Vol. 57, 242, & Vol. 63, 208.

81 According to al-Dhahabī, *Ta'rīkh*, II 265 & 289, he died in this year. However, he also places his death a year later (II 289) and two years later (II 266 & 289). See also Ibn Khayyāṭ, *Ta'rīkh*, I 215; al-Balādhurī, *Ansāb*, IV B 130; Ibn Kathīr, *Bidāyah*, VIII 83 & 87.

82 Al-Zubayrī, *Nasab Quraish*, 132 & 133; Ibn Khayyāṭ, *Ta'rīkh*, I 213; al-Ṭabarī, *Ta'rīkh*, II 180; Ibn 'Asākir, *TMD*, Vol. 57, 242, & Vol. 63, 207-208.

83 'Uthmān's father, 'Affān, and Marwān's father, al-Ḥakam, were brothers: al-Zubayrī, *Nasab Quraish*, 100. Marwān and the current caliph shared a great-grandfather in Umayyah: *Nasab Quraish*, 98, 100 & 121, 123-124, 159.

84 Al-Jahshiyārī, *Kitāb al-wuzarā'*, 21.

85 Al-Ya'qūbī, *Ta'rīkh*, II 60.

86 Al-Ya'qūbī, *Ta'rīkh*, II 71.

87 Ibn Khayyāṭ, *Ta'rīkh*, I 152.

88 Al-Zubayrī, *Nasab Quraish*, 98-99 & 176; al-Dhahabī, *Ta'rīkh*, II 287.

89 Al-Zubayrī, *Nasab Quraish*, 176; al-Balādhurī, *Ansāb*, IV A 39-43 & B 130; Ibn 'Asākir, *TMD*, Vol. 21, 107; al-Dhahabī, *Ta'rīkh*, II 287.

90 Al-Dhahabī, *Ta'rīkh*, II 287.

91 While governor of Medina, Marwān was said to have cursed 'Alī whereas Sa'īd did not: al-Dhahabī, *Ta'rīkh*, II 288 & III 72; Ibn Kathīr, *Bidāyah*, VIII 84.

of governor for the city which had witnessed 'Uthmān's murder. And so, for nearly fifteen years of his reign, Mu'āwiyah relied on two men who were closely related to 'Uthmān to govern Medina. In doing so, he effectively made Marwān and Sa'īd the living embodiment of the ideology underpinning his rule.

It was a point the caliph chose not to limit to Medina. By appointing Marwān and Sa'īd to lead the *ḥajj* for him, and on such a recurrent basis, Mu'āwiyah was able to communicate his message to the cross-section of the Muslim community gathered in Mecca for their pilgrimage.

However, the very reasons which made Marwān and Sa'īd useful to Mu'āwiyah also gave him cause for concern. Marwān and Sa'īd were with 'Uthmān to the bitter end on the *Yawm al-Dār*, whereas Mu'āwiyah was nowhere to be seen. If 'Uthmān's fate provided the legitimacy for Umayyad rule, then the political claims of men who had stayed with him right to the end could be considered more valid than the current caliph's. Or his son's.[92] While Mu'āwiyah was content to use their political merits to legitimize his own authority, he had no wish to see them use their position as a springboard to further their own careers. His aim in rotating so prestigious a governorship as that of the Prophet's City – and leadership of the *ḥajj* – between the two of them was one of the oldest political tricks in the book: to divide and conquer.

He executed this strategy in several ways. When Sa'īd was governor, the caliph wrote to him ordering him to demolish Marwān's house. Sa'īd refused and the refusal was said to have cost him his job.[93] He was also ordered to confiscate Marwān's property but declined on the grounds of their close kinship. He wisely decided to keep all the correspondence he received from the caliph on this matter.[94]

Marwān, when re-instated as governor, found himself on the receiving end of similar orders from the caliph. His reaction, however, was different from Sa'īd's and he agreed to the caliph's request.[95] It was only when Marwān went to carry out the caliph's orders and Sa'īd produced Mu'āwiyah's letters that the two men realized what was going on. Indignant, Sa'īd wrote to the caliph to complain.[96] But Mu'āwiyah was unmoved. To keep these men

92 Hammarneh, "Marwan b. al-Hakam and the Caliphate", 205-206.

93 Al-Balādhurī, *Ansāb*, IV A 25; al-Ṭabarī, *Ta'rīkh*, II 164; Hammarneh, "Marwan b. al-Hakam and the Caliphate", 205.

94 Al-Balādhurī, *Ansāb*, IV A 25; al-Ṭabarī, *Ta'rīkh*, II 164.

95 Al-Ṭabarī, *Ta'rīkh*, II 164.

96 Al-Ṭabarī, *Ta'rīkh*, II 164-165.

unsure of their positions and suspicious of one another was in his long-term interests, as the timing of these incidents indicates: they occurred against the backdrop of Muʿāwiyah's promotion of his son Yazīd as his successor.[97]

The caliph's canvassing on behalf of his son did not stop there. Nor did his double-dealing. One report suggests he went so far as to offer Marwān the position of Yazīd's heir. Marwān was said to have travelled to Syria to discuss the matter with the caliph, only to find upon his return to the Ḥijāz that he had lost the governorship of the Holy City for the second time.[98]

This sacking reportedly happened in 57/677, the same year the caliph removed another of his son's potential rivals from an important governorship. The man in question was Saʿīd, a son of none other than the Umayyad martyr figure ʿUthmān, and the governorship that of the strategically vital province of Khurāsān.[99]

Perhaps the way Saʿīd had played upon his family connections to secure the appointment in the first place had given Muʿāwiyah reason to worry over his longer-term ambitions. In addition to lobbying for the governorship, Saʿīd told Muʿāwiyah in no uncertain terms that he was more worthy of the caliphate than Yazīd would ever be.[100] The challenge veiled in his words was not lost on the caliph and he consented to Saʿīd's request for the governorship.

But in 57/677, the year after Muʿāwiyah had secured sufficient support for Yazīd's succession, he dispensed with Saʿīd in Khurāsān and Marwān in Medina in favour of men of less independent political inclination: Marwān was replaced by the caliph's nephew, al-Walīd b. ʿUtbah, and Saʿīd by the caliph's pseudo-nephew, ʿUbayd Allāh b. Ziyād.[101] The double sacking suggesting that the caliph no longer felt the need to appease either man politically.

The experiences of Muʿāwiyah's governors of Medina show that, important though their position was, occupancy of this governorship did not always translate into leadership of the *ḥajj*.

There were, for example, several occasions during Marwān's two governorships when the caliph did not invite him to lead it. During the first governorship (42/662-663 to 49/669), Muʿāwiyah gave leadership of the ritual

97 Ibn Khayyāṭ, *Taʾrīkh*, I 199-205; al-Ṭabarī, *Taʾrīkh*, II 173-177.
98 Al-Masʿūdī, *Murūj*, 1830.
99 Al-Dhahabī, *Taʾrīkh*, II 265.
100 Al-Ṭabarī, *Taʾrīkh*, II 177. For Saʿīd's appointment to the governorship, see al-Balādhurī, *Ansāb*, V 118; Ibn Aʿtham, *Futūḥ*, IV 184-185; Ibn Kathīr, *Bidāyah*, VIII 78. For his descent, see al-Zubayrī, *Nasab Quraish*, 104.
101 Ibn Khayyāṭ, *Taʾrīkh*, I 213; al-Dhahabī, *Taʾrīkh*, II 265.

to prominent members of his own Sufyānid family: to his brothers 'Anbasah or 'Utbah (42/663, 46/667 and 47/668), and in 44/665 he led it himself.

This pattern was repeated during Marwān's second term as governor (54/674 to 57/677). 56/676 was the one year of this governorship when Marwān did not lead the *ḥajj*. That year, the caliph appointed his nephew al-Walīd b. 'Utbah to lead it for him.

Sa'īd fared no differently. His term ran from 49/669 to 54/674, during which he led the *ḥajj* three times. The two years when he was not invited to lead it, 50/670-671 and 51/671, it was the most senior Sufyānids of all who did so: the caliph and his successor son.

Al-Walīd's situation as governor was slightly different from Marwān's and Sa'īd's. As one of the caliph's nephews, he was more closely related to the caliph; yet even he does not seem to have led all the *ḥajj* seasons of his governorship. He was still governor of Medina during what would turn out to be the last *ḥajj* season of Mu'āwiyah's reign, 59/679, leadership of which the caliph may have given to another of his nephews: 'Uthmān b. Muḥammad b. Abī Sufyān.[102]

The men who led the *ḥajj* for the caliph thus fall into two groups: those who led it because of their relationship to the caliph and those who did so because they occupied the governorship of Medina.

All were Umayyads but the latter group were not as closely related to the caliph as the former and were not therefore as close to the political centre. Marwān and Sa'īd were figures of some standing within the Umayyad family but when it came to leadership of one of the most important religious rituals, the caliph gave precedence to his brothers, his successor son, and his nephews over his official representative in the Holy City.

What Mu'āwiyah's pattern of *ḥajj* leadership shows is that he did not wish his governors in Medina, particularly Marwān and Sa'īd, to become too comfortable in their positions because the branch of the Umayyad family which mattered most to him was his own.

CONSPICUOUS BY THEIR ABSENCE: WHO DID NOT LEAD THE *ḤAJJ*

Mu'āwiyah's pattern of appointments for leadership of the *ḥajj* reveals a great deal about how he understood his power. It also gives an insight into the ideology underpinning his legitimacy and indicates who he relied upon

102 For his descent, see al-Zubayrī, *Nasab Quraish*, 134.

to support him politically. But as well as noting who did lead the *ḥajj* for Muʿāwiyah, it is also worth noting who did *not*, as this too sheds light on how he interpreted his authority.

He did not turn to any of the Islamic old guard. No goodwill gesture was made to the *Anṣār*, the *Ṣaḥābah* or the Prophet's family. And they were not alone. No sons of former caliphs were invited to lead the *ḥajj*. Not even one of the sons of the Umayyad martyr *par excellence,* ʿUthmān. Likewise, no *ashrāf*, tribal leaders, and no military men were called upon to present themselves in Mecca.[103] Nor were any governors of strategically important provinces; not even the caliph's "brother" Ziyād b. Abīhi, who governed Iraq.

What these men had in common was an ability to access a power base or constituency independent of the caliph. As such, there was little chance Muʿāwiyah would have invited any of them onto a platform as high-profile as the *ḥajj*.

Only one *ḥajj* in Muʿāwiyah's caliphate – the first – was not led by a member of the Umayyad family. In 40/661, the caliph appointed his brother ʿUtbah to lead the ritual but before ʿUtbah could reach the Holy City, al-Mughīrah b. Shuʿbah, a governor in Iraq who happened to be in the Ḥijāz at the time, took advantage of his presence on the ground and led the pilgrimage on a forged authorization.[104] Knowing the caliph's brother was on his way, al-Mughīrah was said to have rushed through some of the rituals in order to complete the pilgrimage before his rival's imminent arrival.[105] As for the caliph, he did not allow leadership of the *ḥajj* to fall outside the Umayyad family again.

And perhaps most importantly of all, this caliph, like his four predecessors, did not appoint any religious figure to lead the *ḥajj*; showing that he, like the *Rāshidūn* before him, saw the *ḥajj* as a religious ritual which required political leadership.

103 For the role of the *ashrāf* in the Sufyānid polity, see Hawting, *First Dynasty*, 36; Crone, *Slaves on Horses*, 29-33.

104 Ibn Khayyāṭ, *Taʾrīkh*, I 187; al-Ṭabarī, *Taʾrīkh*, II 4; al-Masʿūdī, *Murūj*, 3632; al-Fāsī, *Akhbār Makkah* II 235. The verb used is *iftaʿala*: to forge, falsify or fabricate.

105 Al-Ṭabarī, *Taʾrīkh*, II 4.

FOUR

The Caliphate in Transition: The *Ḥajj* as a Barometer of Political Change

Yazīd b. Mu'āwiyah became caliph in 60/680 and his caliphate covered four *ḥajj* seasons: from 60/680 to 63/683. Political consensus proved elusive for him and his authority was challenged on more than one occasion at the *ḥajj*. He eventually lost control of it to 'Abd Allāh bin al-Zubayr in 63/683. But he, too, would discover what it was like to be challenged at the *ḥajj*: it happened to him in 68/688. Table 3 shows who led the *ḥajj* during these politically turbulent years.

Table 3

Year	***Ḥajj leader***	***Relationship to caliph***	***Governor of Medina?***
60/680	'Amr b. Sa'īd b. al-'Āṣ[1]	cousin	yes
61/681	al-Walīd b. 'Utbah b. Abī Sufyān[2]	cousin	yes

1 Ibn Khayyāṭ, *Ta'rīkh*, I 221, 224 & 249; al-Ya'qūbī, *Ta'rīkh*, II 169; al-Ṭabarī, *Ta'rīkh*, II 295; al-Mas'ūdī, *Murūj*, 3634; Ibn 'Asākir, *TMD* Vol. 46, 36 & 37, & Vol. 63, 207.

2 Ibn Khayyāṭ, *Ta'rīkh*, I 225 & 249; al-Ya'qūbī, *Ta'rīkh*, II 169; al-Ṭabarī, *Ta'rīkh*, II 399; al-Mas'ūdī, *Murūj*, 3635; Ibn 'Asākir, *TMD*, Vol. 40, 23, & Vol. 63, 208.

62/682	al-Walīd[3] *or* 'Uthmān b. Muḥammad b. Abī Sufyān[4] ***Also seeking leadership:*** 'Abd Allāh b. al-Zubayr;[5] Najdah b. 'Āmir[6]	cousin cousin Both saw the caliphate as theirs	yes x x x
63/683	'Abd Allāh b. al-Zubayr[7]	alternative caliph	x
64/684	'Abd Allāh b. al-Zubayr[8] *or* Yaḥyā b. Ṣafwān[9]	alternative caliph x	- x
65/685	'Abd Allāh b. al-Zubayr[10]	alternative caliph	-
66/686	'Abd Allāh b. al-Zubayr[11] ***Also seeking leadership:*** Ibn al-Ḥanafiyyah; Najdah b. 'Āmir; the Banū Umayyah[12]	alternative caliph All three saw the caliphate as theirs	x x x x

3 Ibn Khayyāṭ, *Ta'rīkh*, I 249; al-Ya'qūbī, *Ta'rīkh*, II 169; al-Ṭabarī, *Ta'rīkh*, II 405; al-Mas'ūdī, *Murūj*, 3635; Ibn 'Asākir, *TMD*, Vol. 40, 23, & Vol. 63, 208.
4 Ibn Khayyāṭ, *Ta'rīkh*, I 227; al-Dhahabī, *Ta'rīkh*, II 353.
5 Al-Ṭabarī, *Ta'rīkh*, II 402.
6 Al-Ṭabarī, *Ta'rīkh*, II 402.
7 Ibn Khayyāṭ, *Ta'rīkh*, I 245 & 249; al-Ya'qūbī, *Ta'rīkh*, II 187; al-Ṭabarī, *Ta'rīkh*, II 422; al-Mas'ūdī, *Murūj*, 3635; Ibn 'Asākir, *TMD*, Vol. 28, 212.
8 Ibn Khayyāṭ, *Ta'rīkh*, I 248 & 249; al-Ya'qūbī, *Ta'rīkh*, II 187; al-Ṭabarī, *Ta'rīkh*, II 537; al-Mas'ūdī, *Murūj*, 3635; Ibn 'Asākir, *TMD*, Vol. 28, 212 & 213.
9 Al-Ya'qūbī, *Ta'rīkh*, II 187.
10 Ibn Khayyāṭ, *Ta'rīkh*, I 249 & 257; al-Ya'qūbī, *Ta'rīkh*, II 187; al-Ṭabarī, *Ta'rīkh*, II 592-593; al-Mas'ūdī, *Murūj*, 3635; Ibn 'Asākir, *TMD*, Vol. 28, 212 & 213.
11 Ibn Khayyāṭ, *Ta'rīkh*, I 249 & 259; al-Ya'qūbī, *Ta'rīkh*, II 187; al-Ṭabarī, *Ta'rīkh*, II 700; al-Mas'ūdī, *Murūj*, 3635; Ibn 'Asākir, *TMD*, Vol. 28, 212 & 213.
12 Al-Fāsī, *Akhbār Makkah*, II 235. For Najdah's pilgrimage, see also Ibn Khayyāṭ, *Ta'rīkh*, I 260.

67/687	'Abd Allāh b. al-Zubayr[13]	alternative caliph	-
68/688	'Abd Allāh b. al-Zubayr[14] ***Also seeking leadership:*** Banū Umayyah; Muḥammad b. al-Ḥanafiyyah; Najdah b. 'Āmir[15]	alternative caliph All three saw the caliphate as theirs	- x x x

YAZĪD AND LEADERSHIP OF THE *ḤAJJ*: THE *ḤARAM* AS AN IDEOLOGICAL BATTLEGROUND

Two very different policies for the *ḥajj* were in evidence during the decade of the 60s/680s, representing two very different visions for the caliphate: that of the Umayyad caliph, Yazīd, and that of 'Abd Allāh b. al-Zubayr, who successfully rebelled against him.[16]

The decade began with the *ḥajj* under the control of Syrian-based Yazīd b. Mu'āwiyah. He maintained continuity with his father's policies by following Mu'āwiyah's practice of appointing Umayyads to the governorship of Medina. Yazīd's governors were his cousins al-Walīd b. 'Utbah and 'Amr b. Sa'īd b. al-'Āṣ, both of whom had prior connections to the politics of the Ḥijāz and the pilgrimage: al-Walīd had led the ritual for Mu'āwiyah, as had 'Amr's father, Sa'īd, the former governor of Medina.

The sense of continuity from father to son was, however, not without its problems. Yazīd was the first ruler in Islam to inherit power from his father but he also inherited his father's unresolved political problems. His first concern as caliph, therefore, was to receive the *bay'ah*, the oath of allegiance, from those who had previously withheld it.[17] But the men who had not felt

13 Ibn Khayyāṭ, *Ta'rīkh*, I 249 & 260; al-Ya'qūbī, *Ta'rīkh*, II 187; al-Ṭabarī, *Ta'rīkh*, II 752; al-Mas'ūdī, *Murūj*, 3635; Ibn 'Asākir, *TMD*, Vol. 28, 212 & 213.

14 Ibn Khayyāṭ, *Ta'rīkh*, I 249 & 261; al-Mas'ūdī, *Murūj*, 3635; Ibn 'Asākir, *TMD*, Vol. 28, 212 & 213; al-Dhahabī, *Ta'rīkh*, III 171; al-Fāsī, *Akhbār Makkah*, II 235.

15 Al-Ya'qūbī, *Ta'rīkh*, II 187; al-Ṭabarī, *Ta'rīkh*, II 781-783.

16 *EI* 2nd edition, s.v. 'Abd Allāh b. al-Zubayr.

17 Al-Balādhurī, *Ansāb*, IV B 12-13; al-Ṭabarī, *Ta'rīkh*, II 216-217.

inclined to acknowledge Yazīd as heir apparent during his father's lifetime felt even less inclined to do so upon his passing. They viewed the transition of power from father to son as an opportunity to retrieve the political influence they had lost. As these men were resident in the Ḥijāz and had more direct access to the Holy Cities than the caliph, the *ḥajj* during this period came to assume a political relevance of the utmost urgency.[18]

As Yazīd's first *ḥajj* season approached in 60/680, two of his main opponents, ʻAbd Allāh b. al-Zubayr and al-Ḥusayn b. ʻAlī, were holding court in the *Ḥarām*.[19] When pressed to give allegiance to Yazīd, they had preferred to make the *hijrah* in reverse and flee from Medina to the security offered by the sanctity of the Kaʻbah in Mecca, leaving Yazīd with the dilemma of how to deal with opponents who were challenging him from the very epicentre of the faith.[20] Even so senior a figure in the Umayyad family as the former governor of Medina (and future caliph) Marwān b. al-Ḥakam felt obliged to advise Yazīd's newly appointed governor of the Holy Cities, ʻAmr b. Saʻīd, not to attack the *Ḥarām* to flush out the rebels.[21] In the history of Islam, no one had ever dared violate the sanctity of the Holy Shrine. The Qur'ān was quite clear on the subject: the only justification for fighting in the Sacred Mosque was defensive.[22]

The rebels' flight from Medina to Mecca was not interpreted as a sign of their political weakness – perhaps because of the Prophet's example of *hijrah* – and residence in the Holy City had advantages for both of them. While the caliph was approximately a month's journey away in Syria, al-Ḥusayn and Ibn al-Zubayr had direct access to the travelling pilgrims as a way of spreading their message of dissent.

And al-Ḥusayn, for one, used it to broaden his range of contacts. Not only did the people of Mecca pay him regular visits, many pilgrims visiting the Holy City to perform the *ʻumrah* did likewise.[23]

Ibn al-Zubayr, for his part, settled so comfortably into his role as "the one

---

18 Hodgson, *Venture of Islam*, vol. 1, 219; Hawting, *First Dynasty*, 46; Kennedy, *Prophet*, 89.

19 *EI* 2nd edition, s.v. al-Ḥuṣayn b. ʻAlī.

20 For al-Ḥusayn in Mecca, see al-Balādhurī, *Ansāb*, IV B 15-16; Ibn Aʻtham, *Futūḥ*, V 34-37; al-Dīnawarī, *Akhbār*, 173-174; al-Yaʻqūbī, *Ta'rīkh*, II 155; al-Ṭabarī, *Ta'rīkh*, II 222-223. For Ibn al-Zubayr, see Ibn Khayyāṭ, *Ta'rīkh*, I 224; al-Balādhurī, *Ansāb*, IV B 13; Ibn Aʻtham, *Futūḥ*, V 20-21; al-Dīnawarī, *Akhbār*, 173; al-Yaʻqūbī, *Ta'rīkh*, II 161; al-Ṭabarī, *Ta'rīkh*, II 219-220. For the two of them, see Wellhausen, *Arab Kingdom*, 146; Hawting, *First Dynasty*, 47.

21 Al-Ṭabarī, *Ta'rīkh*, II 224. See also Wellhausen, *Arab Kingdom*, 147.

22 Qur'ān II, 191. As the verse suggests, their presence in Mecca was not enough to justify an attack by the caliph. From a legal standpoint, such a course of action would be feasible only if the rebels attacked first.

23 Al-Ṭabarī, *Ta'rīkh*, II 233. See also Ibn al-Athīr, *al-Kāmil*, IV 20.

who seeks refuge at the Sanctuary *(al-ʿāʾidh biʾl-bayt)*"[24] that he was reported to have stood apart from the bulk of pilgrims during the *ḥajj* of 60/680 and refused to acknowledge the caliph's appointed leader of the ritual, the governor of Medina ʿAmr b. Saʿīd.[25] His decision to pray only with his own supporters at the *ḥajj* was a calculated snub to the caliph's authority. Public prayer was more than a communal religious act; it functioned as a form of political allegiance, a means of demonstrating loyalty to the caliph. As such, Ibn al-Zubayr would not have wished to pray on behalf of a caliph whose authority he refused to recognize.

Yazīd's authority in the Ḥijāz remained sufficiently tenuous for this situation to repeat itself two years later. In 62/682, he did as he had done the year before and authorized his cousin, al-Walīd b. ʿUtbah b. Abī Sufyān, the governor of Medina, to lead the community of the faithful in the performance of this solemn obligation to God. But for Yazīd, the *ḥajj* of 62/682 did not go as planned. Instead, the *ḥajj* became an ideological battleground where Yazīd's rivals challenged his power and the *ḥajj* became the weapon through which they sought to undermine his credibility. Al-Ṭabarī:

> At the pilgrimage, al-Walīd (b. ʿUtbah b. Abī Sufyān) led the procession (*ifāḍah*) from ʿArafāt and the general body of the people (*ʿāmmah al-nās*) marched in the procession with him. Ibn al-Zubayr made the standing (*wuqūf*) with his followers (*aṣḥāb*) and Najdah made the *wuqūf* with his followers (*aṣḥāb*). Then Ibn al-Zubayr led the procession with his followers, and Najdah led the procession with his followers. None of the three groups went in the procession of the others. Najdah met Ibn al-Zubayr so frequently that the people thought he would give the oath of allegiance to him.[26]

Ibn al-Zubayr and Najdah held radically different points of view, the former espousing the politics of precedence, the latter the politics of piety, yet both set out in 62/682 with the same intention: to declare their political dissent by usurping the caliph's role at the *ḥajj*. That such a consensus could be reached from such opposing political positions suggests that, as had happened at

24 Ibn Khayyāṭ, *Taʾrīkh*, I 224; al-Ṭabarī, *Taʾrīkh*, II 422; al-Masʿūdī, *Murūj*, 1929 & 1939; Wellhausen, *Arab Kingdom*, 148; Hawting, *First Dynasty*, 47; Hoyland, *Seeing Islam*, 197; Robinson, *ʿAbd al-Malik*, 35.

25 Al-Ṭabarī, *Taʾrīkh*, II 222.

26 Al-Ṭabarī, *Taʾrīkh*, II 402; Howard, tr. *Yazīd*, 197. See also Ibn al-Athīr, *al-Kāmil*, IV 102; Ibn Kathīr, *Bidāyah*, VIII 215-216.

the *ḥajj* in 39/660, the rebels understood leadership of the *ḥajj* to equate to leadership of the community itself. Any aspirant to the caliphate was therefore obliged to seek it.

Furthermore, the fact that leadership of the *ḥajj* was appreciated to be a prerogative of power indicated that the performance of this religious ritual held a deep political significance. In the same way that participating in prayers led by the caliph, or his representative, signalled an acceptance of the political status quo, participating in a pilgrimage led by the ruling caliph, or his appointee, likewise implied a willingness to accept his political authority as legitimate.[27] For rebels and their supporters, such a display of obedience was unthinkable: if they were to acquiesce, they would undermine – in the most public way – the validity of their own rebellion. They chose, therefore, to proclaim their own authority and perform the pilgrimage under their own banners.

In doing so, they made full use of the *ḥajj* as a conduit of information in order to spread their message of disobedience. Mecca was the centre of a vast information network spanning the entire Islamic world with the travelling pilgrims acting as the lines of communication. And when these pilgrims left the Holy City to return home after the *ḥajj* of 62/682, they would take with them the impression that the caliph's authority was in crisis.

For Yazīd, as ruling caliph, this *ḥajj* was nothing short of a catastrophe. To be challenged in this particular way and at this particular time was a serious blow to his moral authority and his personal prestige. Just as the arbitration after Ṣiffīn had fatally wounded ʿAlī because it forced him to treat his opponent as an equal, Yazīd had become a caliph who had lost control of the Holiest City in Islam and who was forced to concede his privilege of sole leadership of the *ḥajj*. The only precedent for such a situation was the *ḥajj* of 39/660 when Yazīd's father had challenged ʿAlī for leadership of the pilgrimage. A year later, the caliphate was no longer ʿAlī's but Muʿāwiyah's.

Yazīd's caliphate, in fact, bore more political parallels with ʿAlī's than it did with his father's. Yazīd, like ʿAlī, came to power amidst a constitutional crisis – a crisis he failed to resolve – which compromised his legitimacy. As a result, his power was constantly under threat, particularly in the Ḥijāz, and he was never able to enjoy the degree of authority that Muʿāwiyah had. He was therefore never able to demonstrate his authority in the way that his father had.

27 For an example of a caliph encouraging political dissidents to pray with the community, and thereby acquiesce to the central political authority, see al-Ṭabarī, *Taʾrīkh*, II 27.

This was particularly evident in his approach to the *ḥajj*: he (like 'Alī) did not lead the ritual in person, relying instead on his relatives in the Ḥijāz to do so, and he (like 'Alī) did not endorse a policy of patronage for the Holy Cities in the way that his father and some of the *Rāshidūn* had done. And like 'Ali, Yazīd had to deal with internecine fighting during one of his *ḥajj* seasons: the year after the calamitous *ḥajj* of 62/682, the people of Medina expelled the caliph's recently appointed governor, 'Uthmān b. Muḥammad, publicly cast off their allegiance to the caliph and initiated a siege of the Banū Umayyah resident in the city.[28]

Yazīd had to resort to military means to enforce his political authority in the region:[29] the Battle of the Ḥarrah took place just outside the Holy City of Medina in the holy month of *Dhū al-Ḥijjah* 63/August 683.[30] It was too late for Yazīd's troops to enforce his authority at that year's *ḥajj* and the caliph had no representative at the pilgrimage in 63/683 with the result that, for the first time, Ibn al-Zubayr was able to lead it uncontested.[31] Yazīd thus became the first of the Prophet's successors to rule the caliphate without ruling the Islamic heartland of Mecca.

Yazīd's experiences in the Ḥijāz underlined the pattern which emerged during 'Alī's caliphate in relation to the display of power at the *ḥajj:* when a caliph's authority is secure – as it was for 'Umar, 'Uthmān and Mu'āwiyah – the *ḥajj* offered a high-profile platform where that authority could be demonstrated. But when a caliph's authority is under threat, the *ḥajj* risked becoming transformed into a high-profile weapon directed against the caliph, as happened to 'Alī in 39/660 and Yazīd in 60/680 and 62/682.

Events in the Ḥijāz at this time also showed the importance of neutralizing opposition there, for as soon as Ibn al-Zubayr took control of Mecca, the tactical advantage in the battle for control of the caliphate was his. Yazīd's military actions in the Ḥijāz – as well as the massacre of al-Ḥusayn b. 'Alī and his supporters at Karbalā' – gave Ibn al-Zubayr the opportunity to

---

28 Ibn Khayyāṭ, *Ta'rīkh*, I 228 & 249; Ibn A'tham, *Futūḥ*, V 290-291 & 292; al-Ya'qūbī, *Ta'rīkh*, II 164-165; al-Ṭabarī, *Ta'rīkh*, II 405 & 410; al-Mas'ūdī, *Murūj*, 1922; Ibn 'Asākir, *TMD*, Vol. 40, 24; al-Azraqī, *Akhbār Makkah*, I 139; Dixon, *Umayyad Caliphate*, 17; Hawting, *First Dynasty*, 47-48; Kennedy, *Prophet*, 90.

29 Al-Zubayrī, *Nasab Quraish*, 127; Ibn Khayyāṭ, *Ta'rīkh*, I 227-231 & 249-250; Ibn A'tham, *Futūḥ*, V 292 & 293-294; al-Dīnawarī, *Akhbār*, 196; al-Ya'qūbī, *Ta'rīkh*, II 165; al-Ṭabarī, *Ta'rīkh*, II 407-410; al-Mas'ūdī, *Murūj*, 1923, 1925 & 1929; al-Azraqī, *Akhbār Makkah*, I 139.

30 Ibn Khayyāṭ, *Ta'rīkh*, I 244-245; al-Balādhurī, *Ansāb*, IV B 31-42; Ibn A'tham, *Futūḥ*, V 294-300; al-Dīnawarī, *Akhbār*, 196-197; al-Ṭabarī, *Ta'rīkh*, II 411-423; al-Mas'ūdī, *Murūj*, 1925; al-Azraqī, *Akhbār Makkah*, I 139; Wellhausen, *Arab Kingdom*, 155-157.

31 Ibn A'tham, *Futūḥ*, V 300-302; al-Ya'qūbī, *Ta'rīkh*, II 166-167; al-Ṭabarī, *Ta'rīkh*, II 423-427; al-Mas'ūdī, *Murūj*, 1929-30; al-Azraqī, *Akhbār Makkah*, I 139-140.

accuse a caliph who so blatantly disrespected the City of God and the City of God's Prophet as unfit for the office he held. In the battle for hearts and minds, Ibn al-Zubayr had the message to de-legitimize Yazīd and the means to spread it: in controlling the *ḥajj*, he controlled the most effective propaganda apparatus in Islam.

For the Umayyads in general, and Yazīd in particular, these would prove difficult accusations to counter.

IBN AL-ZUBAYR: REBEL OR RULER?

In 63/683, Yazīd was still widely regarded as caliph but control of the *ḥajj* was no longer his but Ibn al-Zubayr's.

With his authority spreading over increasing parts of the Islamic world, Ibn al-Zubayr wasted no time in adopting a radically different *ḥajj* policy from his Umayyad rival.[32] Not for him was the practice of delegating leadership of the ritual to a relative. On the contrary, he adopted a policy designed to identify him with the sanctuary in the most public way: once fully in control of Mecca, Ibn al-Zubayr – like ʿUmar and ʿUthmān – led every *ḥajj* he could. Based as he was in the Holy City, it was easier for him to do so than it was for a caliph based hundreds of miles away in Syria.

For Ibn al-Zubayr, however, there was a political motivation for leading the *ḥajj* repeatedly: he did not think the caliphate should be based hundreds of miles away in Syria, he wanted it brought back to the Ḥijāz.[33] In rebelling, he aimed to re-establish the political primacy of the Ḥijāz and of the early Islamic elite who resided there. Ibn al-Zubayr hailed from the Prophet's tribe, Quraysh,[34] and his Islamic credentials were impeccable: the Prophet's aunt, Ṣafiyyah bt. ʿAbd al-Muṭṭalib, was his grandmother[35] and his father, al-Zubayr b. al-ʿAwwām, was one of the earliest converts.[36] A *Muhājir*, emigrant, of the first order, al-Zubayr had taken part in the original *hijrah* to Ethiopia and was believed to be the fourth or fifth convert to Islam.[37] Ibn al-Zubayr himself was believed to be the first child born

32 Ibn Khayyāṭ, *Ta'rīkh*, I 255; al-Dīnawarī, *Akhbār*, 212; al-Yaʿqūbī, *Ta'rīkh*, II 170-171; al-Ṭabarī, *Ta'rīkh*, II 467; al-Masʿūdī, *Murūj*, 1957; al-Fāsī, *Akhbār Makkah*, II 169-170; Hawting, *First Dynasty*, 48.

33 Wellhausen, *Arab Kingdom*, 164 & 200; Crone, *Slaves on Horses*, 34.

34 For details of his life, see al-Dhahabī, *Ta'rīkh*, III 167-175.

35 Landau-Tasseron, *Biographies*, 105, 169 & 198-199.

36 Landau-Tasseron, *Biographies*, 27-28 & 105.

37 Landau-Tasseron, *Biographies*, 105. See Rodinson, *Mohamed*, 113-114, for an alternative view of the

amongst the *Muhājirūn* after the *hijrah* to Medina.[38] Al-Zubayr was one of the members of the *shūrā* which elected ʿUthmān caliph[39] and his son had endorsed that position by staying with ʿUthmān on the *Yawm al-Dār*.[40]

The rebel's impressive credentials were not limited to his father's side of the family. His mother, Asmāʾ, was a daughter of the first caliph, Abū Bakr,[41] and he was close to his maternal aunt, the Prophet's wife ʿĀʾishah, on whose side he fought against ʿAlī during the Battle of the Camel in 36/656.[42]

In many ways, ʿAbd Allāh b. al-Zubayr was the very embodiment of the first generation of believers and when he assumed personal leadership of the *ḥajj* at the first available opportunity, he was emulating the practice of the very caliphs whose agenda he was trying to resurrect.[43]

Control of the *Ḥaramayn* also enabled him to assume the caliphal privilege of bestowing patronage on the sanctuary. It had been damaged during the battle with Yazīd's forces[44] and in 64/684, Ibn al-Zubayr undertook a programme of renovations which would repair this damage and leave his mark on the architectural landscape of the Holy City.

To begin with, he had the Kaʿbah demolished until it was razed to the ground.[45] Foundations were dug out and, citing a *ḥadīth* of the Prophet as his motivation, Ibn al-Zubayr had part of the *Ḥijr* joined to the Kaʿbah. Two doors – one an entrance and one an exit – were also added to the structure.[46] That Ibn al-Zubayr had to refer to the example of the Prophet to justify some of the proposed renovations showed how contentious changes within the *Ḥarām* could be. That he persevered with those changes showed his determination to assert his authority as the man in charge of Mecca.

---

merits of participating in the first *hijrah* to Ethiopia.

38 Ibn ʿAsākir, *TMD*, Vol. 28, 151 & 159; al-Dhahabī, *Taʾrīkh*, III 167-168; Hawting, *First Dynasty*, 49; Robinson, *ʿAbd al-Malik*, 13-14 & 17.

39 Al-Ṭabarī, *Taʾrīkh*, I 2724.

40 Al-Ṭabarī, *Taʾrīkh*, I 3005, 3009 & 3014.

41 Ibn ʿAsākir, *TMD*, Vol. 28, 151; Ibn Kathīr, *Bidāyah*, VIII 332. For details of her life, see al-Dhahabī, *Taʾrīkh*, III 133-137.

42 For the battle, see al-Ṭabarī, *Taʾrīkh*, I 3181-3218. He was also related through marriage to the third caliph ʿUthmān: the mother of Ibn al-Zubayr's son, Bakr, was ʿĀʾishah bt. ʿUthmān; see Zubair ibn Bakkār, *Jamharat Nasab Quraish*, I 33.

43 Blankinship, *Jihad*, 27.

44 Wellhausen, *Arab Kingdom*, 165-166.

45 Ibn Khayyāṭ, *Taʾrīkh*, I 256; al-Balādhurī, *Futūḥ*, 46-47; al-Dīnawarī, *Akhbār*, 212; al-Yaʿqūbī, *Taʾrīkh*, II 176; al-Ṭabarī, *Taʾrīkh*, II 537; al-Azraqī, *Akhbār Makkah*, I 142-145, 150-151 & 153; Peters, *Mecca*, 98, & *Hajj*, 60-65.

46 Al-Balādhurī, *Futūḥ*, 47; al-Yaʿqūbī, *Taʾrīkh*, II 177; al-Ṭabarī, *Taʾrīkh*, II 537 & 592; al-Masʿūdī, *Murūj*, 1956; al-Azraqī, *Akhbār Makkah*, I 142-145; Gaudefroy-Demombynes, *Pèlerinage*, 37-38.

Control of the *Ḥaramayn*, however, may have given him more than the right to lead the *ḥajj* and bestow his patronage in Mecca. According to one report, it equated to nothing less than the caliphate itself.

Al-Yaʿqūbī:

> People say that the caliphate (*al-khilāfah*) belongs (*taḥaqqu li*) to whoever controls the Two Sanctuaries (*al-Ḥaramayn*) and leads (*aqāma*) the *ḥajj* for people.[47]

When Ibn al-Zubayr took control of the *ḥajj* and led it uncontested for the first time in 63/683, he did not control both of the Holy Cities. By the *ḥajj* of 64/684, that had changed and he led that year's *ḥajj* with both Mecca and Medina firmly under his control. If al-Yaʿqūbī's account accurately demonstrated a commonly held view that the caliphate belonged to the person who controlled the *Ḥaramayn* and led the *ḥajj*, then in 64/684, Ibn al-Zubayr was not merely a contender to be caliph, he *was* the caliph.

The issue of whether or not he should be regarded as such strikes at the very heart of what a caliph was and what his responsibilities should be. If, as Lapidus suggests, the caliph was expected to be the guarantor of the divine will, then it follows that his primary concern, as Commander of the Faithful, was to ensure that the Muslim community could perform all of their obligations to God. One of which was the *ḥajj*. On that count alone, Ibn al-Zubayr would clearly qualify as caliph.

That Ibn al-Zubayr is so often *not* regarded as a caliph is largely due to the attitude taken by the Muslim sources who – with the exception of al-Yaʿqūbī – organize their histories and genealogies as if Marwān b. al-Ḥakam were the caliph and ʿAbd Allāh bin al-Zubayr the rebel. Because history belongs to the winners, it is not difficult to see why the Muslim sources, writing as they did from their ninth-century vantage point, adopted such a position, one which modern scholarship usually endorses.[48]

The situation may, however, have looked different to those experiencing it. More people acknowledged Ibn al-Zubayr as caliph than the Umayyads – at one point, their authority was only recognized in Jordan[49] – and the caliphal privileges of leading the *ḥajj*, striking coinage and appointing governors were Ibn al-Zubayr's.[50]

---

47 Al-Yaʿqūbī, *Taʾrīkh*, II 188. See also Robinson, *ʿAbd al-Malik*, 37.

48 Hodgson, *Venture of Islam*, vol. 1, 221, & Robinson, *ʿAbd al-Malik*, 31-38, are exceptions.

49 Al-Balādhurī, *Ansāb*, V 188.

50 Hawting, *First Dynasty*, 48; Robinson, *ʿAbd al-Malik*, 35-36.

It could be argued that his status as caliph was confirmed by his Umayyad rivals who, rather than spending *Dhū al-Ḥijjah* 64 AH fighting Ibn al-Zubayr for leadership of the *ḥajj*, spent it fighting each other for leadership of their family. Marwān b. al-Ḥakam, the former governor of Medina, emerged as leader in the wake of Muʿāwiyah II's sudden death[51] with Muʿāwiyah II's younger brother Khālid his immediate successor.[52] Next in line was ʿAmr b. Saʿīd b. al-ʿĀṣ, another former governor of the Holy Cities.[53]

The nomination of Marwān was not welcomed by everyone in the Umayyad power structure and the governor of Damascus, al-Ḍaḥḥāk b. Qays al-Fihrī decided to support Ibn al-Zubayr.[54] He publicly renounced Marwān and the two sides took their differences to the battlefield. The battle of Marj Rāhiṭ[55] took place during the holy month of *Dhū al-Ḥijjah* in 64 AH.[56]

Thus preoccupied with their political infighting, the Umayyads were unable to challenge Ibn al-Zubayr for leadership of that year's *ḥajj*. Their subsequent absence from Mecca, in effect, a tacit admission of the new political reality which saw the roles of ruler and rebel reversed.

ALTERNATIVE USES OF THE *ḤAJJ*: THE *ḤARAM* AS THE CENTRE OF AN INFORMATION NETWORK

The *ḥajj* during this period came to have uses above and beyond its obvious religious functions. It was, for example, a means for rebels to communicate with one another. During Yazīd's caliphate, we have seen how al-Ḥusayn b. ʿAlī made use of his time in Mecca to meet with his supporters. Once Ibn

51 Al-Ṭabarī, *Taʾrīkh*, II 476. For a slightly different version of events, see al-Masʿūdī, *Murūj*, 1961-62, where the details of the succession are similar but the role played by Marwān and ʿAmr is much more active. See also Ibn Khayyāṭ, *Taʾrīkh*, I 255; al-Yaʿqūbī, *Taʾrīkh*, II 171; Wellhausen, *Arab Kingdom*, 182; Dixon, *Umayyad Caliphate*, 19; Bligh-Abramski, *From Damascus to Baghdad*, 74.

52 Al-Yaʿqūbī, *Taʾrīkh*, II 171; al-Ṭabarī, *Taʾrīkh*, II 476; al-Masʿūdī, *Murūj*, 1962; Ibn ʿAsākir, *TMD*, Vol. 46, 44; Dixon, *Umayyad Caliphate*, 19; Bligh-Abramski, *From Damascus to Baghdad*, 74; Hammarneh, "Marwan b. al-Hakam and the Caliphate", 222.

53 Al-Zubayrī, *Nasab Quraish*, 179 (where he is cited as ʿAbd al-Malik's successor); al-Yaʿqūbī, *Taʾrīkh*, II 171; al-Ṭabarī, *Taʾrīkh*, II 476; Ibn ʿAsākir, *TMD*, Vol. 46, 44; Dixon, *Umayyad Caliphate*, 19; Bligh-Abramski, *From Damascus to Baghdad*, 74; Hammarneh, "Marwan b. al-Hakam and the Caliphate", 222.

54 Al-Ṭabarī, *Taʾrīkh*, II 468-474; al-Masʿūdī, *Murūj*, 1965-67; Chejne, *Succession*, 46; Crone, *Slaves on Horses*, 35.

55 Ibn Aʿtham, *Futūḥ*, V 314; al-Balādhurī, *Ansāb*, V 136-146; al-Yaʿqūbī, *Taʾrīkh*, II 171-172; al-Ṭabarī, *Taʾrīkh*, II 481; Robinson, *ʿAbd al-Malik*, 2.

56 Ibn Khayyāṭ, *Taʾrīkh*, I 255; al-Yaʿqūbī, *Taʾrīkh*, II 171-172; al-Ṭabarī, *Taʾrīkh*, II 474-487; Ibn Kathīr, *Bidāyah*, VIII 241-244 (where a range of dates is given for the battle: from *Dhū al-Qaʿdah* 64 to *Muḥarram* 65/June 684 through to September 684); Kennedy, *Prophet*, 91-92.

al-Zubayr took control of the *ḥajj*, he soon learnt that his rivals could make use of it to further their own agenda. Such a state of affairs should perhaps have come as no surprise to him: in the aftermath of ʿUthmān's murder years earlier, his father had used the pretext of the *ʿumrah* to flee Medina for Mecca where he planned to meet up with opponents of ʿAlī.

Ibn al-Zubayr was particularly concerned by the activities of one al-Mukhtār b. Abī ʿUbayd,[57] an ʿAlid sympathizer from al-Kūfah, who initially joined Ibn al-Zubayr and distinguished himself in the defence of the Kaʿbah in 64/683,[58] but problems arose when al-Mukhtār wanted more power than Ibn al-Zubayr was prepared to give him.[59] As soon as al-Mukhtār realized his position with Ibn al-Zubayr was not going to change, he started asking pilgrims from his former city about conditions there and was informed that a group of men were looking for someone to lead them.[60] Al-Mukhtār headed back to al-Kūfah where, before long, he would be re-engaged with power politics.[61]

The change in al-Mukhtār's situation happened as a direct result of the mobility at the very heart of the *ḥajj* and the *ʿumrah*. The route to Mecca enabled people to travel freely across the Islamic world, carrying with them the ideas and information of their choice. In the Holy City, and within the context of the *ḥajj* and *ʿumrah*, contacts were made and alliances were formed which might not otherwise have had the chance to come into being. The problem this presented for the caliph, eager to have his authority demonstrated during the *ḥajj*, was how to monitor the movement of people which the *ḥajj* facilitated and how to gauge the real intentions of the pilgrims arriving in Mecca – two virtually impossible tasks.

Proof of just how impossible these tasks were may be discerned by the fact they kept recurring. In 66/686, Ibn al-Zubayr was so concerned by the arrival in Mecca of al-Ḥusayn's half-brother Muḥammad b. al-Ḥanafiyyah,[62] suspecting he had come with purposes other than pilgrimage in mind, that he adopted extreme measures against him: he had the ʿAlid and his supporters locked up in the *Ḥarām* and threatened with death if they did not acknowledge him as caliph.[63]

---

57 *EI*, 1st edition, s.v. al-Mukhtār b. Abī ʿUbayd.

58 Al-Ṭabarī, *Taʾrīkh*, II 514-517; al-Masʿūdī, *Murūj*, 1930.

59 Al-Yaʿqūbī, *Taʾrīkh*, II 174; al-Ṭabarī, *Taʾrīkh*, II 528-531 (in particular 531).

60 Al-Ṭabarī, *Taʾrīkh*, II 531. See also Ibn Aʿtham, *Futūḥ*, VI 53-58 (in particular 53).

61 Al-Ṭabarī, *Taʾrīkh*, II 598-642. For another version of these events where the basic facts are more or less the same (i.e. al-Mukhtār goes to work for the ʿAlids) but the process of how he achieved it is different, see al-Masʿūdī, *Murūj*, 1935-37. See also Ibn Aʿtham, *Futūḥ*, VI 54.

62 He had refused to give the oath of allegiance to Ibn al-Zubayr: al-Balādhurī, *Ansāb*, V 188; al-Dhahabī, *Taʾrīkh*, III 170.

63 The account here is largely taken from al-Ṭabarī, *Taʾrīkh*, II 693-695. Other versions of Ibn

They appealed to none other than al-Mukhtār for help[64] and he quickly rallied his forces and rode to their rescue.[65] He and his men arrived in Mecca brandishing clubs rather than swords because of the Qur'ānic prohibition on weapons in the *Ḥarām*. With their rallying cry of "Vengeance for al-Ḥusayn", they freed the trapped men and prepared to avenge themselves on 'Abd Allāh bin al-Zubayr.

Ibn al-Ḥanafiyyah, however, restrained them by refusing to sanction fighting in "God's Precinct *(Ḥarām Allāh)*" and the matter, for the moment, ended there.[66] Ibn al-Zubayr retained his control of the Holy City, and the *ḥajj* to it, and continued his practice of leading it in person: doing so in this year and the following year, 67/687.

But in 68/688, the problems of policing the *ḥajj* would again become apparent.

THE *ḤAJJ* OF 68 AH: A PLATFORM FOR REBELLION

The most high-profile use of the *ḥajj* during this period was as a platform for political rivalries. Previous *ḥajj* seasons – most notably those of 10/632 and 39/660 – had shown that leadership of the *ḥajj* was understood to equate to leadership of the community.

In 68/688, the pilgrimage yet again assumed centre stage as the platform where each of the contenders for power made their claim to lead the community. And in this year, Ibn al-Ḥanafiyyah was one of them:

> In the year 68/688, four banners (*alwīyah*) stood at 'Arafāt: Ibn al-Ḥanafiyyah with his companions (*aṣḥāb*) stood with a banner...; Ibn al-Zubayr stood with a banner at the present standing place of the *Imām*; then Ibn al-Ḥanafiyyah led his companions forward so that they stood opposite Ibn al-Zubayr; behind these two was Najdah the *Ḥarūrī* (*Khārijī*), and the banner of the Banū Umayyah was to the left of the two.

---

al-Zubayr's treatment of Ibn al-Ḥanafiyyah differ in some of the details but not in the main facts, which are: Ibn al-Zubayr pressed the 'Alid for the oath of allegiance; he refused and Ibn al-Zubayr resorted to violence to force it from him. Ibn Khayyāṭ, *Ta'rīkh*, I 258-259; Ibn A'tham, *Futūḥ*, VI 125-130; al-Ya'qūbī, *Ta'rīkh*, II 178-179.

64 Ibn A'tham, *Futūḥ*, VI 131-137; al-Ya'qūbī, *Ta'rīkh*, II 178; al-Ṭabarī, *Ta'rīkh*, II 693-694.

65 Al-Ya'qūbī, *Ta'rīkh*, II 178-179; al-Ṭabarī, *Ta'rīkh*, II 694.

66 Al-Ya'qūbī, *Ta'rīkh*, II 179; al-Ṭabarī, *Ta'rīkh*, II 694-695; al-Mas'ūdī, *Murūj*, 1942. See Crone, "The Significance of Wooden Weapons in al-Mukhtār's Revolt and the 'Abbāsid Revolution" in Netton, ed. *Studies in Honour of Clifford Edmund Bosworth*, vol. I, 174-187. I am grateful to Professor G.R. Hawting for drawing my attention to this article.

> The first banner to return from ʿArafāt was that of Muḥammad b. al-Ḥanafiyyah; he was followed by Najdah, then by the banner of the Banū Umayyah, and then by the banner of Ibn al-Zubayr, with the people (*al-nās*) following it.[67]

With four rival groups competing to show their political supremacy at ʿArafāt, an intermediary had to liaise between them to ensure that the pilgrims' *ḥajj* would not be invalidated by an outbreak of fighting.[68]

In religious terms, the *wuqūf*, the standing at ʿArafāt on the second day of the *ḥajj* – the ninth day of the month of *Dhū al-Ḥijjah* – is one of the obligatory rites of the pilgrimage, the omission of which renders a *ḥajj* invalid. Its importance is such that the Prophet is quoted as saying that the *ḥajj* is ʿArafāt.

Furthermore, ʿArafāt is where Muḥammad delivered his *khuṭbah* during the Farewell *Ḥajj* which set the seal on the rituals to be observed for all future pilgrimages. It also set the seal on his career as the founder of a religion and the founder of a political entity based on that religion. It is this convergence of the Prophet with the politician which infuses ʿArafāt with political, as well as spiritual, significance.

When performing the *ḥajj*, pilgrims try to enact its rituals in accordance with what they believe the Prophet to have done. His behaviour is the template they follow. For those claiming the right to succeed to the Prophet's political authority, there is a similar motivation. But what they seek to emulate at ʿArafāt, in addition to the Prophet's piety, is his political leadership of the *ummah* and the right to be considered his legitimate successor; hence the presence at ʿArafāt in 68/688 of banners representing all four contenders for the caliphate.

---

67 Al-Ṭabarī, *Taʾrīkh*, II 781-782; Fishbein, tr. *The Victory of the Marwānids*, 152. Al-Yaʿqūbī, *Taʾrīkh*, II 180-181, sums the situation up thus: "For every tribe, there was a Commander of the Faithful." See also Goitein, *Studies in Islamic History and Institutions*, 135-148; Dixon, *The Umayyad Caliphate*, 172.

68 Al-Ṭabarī, *Taʾrīkh*, II 782-783.

FIVE

The Return of the Umayyads and the Reintroduction of the Sufyānid *Ḥajj* Policy

After the disputed *ḥajj* of 68/688, Ibn al-Zubayr managed to retain sole control of the ritual until 71/691. But the following year he was under attack in Mecca by a military expedition sent by ʿAbd al-Malik and was unable to perform all aspects of the ritual.[1] Soon afterwards, he was defeated and killed and ʿAbd al-Malik was acknowledged as caliph throughout the Islamic world; a position he held until his death in 86/705. Table 4 shows who led the *ḥajj* during the last years of Ibn al-Zubayr's period in power, 69/689 to 71/691. It also shows ʿAbd al-Malik's choice of *ḥajj* leaders for the years of his caliphate.

Table 4

Year	*Ḥajj leader*	*Relationship to caliph*	*Governor of Medina?*
69/689	ʿAbd Allāh b. al-Zubayr[2]	alternative caliph	-
70/690	ʿAbd Allāh b. al-Zubayr[3]	alternative caliph	-

1 *EI* 2nd edition, s.v. ʿAbd al-Malik.

2 Ibn Khayyāṭ, *Taʾrīkh*, I 249; al-Yaʿqūbī, *Taʾrīkh*, II 187; al-Ṭabarī, *Taʾrīkh*, II 796; al-Masʿūdī, *Murūj*, 3635; Ibn ʿAsākir, *TMD*, Vol. 28, 212 & 213.

3 Ibn Khayyāṭ, *Taʾrīkh*, I 249 & 262; al-Yaʿqūbī, *Taʾrīkh*, II 187; al-Ṭabarī, *Taʾrīkh*, II 797; al-Masʿūdī, *Murūj*, 3635; Ibn ʿAsākir, *TMD*, Vol. 28, 212 & 213.

71/691	'Abd Allāh b. al-Zubayr[4]	alternative caliph	-
72/692	al-Ḥajjāj b. Yūsuf[5]	x	Mecca
73/693	al-Ḥajjāj b. Yūsuf[6]	x	Mecca
74/694	al-Ḥajjāj b. Yūsuf[7]	x	yes
75/695	CALIPH[8]	-	-
76/696	Abān b. 'Uthmān[9]	(distant) cousin	yes
77/697	Abān b. 'Uthmān[10]	(distant) cousin	yes
78/698	al-Walīd b. 'Abd al-Malik[11] *or* Abān b. 'Uthmān[12] *or* 'Abd al-Malik[13]	caliph's son (distant) cousin caliph	- yes -
79/699	Abān b. 'Uthmān[14]	(distant) cousin	yes
80/700	Abān b. 'Uthmān[15] *or* Sulaymān b. 'Abd al-Malik[16]	(distant) cousin caliph's son	yes -

4 Ibn Khayyāṭ, *Ta'rīkh*, I 249 & 264; al-Ya'qūbī, *Ta'rīkh*, II 187; al-Ṭabarī, *Ta'rīkh*, II 818; al-Mas'ūdī, *Murūj*, 3635; Ibn 'Asākir, *TMD*, Vol. 28, 212 & 213.

5 Ibn Khayyāṭ, *Ta'rīkh*, I 264; al-Ya'qūbī, *Ta'rīkh*, II 203; al-Ṭabarī, *Ta'rīkh*, II 830; al-Mas'ūdī, *Murūj*, 3635; Ibn 'Asākir, *TMD*, Vol. 12, 117 & 118.

6 Ibn Khayyāṭ, *Ta'rīkh*, I 266 & 301; al-Ya'qūbī, *Ta'rīkh*, II 203; al-Ṭabarī, *Ta'rīkh*, II 853; al-Mas'ūdī, *Murūj*, 3635; Ibn 'Asākir, *TMD*, Vol. 12, 117 & 118.

7 Ibn Khayyāṭ, *Ta'rīkh*, I 268 & 301; al-Ya'qūbī, *Ta'rīkh*, II 203; al-Ṭabarī, *Ta'rīkh*, II 862; al-Mas'ūdī, *Murūj*, 3635; Ibn 'Asākir, *TMD*, Vol. 12, 117 & 118.

8 Ibn Khayyāṭ, *Ta'rīkh*, I 268, 270 & 301; al-Ya'qūbī, *Ta'rīkh*, II 203; al-Ṭabarī, *Ta'rīkh*, II 873, 877 & 881; al-Mas'ūdī, *Murūj*, 3635; Ibn 'Asākir, *TMD*, Vol. 12, 118, & Vol. 37, 133.

9 Ibn Khayyāṭ, *Ta'rīkh*, I 301; al-Ya'qūbī, *Ta'rīkh*, II 203; al-Ṭabarī, *Ta'rīkh*, II 940 & 1032; al-Mas'ūdī, *Murūj*, 3635; Ibn 'Asākir, *TMD*, Vol. 6, 155 & 156.

10 Ibn Khayyāṭ, *Ta'rīkh*, I 275 & 301; al-Ya'qūbī, *Ta'rīkh*, II 203; al-Ṭabarī, *Ta'rīkh*, II 1032; al-Mas'ūdī, *Murūj*, 3635; Ibn 'Asākir, *TMD*, Vol. 6, 155 & 156.

11 Ibn Khayyāṭ, *Ta'rīkh*, I 276 & 301; al-Ṭabarī, *Ta'rīkh*, II 1035; Ibn 'Asākir, *TMD*, Vol. 6, 156, & Vol. 63, 169, 170 & 171; al-Dhahabī, *Ta'rīkh*, III 126 & IV 65; Ibn Kathīr, *Bidāyah*, IX 22.

12 Al-Ya'qūbī, *Ta'rīkh*, II 203; al-Mas'ūdī, *Murūj*, 3635; Ibn al-Athīr, *al-Kāmil*, IV 448.

13 Al-Fāsī, *Akhbār Makkah*, II 235-236.

14 Ibn Khayyāṭ, *Ta'rīkh*, I 277 & 301; al-Ya'qūbī, *Ta'rīkh*, II 203; al-Ṭabarī, *Ta'rīkh*, II 1039; al-Mas'ūdī, *Murūj*, 3635; Ibn 'Asākir, *TMD*, Vol. 6, 155 & 156.

15 Ibn Khayyāṭ, *Ta'rīkh*, I 278 & 301; al-Ya'qūbī, *Ta'rīkh*, II 203; al-Ṭabarī, *Ta'rīkh*, II 1046-47; al-Mas'ūdī, *Murūj*, 3635; Ibn 'Asākir, *TMD*, Vol. 6, 155 & 156; Ibn al-Athīr, *al-Kāmil*, IV 456; Ibn Kathīr, *Bidāyah*, IX 32.

16 Al-Ṭabarī, *Ta'rīkh*, II 1046-47; Ibn Kathīr, *Bidāyah*, IX 32.

81/701	Sulaymān b. 'Abd al-Malik[17] *or* Isḥāq b. 'Īsā[18]	caliph's son x	- x
82/702	Abān b. 'Uthmān[19]	(distant) cousin	yes
83/703	Hishām b. Ismā'īl al-Makhzūmī[20] *or* Abān b. 'Uthmān[21]	father-in-law (distant) cousin	yes x
84/703	Hishām b. Ismā'īl[22]	father-in-law	yes
85/704	Hishām b. Ismā'īl[23]	father-in-law	yes

A TALE OF TWO HOLY CITIES: MECCA, JERUSALEM AND THE *ḤAJJ*

Ibn al-Zubayr succeeded in emerging from the disputed *ḥajj* of 68/688 with sufficient political authority to lead the next three *ḥajj* seasons uncontested. According to al-Ya'qūbī, he was helped in this by the unlikeliest of sources: his Umayyad rival 'Abd al-Malik.[24]

In al-Ya'qūbī's account, 'Abd al-Malik is said to have banned the people of Syria from travelling to Mecca because Ibn al-Zubayr was taking advantage of the *ḥajj* to impose the oath of allegiance on the pilgrims. When the people of Syria raised a hue and cry at the prospect of being prevented from going to Mecca to fulfil their obligation to God, 'Abd al-Malik responded by quoting a *ḥadīth* of the Prophet which commended three mosques, one of which, Jerusalem, fell within the territory he controlled, and reminded his fellow Muslims that Jerusalem was the scene of the Prophet's ascent to heaven. The

17 Ibn Khayyāṭ, *Ta'rīkh*, I 280 & 302; al-Ya'qūbī, *Ta'rīkh*, II 203; al-Ṭabarī, *Ta'rīkh*, II 1063; al-Mas'ūdī, *Murūj*, 3636; Ibn 'Asākir, *TMD*, Vol. 6, 156; Ibn al-Athīr, *al-Kāmil*, IV 466; Ibn Kathīr, *Bidāyah*, IX 178.

18 Ibn Kathīr, *Bidāyah*, IX 37.

19 Ibn Khayyāṭ, *Ta'rīkh*, I 289 & 302; al-Ya'qūbī, *Ta'rīkh*, II 203; al-Ṭabarī, *Ta'rīkh*, II 1085; al-Mas'ūdī, *Murūj*, 3636; Ibn 'Asākir, *TMD*, Vol. 6, 155 & 156.

20 Ibn Khayyāṭ, *Ta'rīkh*, I 290 & 302; al-Ya'qūbī, *Ta'rīkh*, II 203; al-Ṭabarī, *Ta'rīkh*, II 1127; al-Mas'ūdī, *Murūj*, 3636.

21 Ibn 'Asākir, *TMD*, Vol. 6, 155.

22 Ibn Khayyāṭ, *Ta'rīkh*, I 291 & 302; al-Ya'qūbī, *Ta'rīkh*, II 203; al-Ṭabarī, *Ta'rīkh*, II 1132; al-Mas'ūdī, *Murūj*, 3636.

23 Ibn Khayyāṭ, *Ta'rīkh*, I 292 & 302; al-Ya'qūbī, *Ta'rīkh*, II 203; al-Ṭabarī, *Ta'rīkh*, II 1171; al-Mas'ūdī, *Murūj*, 3636.

24 Al-Ya'qūbī, *Ta'rīkh*, II 177-178. See also Ibn Kathīr, *Bidāyah*, VIII 280-281.

rock upon which the Prophet had placed his foot was domed and decorated in suitably grand style; custodians were appointed to guard it and people began performing the *ṭawāf* around it just as they did around the Ka'bah in Mecca.[25]

This account, however, does not address many of the issues relating to the origins of the Dome of the Rock. Because its design more closely resembles a Byzantine structure than a congregational mosque and because the Qur'ānic verses decorating its interior repeatedly refer to God's unity as opposed to the trinity, it has been suggested that it was built as a concrete assertion of Muslim hegemony over the Christian city of Jerusalem rather than an alternative *Ḥarām* to the one in Mecca.[26]

Al-Duri, for example, considers the *hadīth* quoted by 'Abd al-Malik in al-Ya'qūbī to be highly dubious[27] and Rabbat points out that it would have been problematic for 'Abd al-Malik, as a Muslim caliph, to put Jerusalem in Mecca's place.[28] Such a comment, however, is predicated on the belief that the *ḥajj* had already become established as one of the pillars of the faith, a view not endorsed by everyone.[29]

The debate as to why the Dome of the Rock was built thus feeds into the status of Mecca as the sacred centre of Islam and the time scale of the development of the *ḥajj*. While the latter falls outside the scope of this study, the position of Mecca as the religious centre of Islam is directly relevant to the politics of pilgrimage. For, if we set the debate about the Dome of the Rock as a possible alternative *Ḥarām* within the context of policies which the early caliphs adopted for the *ḥajj*, a pattern emerges which suggests that Mecca was indeed acknowledged as the spiritual centre of Islam; a state of affairs which makes it unlikely – if not impossible – that the Dome of the Rock was constructed to be an alternative *Ḥarām*.

We have seen that Muslim tradition connects the Prophet with the

---

25 Al-Ya'qūbī, *Ta'rīkh*, II 178. See also Wellhausen, *Arab Kingdom*, 212- 213.

26 For a fuller examination of why the Dome of the Rock was built, see Goitein, "The Historical Background to the Erection of the Dome of the Rock", *JOAS*, 70, 1950, 104-108, & "The sanctity of Jerusalem and Palestine in early Islam" in his *Studies in Islamic history and institutions,* 135-148; Grabar, "The Umayyad Dome of the Rock in Jerusalem" & "The Meaning of the Dome of the Rock in Jerusalem"; Kessler, "'Abd al-Malik's Inscription in the Dome of the Rock: A Reconsideration", 11, note 20; Dixon, *Umayyad Caliphate*, 22-23 & 24; Hawting, *First Dynasty*, 59-61; Rabbat, "The Meaning of the Umayyad Dome of the Rock", 14-15, 16, 17 & 18; Elad, "Why did 'Abd al-Malik build the Dome of the Rock? A Re-examination of the Muslim Sources", in *Bayt al-Maqdis: 'Abd al-Malik's Jerusalem*, & *Medieval Jerusalem*, 147, 148, 158 & 160; van Ess, J., "'Abd al-Malik and the Dome of the Rock: An Analysis of Some Texts" in *Bayt al-Maqdis*; Hoyland, *Seeing Islam*; 569; Lapidus, *Islamic Societies*, 69 & 71; Robinson, *'Abd al-Malik*, 3-9.

27 Al-Duri, *Rise of Historical Writing*, 117.

28 Rabbat, "The Meaning of the Umayyad Dome of the Rock", 17.

29 Hawting, *First Dynasty*, 55 & 61; Robinson, *'Abd al-Malik*, 38 & 96.

pilgrimage in the most public way – by his leadership of the Farewell Pilgrimage in 10/632 – and that the majority of the *Rāshidūn* caliphs, 'Umar and 'Uthmān in particular, maintained this connection between leadership of the community and leadership of its rituals. That sense of continuity did not stop with them. Mu'āwiyah made sure to demonstrate his authority in Mecca: he led the *ḥajj* twice; used the ritual as a springboard to launch his son's caliphal career; had the Ka'bah draped in silk; employed slaves to guard it; and had dams built in the region.[30] Even the *kiswah* he gave to cover the Ka'bah was an expression of his authority and bore his name as caliph. Such actions from the man who willingly transferred the political and administrative centre of the caliphate to Syria suggest that Mecca enjoyed a status which compelled him, as caliph, to present himself in the Holy City. That Mu'āwiyah's sojourns there coincided with the *ḥajj* (or *'umrah*) would further suggest the status which the city enjoyed was a religious one which he, as Commander of the Faithful, was obliged to respect and uphold.

The centrality of Mecca to Islam is demonstrated further by the policies the Umayyads adopted for the *ḥajj* after Ibn al-Zubayr's rebellion. 'Abd al-Malik, as we shall see below, came to the Ḥijāz in 75/695 to lead the *ḥajj*. Post-*fitnah*, there was arguably no reason for him to endorse the city in this way unless Mecca was understood to occupy a position of some significance in Islam. He could simply have chosen, instead, to go to his "alternative *Ḥarām*" in Jerusalem.

In addition, 'Abd al-Malik's endorsement of Mecca went beyond his own *ḥajj*: he, like Mu'āwiyah, used the ritual as a springboard to promote the caliphal careers of his chosen successor sons. And once the caliphate was theirs, his sons adopted the twin-track policy of leading the *ḥajj* and appointing their successor sons to do so.

That the Marwānid branch of the Umayyad family adopted the same policies for the *ḥajj* as the Sufyānid branch before them indicates that, as a political dynasty, the Umayyads understood the critical importance of the Holy City of Mecca – and the *ḥajj* to it – from the very beginning of their time in power.

THE *ḤAJJ* OF 72 AH: A BAROMETER OF POLITICAL CHANGE

Ibn al-Zubayr was keen to publicize his enthusiasm for the House of God and adopted a *ḥajj* policy which identified him with the Holy Places in

30 King, *Introduction*, in King, & Cameron, eds. *The Byzantine and Early Islamic Near East Vol. II*, 192-193. Peters, *Mecca*, 96.

a high-profile way.[31] Such was his commitment to the Ḥijāz that he even turned down the offer of recognition as caliph from Yazīd's forces after the latter's death if he agreed to move to Syria.[32]

Yet, it was to be at the *ḥajj* that it would become clear his grip on power was slipping. In *Dhū al-Qaʿdah* 72/March 692[33] al-Ḥajjāj launched a surprise attack against him having used the *ḥajj* as cover to move his troops into position.[34] A month later, and for the first time in almost a decade, Ibn al-Zubayr did not lead the *ḥajj*. Instead, it was al-Ḥajjāj, representing the Umayyads, who is recorded as leading that year's *ḥajj*.

He did not, however, perform all the required rituals. He did not perform the *ṭawāf*, nor did he adopt the *iḥrām*; both of which are obligatory rites of the *ḥajj*. Furthermore, while he was present at ʿArafāt as required, instead of the regulation *iḥrām* he wore a coat of mail, a neck protector and a sword.[35] For his part, Ibn al-Zubayr also omitted one of the most important obligatory rituals: as a result of the attack, he and his men were not present at ʿArafāt.[36]

This religious stalemate in Mecca reflected the wider political stalemate: Ibn al-Zubayr still controlled the Holy City but no longer enjoyed the authority he once had; al-Ḥajjāj, by contrast, had the power to keep up the attack against his rival but could not yet convert it into victory. On balance, however, it was al-Ḥajjāj who emerged from the *ḥajj* in 72/692 holding the political advantage. Leadership of the *ḥajj* had been Ibn al-Zubayr's to lose; any diminution of the latter's authority was therefore a gain for the Umayyads. In that regard, the situation had parallels with the pilgrimages of 39/660 and 62/682.

The eventual defeat of Ibn al-Zubayr spelt the end of an era. He had rebelled in defence of the political model adopted by ʿUmar and ʿUthmān and for over a decade, he had succeeded. But attempts to resurrect the ideal of the Ḥijāz-based caliphate were to die along with him. The Umayyads would face many political challenges and threats during the rest of their era

31 Hoyland, *Seeing Islam*, 197. I am grateful to Professor Hoyland for drawing this reference to my attention.

32 Wellhausen, *Arab Kingdom*, 166-167.

33 Ibn Khayyāṭ, *Taʾrīkh*, I 266; Ibn Aʿtham, *Futūḥ*, VI 273 & 275-276; al-Dīnawarī, *Akhbār*, 227; al-Yaʿqūbī, *Taʾrīkh*, II 185; al-Ṭabarī, *Taʾrīkh*, II 829-830; al-Masʿūdī, *Murūj*, 2022; Ibn ʿAsākir, *TMD*, Vol. 12, 117; al-Fākihī, *Akhbār Makkah*, II 20; Kennedy, *Prophet*, 98.

34 Al-Balādhurī, *Ansāb*, V 357-358; Peters, *Hajj*, 65-68.

35 Ibn Khayyāṭ, *Taʾrīkh*, I 267; al-Ṭabarī, *Taʾrīkh*, II 830 & 831; al-Masʿūdī, *Murūj*, 2023 & 3635; Ibn ʿAsākir, *TMD*, Vol. 12, 117, & Vol. 28, 213; al-Fākihī, *Akhbār Makkah*, II 25.

36 Ibn Khayyāṭ, *Taʾrīkh*, I 267; al-Ṭabarī, *Taʾrīkh*, II 830; al-Masʿūdī, *Murūj*, 2023; Ibn al-Athīr, *al-Kāmil*, IV 350; Ibn Kathīr, *Bidāyah*, VIII 325 & IX 119.

but they would not come from the early Islamic elite, or their descendants, in the Holy Cities.

The new era began in earnest in 73/693 when al-Ḥajjāj was again appointed to lead the *ḥajj*. That year there would be no dispute over the validity of his pilgrimage: he led all the rituals on behalf of the new political order. And, as if to underline that new order in the most public way and consign Ibn al-Zubayr to history, al-Ḥajjāj received orders from his caliph to remove, quite literally, all traces of Ibn al-Zubayr's period of power:

> ... al-Ḥajjāj dismantled (*naqaḍa*) the structures of the Ka'bah that Ibn al-Zubayr had put up. The latter had incorporated the *Ḥijr* inside the Ka'bah and given the Ka'bah two doors; al-Ḥajjāj returned (*a'āda*) it to its original form (*'alā binā'iha al-awwal*).[37]

The work was completed in 74/693.[38] The restoration of the Ka'bah to its "original form" demonstrated that architectural changes to the *Ḥarām* were not purely symbolic but were designed to represent the authority of the ruling order.[39] Al-Ḥajjāj's actions were a tangible confirmation that not only was the Zubayrī political interregnum over but the man in question was not to be allowed any legacy in the architectural environment of the Holy City he had controlled for so long: he was to be airbrushed from history.

That same year saw the governorship of Medina added to al-Ḥajjāj's responsibilities.[40] Once the renovation work to the Ka'bah was finished, he set out for Medina where he spent the next three months.[41] If the inhabitants of the Prophet's City hoped their new governor would adopt a conciliatory policy towards them in the wake of Ibn al-Zubayr's defeat, they soon discovered such hopes were misplaced. The new Umayyad governor chose, instead, to remind them of where power now lay and to show them how the Umayyads, and their supporters, understood the roots of that power.

In this, the role of their murdered kinsman, the caliph 'Uthmān, was critical. To show just how important it was, al-Ḥajjāj resorted to the politics

37 Al-Ṭabarī, *Ta'rīkh*, II 854; Rowson, tr. *The Marwānid Restoration*, 1. See also al-Dīnawarī, *Akhbār*, 212; Gaudefroy-Demombynes, *Pèlerinage*, 39; Dixon, *Umayyad Caliphate*, 138-139.

38 Al-Ya'qūbī, *Ta'rīkh*, II 191. See also Ibn Khayyāṭ, *Ta'rīkh*, I 268; Ibn A'tham, *Futūḥ*, VI 282; al-Balādhurī, *Futūḥ*, 47; al-Dīnawarī, *Akhbār*, 229; al-Ṭabarī, *Ta'rīkh*, II 854; al-Mas'ūdī, *Murūj*, 1956; al-Azraqī, *Akhbār Makkah*, I 145-146.

39 Peters, *Hajj*, 68.

40 Ibn Khayyāṭ, *Ta'rīkh*, I 294 (where the year of his appointment is given as a year earlier); al-Ṭabarī, *Ta'rīkh*, II 854. He may also have performed the lesser pilgrimage around this time: al-Ṭabarī, *Ta'rīkh*, II 854.

41 Al-Ṭabarī, *Ta'rīkh*, II 854.

of reprisal and conducted something of a witch hunt against anyone who had not helped 'Uthmān in his hour of need. His treatment of some of the *Ṣaḥābah*, the Companions of the Prophet, was particularly brutal.

"What stopped you helping 'Uthmān?" was a question he asked people repeatedly.

If he deemed the response to be less than satisfactory, he punished the offender by branding his hands and/or neck, sometimes with lead, in the way that non-Muslims were often branded to indicate they had paid their taxes.[42] It was a policy intended to humiliate and when, in 74/694, the caliph appointed the man behind it to lead the *ḥajj* for the third year in a row the people of Medina would have understood the message the caliph was sending them. Politically, their time was over and all that remained for a full assertion of Umayyad hegemony in the Ḥijāz was an appearance by the caliph himself in the Holy Cities.

RESTORING PRECEDENT: THE CALIPH'S VICTORY *ḤAJJ* OF 75 AH

'Abd al-Malik was the fifth Umayyad caliph to rule but the first since Mu'āwiyah, the founder of the dynasty, to lead the *ḥajj* in person. His leadership of it in 75/695 was a reminder to everyone who had supported Ibn al-Zubayr that their rebellion had failed.

En route to Mecca, 'Abd al-Malik stopped in Medina, the Holy City his father Marwān had governed. Both there and in Mecca, he delivered the *khuṭbah* in the Mosque during which he acknowledged that there was little love lost between the people of the Holy Cities and the people who, once again, ruled over them. It was perhaps inevitable on this victory *ḥajj* that 'Abd al-Malik would choose to mention his fallen kinsman, 'Uthmān. He contrasted the treatment the Quraysh received from the second caliph, 'Umar b. al-Khaṭṭāb, with that of the third caliph 'Uthmān. Where the former was harsh, the latter was lenient. Then he went further:

> O Quraysh, we know that while you remember the Day of al-Ḥarrah, you will never love us. And while we remember the murder of 'Uthmān, we will never love you.[43]

42 Al-Ṭabarī, *Ta'rīkh*, II 854-855; Ibn al-Athīr, *al-Kāmil*, IV 358-359 & 365; Ibn Kathīr, *Bidāyah*, IX 2.

43 Al-Mas'ūdī, *Murūj*, 2047. It is not clear whether he said this during the *khuṭbah* in Medina or Mecca. See also Ibn Khayyāṭ, *Ta'rīkh*, I 270-271; al-Ya'qūbī, *Ta'rīkh*, II 193 & 194; Ibn al-Athīr, *al-Kāmil*, IV 391-392; Dixon, *Umayyad Caliphate*, 16-17.

It was during this year that 'Abd al-Malik decided to install a new governor in Medina: his paternal uncle Yaḥyā. This appointment, coinciding as it did with 'Abd al-Malik's triumphant return to the Holy Cities, was a blatant political statement.[44] Yaḥyā was the brother of Marwān, the former governor of Medina, who had been forced to flee his home by the inhabitants of the Holy City. Yaḥyā's governorship was thus intended to remind them of their defeat and the Umayyad victory. Like Mu'āwiyah on his first *ḥajj* as caliph in 44/665, 'Abd al-Malik was less concerned with winning the popular support of his political enemies than with securing their obedience.

There were other parallels between 'Abd al-Malik's pilgrimage and Mu'āwiyah's. While Mu'āwiyah was in the Ḥijāz, he had been taken to task by 'Ā'ishah for the killing of a political rival; 'Abd al-Malik was similarly upbraided by a society woman of some standing for killing one of his political rivals, Muṣ'ab b. al-Zubayr, a criticism he shrugged off as owing to political necessity.[45] And 'Abd al-Malik, like Mu'āwiyah before him, tried to remove the Prophet's pulpit from Medina and take it back to Syria. But as happened with Mu'āwiyah, his efforts came to nothing.[46]

'Abd al-Malik took advantage of his time in Mecca to consult a trusted Qur'ān reciter about the validity (or not) of the renovations his rival Ibn al-Zubayr made to the *Ḥarām*.[47] This debate was less of a discussion on the legitimacy of the adjustments Ibn al-Zubayr made to the *Ḥarām* than a coded exchange about Ibn al-Zubayr's political legitimacy vis-à-vis 'Abd al-Malik's.

'Abd al-Malik ruled for another eleven years but he did not lead the *ḥajj* again.[48] His decision not to do so made little difference to his overall political standing. The caliphal *ḥajj* of 75/695 was all about power – *his* power – and having demonstrated it, he had made his point. But his *ḥajj* in 75/695 would not be the end of his family's association with leadership of the pilgrimage. Having fought so hard to win the caliphate, 'Abd al-Malik wanted to secure the succession for his sons. And he made full use of the *ḥajj* to achieve it.

44 Ibn Khayyāṭ, *Ta'rīkh*, I 294; al-Ṭabarī, *Ta'rīkh*, II 863; Ibn 'Asākir, *TMD*, Vol. 64, 119; Ibn Kathīr, *Bidāyah*, IX 7 & 9. For his descent, see al-Zubayrī, *Nasab Quraish*, 159.

45 Al-Ṭabarī, *Ta'rīkh*, II 811-812. 'Ā'ishah had criticized Mu'āwiyah for killing Ḥujr b. 'Adī: al-Ya'qūbī, *Ta'rīkh*, II 141; Ibn Kathīr, *Bidāyah*, VIII 54.

46 Al-Ṭabarī, *Ta'rīkh*, II 92-93.

47 Al-Azraqī, *Akhbār Makkah*, I 218-219.

48 See al-Ṭabarī, *Ta'rīkh*, II 880-881 & Ibn al-Athīr, *al-Kāmil*, IV 391, for details of a possible plot to assassinate the caliph during the pilgrimage.

THE ISSUE OF SUCCESSION: THE *ḤAJJ* SEASONS OF 78 AH AND 81 AH

ʿAbd al-Malik followed the precedent set by Muʿāwiyah I of keeping power within his immediate family. Such a decision was not without its risks: Muʿāwiyah's determination to appoint his son as his successor caused him considerable political difficulty and had, arguably, contributed to the downfall of the Sufyānids.

But for all the difficulties Muʿāwiyah encountered over his succession plans, when the Umayyad family re-grouped as a political unit in the aftermath of Muʿāwiyah II's unexpected death, they chose not to abandon the system of designating an heir but to reinforce it. Their caliph was to have not one, but two, appointed heirs: the so-called "heir and a spare".

Consequently, when the Umayyads agreed upon Marwān as their leader, they gave him two successors: Khālid b. Yazīd and ʿAmr b. Saʿīd b. al-ʿĀṣ. Even when Marwān ditched these arrangements in favour of his own choice of heir, he stuck to the policy of nominating two successors: his sons ʿAbd al-Malik and ʿAbd al-ʿAzīz.[49]

When ʿAbd al-Malik became caliph, he therefore did so with no room for manoeuvre on the succession. But he chose not to do as his father had done and bypass the arrangements he had been given. Instead, he adopted the course of action taken by Muʿāwiyah and built up the profile of the sons he wanted to place in the succession. To that end, he did not move against his brother ʿAbd al-ʿAzīz but confirmed him in his position as governor of Egypt.[50] This was a more tactical decision on the caliph's part than it seemed for ʿAbd al-ʿAzīz's job kept him at a convenient distance from the Umayyad political centre in Syria. With the official heir apparent thus occupied, the caliph embarked on a campaign to raise the profile of his chosen successor sons, al-Walīd and Sulaymān.

To achieve this, he again followed Muʿāwiyah's example and appointed his sons to lead the major offices of state; those most closely associated in the public imagination with leadership of the community. He authorized his immediate successor, al-Walīd, to lead the *ḥajj* in 78/698 and his next-in-line

49 Al-Zubayrī, *Nasab Quraish*, 160; Ibn Khayyāṭ, *Taʾrīkh*, I 257; al-Balādhurī, *Ansāb*, V 183; al-Yaʿqūbī, *Taʾrīkh*, II 173; al-Ṭabarī, *Taʾrīkh*, II 576; al-Jahshiyārī, *Kitāb al-wuzarāʾ*, 34; al-Masʿūdī, *Murūj*, 1969; Ibn ʿAsākir, *TMD*, Vol. 46, 44; Ibn Khaldūn, *Muqaddimah*, 206; Chejne, *Succession*, 47; Dixon, *Umayyad Caliphate*, 19; Bligh-Abramski, *From Damascus to Baghdad*, 74; Hawting, *First Dynasty*, 59; Bacharach, "Marwanid Umayyad Building Activities: Speculations on Patronage", 29.

50 Al-Zubayrī, *Nasab Quraish*, 160; Ibn Khayyāṭ, *Taʾrīkh*, I 300; al-Balādhurī, *Futūḥ*, 229; al-Yaʿqūbī, *Taʾrīkh*, II 191; Wellhausen, *Arab Kingdom*, 222; Zambaur, *Généalogie*, 25; Kennedy, *Prophet*, 99.

son, Sulaymān, to do so in 81/701. The order of succession was clear: ʿAbd al-Malik led the *ḥajj* himself in 75/695; three years later, it was al-Walīd, the first successor; three years after that, it was Sulaymān. Al-Walīd, as the immediate heir apparent, was also authorized to lead the *ṣāʾifah*, the summer campaign.[51] According to Ibn Khayyāṭ, he led it in 79/698, the year after he led the *ḥajj*.[52]

The profile of these particular sons was thrown into sharper relief by who did *not* lead the *ḥajj*. Not once during ʿAbd al-Malik's caliphate did he invite his designated successor, his brother ʿAbd al-ʿAzīz, to lead the ritual. Nor did he ask any of his other brothers to lead it for him.

This caliph preferred to keep leadership of the *ḥajj* restricted to his core circle of power – the caliph himself and his successor sons – or to those on the periphery of power: his governors in the Ḥijāz who relied upon him for their position. This policy made the caliph's intention doubly clear: leading the *ḥajj* was the prerogative of the highest authority in the *ummah,* those in line to succeed to it, and those who were so politically dependent upon the person of the caliph that it was in their interests to reflect his power rather than try to claim it for themselves.

That ʿAbd al-Malik chose to appoint only two of his sons to lead the *ḥajj* – those same sons who happened to be in the running for the succession – demonstrates the connection between leadership of this ritual and leadership of the community. ʿAbd al-Malik had many other sons (according to al-Yaʿqūbī he had fourteen in total)[53] but in political terms, they were not all equal: some were eligible for the caliphate and some were not. The dividing line between the two groups was their maternal descent. Since the days of Abū Bakr's caliphate, membership of the Prophet's tribe of Quraysh had been seen by many in the community as a prerequisite for rule.[54] Likewise, descent from a free-born Arab mother was viewed as one of the criteria for the caliphate.[55] There was no Qurʾānic basis for

51 The caliph made a truce with the Byzantines around 70/689-690 to concentrate his military efforts against Ibn al-Zubayr; these raids resumed in 75/694-695: al-Yaʿqūbī, *Taʾrīkh*, II 203; al-Ṭabarī, *Taʾrīkh*, II 863. According to al-Yaʿqūbī, *Taʾrīkh*, II 203, al-Ṭabarī, *Taʾrīkh*, II 1032, & Ibn al-Athīr, *al-Kāmil*, IV 447, he led the summer campaign in 77/696. He was also sent on campaign in 80/699: al-Ṭabarī, *Taʾrīkh*, II 1047; Ibn Kathīr, *Bidāyah*, IX 32. Ibn ʿAsākir, *TMD*, Vol. 63, 169 & 170, has the caliph's son raiding in 77/696 and 78/697.

52 Ibn Khayyāṭ, *Taʾrīkh*, I 277 & 301. Al-Dhahabī, *Taʾrīkh*, III 127, agrees.

53 Al-Yaʿqūbī, *Taʾrīkh*, II 202. Al-Dhahabī, *Taʾrīkh*, III 281, also mentions fourteen. Al-Ṭabarī, *Taʾrīkh*, II 1174, mentions sixteen. See also al-Zubayrī, *Nasab Quraish*, 161-165.

54 Al-Māwardī, *Aḥkām* 6, has Qurashī descent the seventh of seven conditions necessary to be caliph. Ibn Khaldūn, *Muqaddimah*, 193-196, mentions Qurashī descent as a pre-requisite for the caliphate but acknowledges differing views over it. See also Amabe, *Emergence,* 5.

55 For the concept in practice, see al-Ṭabarī, *Taʾrīkh*, II 1676, where the caliph Hishām tells the rebel

these beliefs but they had been adopted at the time of the *Rāshidūn* and the Umayyads followed suit.[56] Mu'āwiyah's son, Yazīd, was a member of Quraysh and the son of a free-born Arab mother.[57] His son Mu'āwiyah was too.[58] Similarly, Marwān and his successor son, 'Abd al-Malik, were Qurashī and born of free Arab women.[59] 'Abd al-Malik nominated successors who met these criteria: al-Walīd and Sulaymān were full brothers, sons of the same free-born Arab woman of status.[60]

'Abd al-Malik did not, however, wish to limit the caliphate to these two sons. He reportedly told Sulaymān to make sure he passed the caliphate on to his brothers Yazīd and Marwān (and later Hishām).[61] Yazīd and Marwān were the sons of an Umayyad princess (she was the daughter of the second Umayyad caliph Yazīd)[62] and Hishām was the son of an Arab woman of status.[63] All three were therefore eligible for the caliphate but 'Abd al-Malik could not appoint any of them to lead the *ḥajj* because they were too young. Al-Walīd and Sulaymān were both well into their twenties during their father's caliphate and therefore old enough to lead the ritual[64] whereas 'Abd al-Malik's other sons who went on to become caliphs, Yazīd and Hishām, had not yet reached the age when they could legitimately lead the pilgrimage.[65]

As for the rest of the caliph's sons, at least seven of them were born of *ummahāt awlād*, slave women who were not necessarily Arabs.[66] Many of these sons were actively engaged in power politics: 'Abd Allāh, for one, occupied strategic governorships. He was governor of Ḥimṣ,[67] and later of

---

Zayd b. 'Alī that he will never be caliph because he is the son of a slave girl. See also Bligh-Abramski, *From Damascus to Baghdad*, 77-78.

56 Madelung, *Succession*, 57.

57 Al-Zubayrī, *Nasab Quraish,* 127; Ibn Khayyāṭ, *Ta'rīkh*, I 250; al-Ya'qūbī, *Ta'rīkh* II 154.

58 Al-Zubayrī, *Nasab Quraish*, 128; al-Ya'qūbī, *Ta'rīkh*, II 169; al-Dhahabī, *Ta'rīkh*, III 83.

59 Al-Zubayrī, *Nasab Quraish*, 159 & 160; Ibn Khayyāṭ, *Ta'rīkh*, I 255 & 259; al-Ya'qūbī, *Ta'rīkh*, II 187; al-Dhahabī, *Ta'rīkh*, III 71 & 277.

60 Al-Zubayrī, *Nasab Quraish*, 162; Ibn Khayyāṭ, *Ta'rīkh*, I 302 & 314; al-Ya'qūbī, *Ta'rīkh*, II 204 & 216; al-Dhahabī, *Ta'rīkh*, III 281; Dixon, *Umayyad Caliphate*, 113.

61 Al-Zubayrī, *Nasab Quraish*, 162 & 163; al-Ṭabarī, *Ta'rīkh*, II 1317. See Ibn A'tham, *Futūḥ*, VII 202, for a slightly different version of events.

62 Al-Ṭabarī, *Ta'rīkh*, II 1174.

63 Al-Zubayrī, *Nasab Quraish*, 164 & 328; al-Ya'qūbī, *Ta'rīkh*, II 243; al-Dhahabī, *Ta'rīkh*, III 280 & V 170.

64 Al-Walīd was in his 40s – the possibilities range from 42 to 47 – when he died in 96/715: al-Ṭabarī, *Ta'rīkh*, II 1270. Even the youngest age given would have placed him in his 20s when he led the pilgrimage in 78/698. Sulaymān was in his mid-40s when he died in 99/717: Ibn Khayyāṭ, *Ta'rīkh*, I 322, making him in his mid-to-late 20s when he led the pilgrimage in 81/701.

65 Yazīd was in his mid-30s when he died in 105/724: al-Ṭabarī, *Ta'rīkh*, II 1463, making him a teenager at the end of his father's caliphate. Hishām was born in 72/692: al-Ṭabarī, *Ta'rīkh*, II 1466, which meant he too would have been a teenager at the end of his father's caliphate.

66 Al-Zubayrī, *Nasab Quraish*, 164-165; al-Ṭabarī, *Ta'rīkh*, II 1174; Crone, *Slaves on Horses*, 124.

67 Ibn Khayyāṭ, *Ta'rīkh*, I 301.

Egypt,[68] and he led the *ṣā'ifah* in 83/702, 84/703 and 85/704.[69] But there were limits to the political ambitions these sons could harbour. While they could govern a province and lead the *ṣā'ifah*, they were by reason of their birth excluded from the succession and therefore, it seems, from leadership of the *ḥajj*.

In 85/704, 'Abd al-Malik moved to change the succession and tried to persuade his brother to step aside in favour of al-Walīd.[70] The promise that 'Abd al-'Azīz would be appointed al-Walīd's heir apparent did nothing to sway him. 'Abd al-'Azīz knew that time was not on his side and feared that if he agreed to be sidelined once, there would be no guarantee it would not happen again.

The problem was solved for 'Abd al-Malik when, later that same year, 'Abd al-'Azīz died, apparently of natural causes, and the way was now clear for two of the caliph's most high-profile sons, al-Walīd and Sulaymān, to become his heirs.[71]

THE GOVERNORS OF MEDINA AND LEADERSHIP OF THE *ḤAJJ*: THE SUFYĀNID MODEL REVISITED

'Abd al-Malik adopted many of Mu'āwiyah's policies regarding the governorship of Medina and leadership of the *ḥajj*.

First, he maintained the connection between this governorship and leadership of the ritual: nine of his thirteen *ḥajj* seasons were led by his governor of Medina.

Second, 'Abd al-Malik maintained the connection between the governorship of Medina, leadership of the *ḥajj* and the family of the murdered caliph 'Uthmān. The Umayyads continued to see vengeance for 'Uthmān as their political *raison d'etre*; it was their answer to the questions so frequently

68 Ibn Khayyāṭ, *Ta'rīkh*, I 300; al-Ṭabarī, *Ta'rīkh*, II 1165.

69 Ibn Khayyāṭ, *Ta'rīkh*, I 290 & 292; al-Balādhurī, *Futūḥ*, 165; al-Ṭabarī, *Ta'rīkh*, II 1127. Another son, 'Ubayd Allāh, led it in 81/700: al-Ṭabarī, *Ta'rīkh*, II 1047.

70 Al-Ya'qūbī, *Ta'rīkh*, II 201 & 202, gives two different accounts: in one, the caliph sets out to oust his brother (201) and in the other (202), he does not. According to al-Ṭabarī, *Ta'rīkh*, II 1164-71, the caliph set out to depose his brother. In al-Jahshiyārī, *Kitāb al-wuzarā'*, 34, the caliph intended to oust his brother in favour of his sons but was advised against doing so; his brother's timely death solved the problem for him. This is similar to an account in Ibn al-Athīr, *al-Kāmil*, IV 513-515 (513). In another, IV 514, the caliph makes an attempt to sideline his brother, wishing to make him his son's heir, but the plan fails. In al-Dhahabī, *Ta'rīkh*, III 235, the caliph is certainly not sorry to learn of his brother's death: he had resolved to sack him and wasted no time arranging the succession to his liking. Ibn Khayyāṭ, *Ta'rīkh*, I 290, diplomatically glosses over the details of the whole affair. See also Wellhausen, *Arab Kingdom*, 223-224; Chejne, *Succession*, 46-47.

71 Wellhausen, *Arab Kingdom*, 221.

asked about their right to rule and in few places were these questions asked with such frequency as in the Holy City of Medina. As a result, in no place but Medina did the Umayyads so frequently appoint governors with connections to ʿUthmān.

ʿAbd al-Malik chose one of ʿUthmān's sons – Abān – to govern the city and to lead the *ḥajj* for him.[72] This appointment also allowed him to score a political point against his former rival Ibn al-Zubayr. While the latter was a political supporter of ʿUthmān, he was not a blood relative of the murdered caliph in the way the Umayyads were. One of the most obvious ways for the new caliph to show himself as the true heir of the murdered caliph's political legacy was therefore to appoint one of ʿUthmān's relatives – and his own – to govern the city where ʿUthmān met his death.[73]

Abān led the *ḥajj* five times and retained his position for seven (Islamic) years,[74] becoming the longest serving Umayyad appointed governor of Medina since the days when ʿAbd al-Malik's father, Marwān, occupied the post for Muʿāwiyah.

Third, ʿAbd al-Malik maintained the connection between the governorship of Medina, leadership of the *ḥajj*, and the Umayyad family. The only deviations from this policy came during the uncertainty of the *fitnah* when a *mawlā* of ʿUthmān, Ṭāriq b. ʿAmr,[75] and al-Ḥajjāj, ʿAbd al-Malik's military leader, were appointed to the governorship. While Ṭāriq did not occupy the position long and did not lead the *ḥajj*, the significance of appointing a *mawlā* of the murdered caliph to represent Umayyad authority in Medina during the *fitnah* would not have been lost on the city's residents.[76]

Al-Ḥajjāj, by contrast, represented ʿAbd al-Malik in Mecca on a total of three occasions and was the first person from outside the Umayyad family appointed by an Umayyad caliph to lead the *ḥajj*. Previous caliphs, as we have seen, shied away from inviting anyone from the military to lead the *ḥajj*. Al-Ḥajjāj was also one of the few governors of Mecca to be given priority over the governor of Medina when it came to leading the *ḥajj*. This may have been due to the exceptional political and military circumstances in the Ḥijāz following Ibn al-Zubayr's death when the new caliph needed

72 Al-Balādhurī, *Ansāb*, V 120.

73 For his descent, see al-Zubayrī, *Nasab Quraish*, 104. For his appointment, see Ibn Khayyāṭ, *Taʾrīkh*, I 294; al-Ṭabarī, *Taʾrīkh*, II 940.

74 Ibn Khayyāṭ, *Taʾrīkh*, I 294; al-Ṭabarī, *Taʾrīkh*, II 1085; Ibn ʿAsākir, *TMD*, Vol. 6, 157.

75 Ibn Khayyāṭ, *Taʾrīkh*, I 265, places his appointment in 71/690-691; al-Ṭabarī, *Taʾrīkh*, II 818, 834 & 852, has him as governor from 71/690-691 to 73/692-693; Ibn Kathīr, *Bidāyah*, VIII 326, places his appointment in 72/691-692.

76 Ibn Khayyāṭ, *Taʾrīkh*, I 294; al-Ṭabarī, *Taʾrīkh*, II 852 & 854; Zambaur, *Généalogie*, 24.

a strong presence in Mecca to ensure his newly regained authority was not challenged. Al-Ḥajjāj had repeatedly shown he was the man for that job and was therefore appointed to lead the first *ḥajj* of the new era in 73/693. The governorship of Medina was soon added to his responsibilities.[77]

But a year later, with al-Ḥajjāj's work in the Ḥijāz so effectively accomplished, it was time for his military skills to be deployed elsewhere and he was appointed to govern the strategically important province of Iraq.[78] 'Abd al-Malik then returned to the tried and tested Umayyad practice of appointing members of the Umayyad family to the governorship of Medina and leadership of the *ḥajj*: every *ḥajj* from 75/695 to the last of 'Abd al-Malik's caliphate in 85/704 was led by a member of the Umayyad family, whether by birth or marriage.

And fourth, 'Abd al-Malik followed Mu'āwiyah's policy of giving precedence to members of his own family over the incumbent governor of Medina when it came to leading the *ḥajj*. In the post-*fitnah* period, a greater degree of stability was evident in the administration of the Prophet's City than had been the case during the turbulence of Yazīd's caliphate. Governors again occupied the position for lengthy periods of time: 'Abd al-Malik's fourteen (Islamic) years in power saw a total of five men appointed to the governorship of Medina compared to three for Yazīd's four years in power. But, no matter how diligently a governor performed his duties or how loyally he served the caliph who appointed him, leadership of the *ḥajj* was not an automatic privilege of his position. The caliph's immediate family continued to take precedence. Abān b. 'Uthmān, for example, did not lead two of the *ḥajj* seasons of his governorship; the caliph gave leadership of these, 78/698 and 81/701, to his sons al-Walīd and Sulaymān respectively.

The many areas of common ground between the *ḥajj* policy of Mu'āwiyah, the founder of the Umayyad political dynasty, and that of 'Abd al-Malik, the restorer of it, show that within the context of the *ḥajj*, the most tangible differences in policy were not between the different branches of the Umayyads – the Sufyānids and the Marwānids – but between the Umayyads as a unit and the *Rāshidūn* caliphs, 'Umar and 'Uthmān, and Ibn al-Zubayr. These two groupings represented different visions for the caliphate, visions which found expression in their contrasting policies for the *ḥajj*.

77 Ibn Khayyāṭ, *Ta'rīkh*, I 294; al-Ṭabarī, *Ta'rīkh*, II 854; al-Mas'ūdī, *Murūj*, 2029.
78 Ibn Khayyāṭ, *Ta'rīkh*, I 294; Ibn A'tham, *Futūḥ*, VII 3 & 4; al-Ṭabarī, *Ta'rīkh*, II 863.

The one aspect of his *ḥajj* policy which ʿAbd al-Malik developed in distinction from his Umayyad predecessors was his decision to appoint his father-in-law, Hishām b. Ismāʿīl al-Makhzūmī,[79] governor of Medina and to give him leadership of three *ḥajj* seasons. Hishām was the father of ʿAbd al-Malik's wife, ʿĀ'ishah, and the grandfather of the future caliph Hishām who was said to have been named after him.[80]

In appointing him, ʿAbd al-Malik hoped to resolve one of the legacies left by the *fitnah*: how to contain the political aspirations of the former seat of the caliphate without appearing to disrespect the City of the Prophet. The prestige of the Holy City demanded that the caliph appoint someone of suitable standing to govern it. A member of the caliph's family was the ideal choice: it intimated a very personal connection between the caliph and one of the Holiest Cities in Islam; it signalled his ongoing commitment to the region; and it proved that the city still ranked highly on his list of priorities. The question was who could the caliph trust amongst his own family to represent him in the Holy Cities and on the *ḥajj*?

For his political survival, ʿAbd al-Malik had to ensure that no rival and no one with an independent power base could capitalize on the symbolism of Mecca and Medina for their own benefit. He needed governors who were wholly dependent on him and whose interests coincided with his. He was effectively looking for the political equivalent of a *mawlā*. But such an appointment was unlikely in politically settled times. The people of Mecca and Medina may have interpreted it as a snub to the standing of the Holy Cities. The caliph was therefore caught in a contradiction: he had to appoint governors to Mecca and Medina who were men of status but not men of power.

He, and the caliphs who came after him, found the answer by turning to the men on the fringes of the Umayyad family. To in-laws, second cousins, maternal uncles: men who would not have expected appointment to positions of primary importance in the caliphate but who found themselves governing a Holy City and thereby candidates to lead the most prestigious religious event of all. Such men enjoyed all the prestige of belonging to the ruling house but none of the executive power.

79 The timing of this appointment is less than clear: the sources differ as to whether it took place in 82/701 or a year later: al-Zubayrī, *Nasab Quraish*, 328; Ibn Khayyāṭ, *Ta'rīkh*, I 294; al-Yaʿqūbī, *Ta'rīkh*, II 202; al-Ṭabarī, *Ta'rīkh*, II 1085; Ibn al-Athīr, *al-Kāmil*, IV 476 (where the new governor's starting date is given as 82/701) & IV 496 (where it is given as a year later).

80 Al-Zubayrī, *Nasab Quraish*, 164 & 328; al-Ṭabarī, *Ta'rīkh*, II 1174 & 1466; Wellhausen, *Arab Kingdom*, 215.

The caliph's decision to appoint his father-in-law, a man with easy access to him, to govern Medina helped retain the illusion that the Holy City continued to enjoy a political status which it had in fact lost with the demise of Ibn al-Zubayr. 'Abd al-Malik's nomination of a member of his inner family circle to this governorship may have looked like a compliment to its status but the political reality was different. The appointment of an affinal relative like Hishām merely confirmed the ongoing process of de-politicizing the Holy Cities.

For, unlike Ibn al-Zubayr before him, 'Abd al-Malik had no intention of returning the caliphate to its former home or of resurrecting the *ḥajj* policies of 'Umar and 'Uthmān which saw the caliph led the *ḥajj* on an annual basis. Nor did 'Abd al-Malik seem particularly keen to return to his former home in Medina. He came back to the Ḥijāz to lead the *ḥajj* in 75/695 but showed little inclination to do so again. This caliph was determined to remain in Syria and rule from there.

Employing lower-ranking members of his family as governors in the Ḥijāz offered 'Abd al-Malik another political benefit: it enabled him to exclude members of the local elite – the 'Alids, the *Anṣār* and the *Ṣaḥābah* – from positions of political leadership in the Holy Cities. Many of these people were employed in the judiciary in Medina but they were kept out of the political decision-making process. No one, other than the caliph's personal choice of nominee, was to be allowed to benefit from the prestige of political association with the Prophet's City. And if the governor of Medina were to be honoured by the caliph with leadership of the *ḥajj*, it was his job to ensure that any political capital accrued from it was to go to the caliph and the caliph alone.

SIX

A House Dividing
The Successor Sons of 'Abd al-Malik: al-Walīd and Sulaymān

Al-Walīd[1] became caliph in 86/705, a position he retained until his death in 96/715. He was succeeded by his brother Sulaymān[2] who remained caliph until his death in 99/717. Table 5 shows their choices of *ḥajj* leaders for their respective caliphates.

Table 5

Year	*Ḥajj leader*	*Relationship to caliph*	*Governor of Medina?*
al-Walīd			
86/705	Hishām b. Ismā'īl[3] *or* al-'Abbās b. al-Walīd[4]	x son	yes x
87/706	'Umar b. 'Abd al-'Azīz[5]	cousin	yes

1 *EI* 2nd edition, s.v. Walīd b. 'Abd al-Malik.
2 *EI* 2nd edition, s.v. Sulaymān b. 'Abd al-Malik.
3 Ibn Khayyāṭ, *Ta'rīkh*, I 316; al-Ya'qūbī, *Ta'rīkh*, II 215; al-Ṭabarī, *Ta'rīkh*, II 1182.
4 Al-Mas'ūdī, *Murūj*, 3636.
5 Ibn Khayyāṭ, *Ta'rīkh*, I 304 & 316; al-Ya'qūbī, *Ta'rīkh*, II 215; al-Ṭabarī, *Ta'rīkh*, II 1191; al-Mas'ūdī, *Murūj*, 3636; Ibn 'Asākir, *TMD*, Vol. 45, 140.

88/707	'Umar b. al-Walīd[6] *or* 'Umar b. 'Abd al-'Azīz[7] *or* CALIPH[8]	caliph's son cousin -	x yes -
89/708	'Umar b. 'Abd al-'Azīz[9]	cousin	yes (& Mecca)
90/709	'Umar b. 'Abd al-'Azīz[10]	cousin	yes (& Mecca)
91/710	CALIPH[11]	-	-
92/711	'Umar b. 'Abd al-'Azīz[12]	cousin	yes (& Mecca)
93/712	'Abd al-'Azīz b. al-Walīd[13] *or* 'Umar b. 'Abd al-'Azīz[14] *or* 'Uthmān b. al-Walīd[15]	caliph's son cousin caliph's son	x x x
94/713	Maslamah b. 'Abd al-Malik[16] *or* 'Abd al-'Azīz b. al-Walīd[17] *or* al-'Abbās b. al-Walīd[18]	half-brother caliph's son caliph's son	x x x

6 Ibn Khayyāṭ, *Ta'rīkh*, I 305 & 316; al-Ṭabarī, *Ta'rīkh*, II 1197; Ibn 'Asākir, *TMD*, Vol. 45, 139; Ibn al-Athīr, *al-Kāmil*, IV 534.

7 Al-Ṭabarī, *Ta'rīkh*, II 1196; Ibn 'Asākir, *TMD*, Vol. 45, 139; Ibn al-Athīr, *al-Kāmil*, IV 534; Ibn Kathīr, *Bidāyah*, IX 75.

8 Al-Mas'ūdī, *Murūj*, 3636.

9 Ibn Khayyāṭ, *Ta'rīkh*, I 306 & 316; al-Ya'qūbī, *Ta'rīkh*, II 215; al-Ṭabarī, *Ta'rīkh*, II 1200; al-Mas'ūdī, *Murūj*, 3636; Ibn 'Asākir, *TMD*, Vol. 45, 139 & 140.

10 Ibn Khayyāṭ, *Ta'rīkh*, I 306 & 316; al-Ya'qūbī, *Ta'rīkh*, II 215; al-Ṭabarī, *Ta'rīkh*, II 1208; al-Mas'ūdī, *Murūj*, 3636; Ibn 'Asākir, *TMD*, Vol. 45, 139 & 140.

11 Ibn Khayyāṭ, *Ta'rīkh*, I 307 & 316; al-Dīnawarī, *Akhbār*, 235; al-Ya'qūbī, *Ta'rīkh*, II 206; al-Ṭabarī, *Ta'rīkh*, II 1232; al-Mas'ūdī, *Murūj*, 3637; Ibn 'Asākir, *TMD*, Vol. 45, 139, & Vol. 63, 170 & 171; al-Fāsī, *Akhbār Makkah*, II 236.

12 Ibn Khayyāṭ, *Ta'rīkh*, I 316; al-Ya'qūbī, *Ta'rīkh*, II 215; al-Ṭabarī, *Ta'rīkh*, II 1235; al-Mas'ūdī, *Murūj*, 3637; Ibn 'Asākir, *TMD*, Vol. 45, 139 & 140.

13 Ibn Khayyāṭ, *Ta'rīkh*, I 309 & 316; al-Ṭabarī, *Ta'rīkh*, II 1255; al-Mas'ūdī, *Murūj*, 3637; Ibn 'Asākir, *TMD*, Vol. 36, 372; Ibn al-Athīr, *al-Kāmil*, IV 578.

14 Al-Ya'qūbī, *Ta'rīkh*, II 215; Ibn 'Asākir, *TMD*, Vol. 45, 139; Ibn Kathīr, *Bidāyah*, IX 194.

15 Al-Mas'ūdī, *Murūj*, 3637.

16 Ibn Khayyāṭ, *Ta'rīkh*, I 310 & 316; al-Ya'qūbī, *Ta'rīkh*, II 215; al-Ṭabarī, *Ta'rīkh*, II 1266; al-Mas'ūdī, *Murūj*, 3637; Ibn 'Asākir, *TMD*, Vol. 58, 32 & 33.

17 Al-Ṭabarī, *Ta'rīkh*, II 1266.

18 Ibn Kathīr, *Bidāyah*, IX 97.

95/714	Bishr b. al-Walīd[19] *or* Abū Bakr b. Muḥammad[20] *or* CALIPH[21]	caliph's son x -	x x -
Sulaymān			
96/715	Abū Bakr b. Muḥammad[22]	x	yes
97/716	CALIPH[23]	-	-
98/717	'Abd al-'Azīz b. 'Abd Allāh b. Khālid b. Asīd[24]	distant relative	governor of Mecca

POWER AND PATRONAGE: THE CALIPHAL *ḤAJJ* OF 91 AH

The Umayyad grip on power was secure when al-Walīd succeeded his father in *Shawwāl* 86/October 705. He was the sixth Umayyad caliph but the first since the founder of the dynasty, Mu'āwiyah, to rule in times of political stability. He took advantage of it to endorse two key areas of policy: the *ḥajj* and the *jihād*. His caliphate witnessed the high-water mark of the conquests in the name of Islam: he was the caliph who oversaw the expansion of the Muslim territories to al-Andalus in the west and to Samarqand, Bukhārā and al-Hind in the east.[25] His governor of Khurāsān, Qutaybah b. Muslim, was militarily strong enough to dispatch a delegation to the king of China.[26]

19 Ibn Khayyāṭ, *Ta'rīkh*, I 313 & 316; al-Ṭabarī, *Ta'rīkh*, II 1269; al-Mas'ūdī, *Murūj*, 3637; Ibn 'Asākir, *TMD*, Vol. 10, 268 & 269.

20 Al-Ya'qūbī, *Ta'rīkh*, II 215.

21 Al-Fāsī, *Akhbār Makkah*, II 236.

22 Ibn Khayyāṭ, *Ta'rīkh*, I 318 & 325; al-Ya'qūbī, *Ta'rīkh*, II 225; al-Ṭabarī, *Ta'rīkh*, II 1305; al-Mas'ūdī, *Murūj*, 3637; Ibn 'Asākir, *TMD*, Vol. 66, 45.

23 Ibn Khayyāṭ, *Ta'rīkh*, I 320 & 325; al-Balādhurī, *Ansāb*, VI B 184; al-Ya'qūbī, *Ta'rīkh*, II 225; al-Ṭabarī, *Ta'rīkh*, II 1314; al-Mas'ūdī, *Murūj*, 3637; al-Fāsī, *Akhbār Makkah*, II 236.

24 Ibn Khayyāṭ, *Ta'rīkh*, I 321 & 325; al-Ya'qūbī, *Ta'rīkh*, II 225; al-Ṭabarī, *Ta'rīkh*, II 1335; al-Mas'ūdī, *Murūj*, 3637; Ibn 'Asākir, *TMD*, Vol. 36, 296 & 297.

25 Ibn Khayyāṭ, *Ta'rīkh*, I 308 & 309; al-Dīnawarī, *Akhbār*, 235; al-Ṭabarī, *Ta'rīkh*, II 1235, 1241-52 & 1271; Ibn al-Athīr, *al-Kāmil*, IV 542-543, 556-567 & 571-576; Quṭb al-Dīn, *Akhbār Makkah*, III 86 (where parallels are drawn with the achievements of 'Umar); Wellhausen, *Arab Kingdom*, 224.

26 Al-Ṭabarī, *Ta'rīkh*, II 1276-79.

Al-Walīd's achievements in the Ḥijāz were no less impressive. The settled political circumstances of his accession allowed him to demonstrate his authority and bestow his patronage as he wished. He took his father's building project, the Dome of the Rock, as his example and went a stage further and developed caliphal patronage into an entire programme.[27] His name would forever be associated with the Holy City of Medina thanks to the huge building programme he sponsored there.[28] He was not the first caliph to build in the Holy City – 'Umar and 'Uthmān did so – but no one had previously developed the Prophet's Mosque on such a scale.[29]

Aside from the political benefits of such patronage, a very practical reason may have motivated al-Walīd to expand the Mosque. The number of Muslims had increased since the days of 'Umar and 'Uthmān and more space would have been needed to facilitate the greater number of worshippers. In addition, the Muslim community itself was now into its third generation and would have been considerably larger than it had been in the days of the *Rāshidūn*.

Work began on the project in 88/707, a year which al-Mas'ūdī records al-Walīd leading the *ḥajj*. As part of the renovations, the caliph ordered, somewhat controversially, that the *qiblah* wall be moved forward. That he recognized the difficulties of such an innovation may be seen in the advice he gave to his governor of the Holy City, his cousin 'Umar b. 'Abd al-'Azīz: al-Walīd suggested that 'Umar play upon the name of his maternal grandfather, the second caliph 'Umar, to push the project forward. And if that failed, an array of financial incentives was to be offered to overcome local opposition.[30]

The caliph's analysis of what was needed proved correct; demolition work soon began and not long afterwards, workmen sent by al-Walīd arrived in the Holy City to start construction of the new structure.[31]

In an unusual twist of imperial politics, the caliph turned to none other than the Byzantine emperor for assistance with these renovations. Out of respect, perhaps, to their positions as two of the most powerful men in the

---

27 Al-Ṭabarī, *Ta'rīkh*, II 1272-73; Ibn al-Athīr, *al-Kāmil*, V 9 & 10; Wellhausen, *Arab Kingdom*, 225; Peters, *Hajj*, 69; Blankinship, *Jihad*, 82 & 95; Bacharach, "Marwanid Umayyad Building Activities: Speculations on Patronage", 32; Hoyland, *Seeing Islam*, 567-568, 569 & 651; Flood, *The Great Mosque of Damascus*, 9; Hitti, *History*, 221-222; Lapidus, *Islamic Societies*, 71.

28 Sauvaget, *La mosquée de Médine*; Bisheh, *The Mosque of the Prophet*; Peters, *Mecca*, 102-105.

29 Al-Ṭabarī, *Ta'rīkh*, II 1192-93. See also Ibn Khayyāṭ, *Ta'rīkh*, I 304; al-Balādhurī, *Futūḥ*, 6-7; al-Dīnawarī, *Akhbār*, 234; al-Ya'qūbī, *Ta'rīkh*, II 206; al-Mas'ūdī, *Murūj*, 2115; Quṭb al-Dīn, *Akhbār Makkah*, II 85-86.

30 Al-Ṭabarī, *Ta'rīkh*, II 1193. For 'Umar's descent from the caliph of the same name, see al-Zubayrī, *Nasab Quraish*, 168; al-Ṭabarī, *Ta'rīkh*, II 1362; Wellhausen, *Arab Kingdom*, 267.

31 Al-Ṭabarī, *Ta'rīkh*, II 1193-94.

world, the emperor responded positively and sent al-Walīd one hundred thousand *mithqāls* of gold, one hundred workers and forty loads of mosaic.[32] And his generosity did not stop there. He ordered that any mosaic found in ruined cities should be sent to the caliph for use in Medina. What made this gift giving all the more extraordinary is that it took place against the backdrop of continued Muslim raids on Byzantine territory; raids led by such senior members of the ruling family as the caliph's brother, Maslamah, and the caliph's son, al-'Abbās.[33]

Al-Walīd's programme of patronage extended to a number of projects in the Ḥijāz. He was mindful of the hardships which pilgrims endured en route to the Holy Cities, particularly if the *ḥajj* fell in the heat of summer, and ordered his governor of Medina to have wells dug in the Ḥijāz.[34] Mountain passes were made easier to cross[35] and a drinking fountain was constructed in the Holy City.[36] As if to vindicate al-Walīd's concerns about the potential scarcity of water in the Ḥijāz, Mecca ran short of water in the very year he set these projects in motion.[37]

This patronage of water wells in the Holy Cities, and the routes to them, was more than a mere display of caliphal generosity; it was a political necessity for any caliph who sought to secure the goodwill of the pilgrims. Al-Walīd's patronage of water wells in the Ḥijāz was such a priority policy that his governor of Mecca, Khālid b. 'Abd Allāh al-Qasrī, saw fit to refer to it in glowing terms during a *khuṭbah* in Mecca when he compared the caliph to the Prophet Ibrāhīm.[38]

During the caliphate of al-Walīd's father, the completion of renovations to the *Ḥarām* had been the catalyst for 'Abd al-Malik to travel to the Ḥijāz and lead the *ḥajj*. During al-Walīd's, the completion of the renovations to the Prophet's Mosque paved the way for him to do the same.[39] The motivation between the two caliphal pilgrimages, however, could not have been more different. If 'Abd al-Malik's *ḥajj* in 75/695 had been about the demonstration of his power, al-Walīd's in 91/710 was about the bestowal of caliphal patronage. On his *ḥajj*, 'Abd al-Malik sought to remind the inhabitants of the Holy Cities, many of whom had sided against him in the *fitnah*, of his victory over

32 Al-Dīnawarī, *Akhbār*, 234; al-Ya'qūbī, *Ta'rīkh*, II 206; al-Ṭabarī, *Ta'rīkh*, II 1194.
33 Ibn Khayyāṭ, *Ta'rīkh*, I 305 & 317; al-Ya'qūbī, *Ta'rīkh*, II 215; al-Ṭabarī, *Ta'rīkh*, II 1192 & 1194.
34 Al-Ṭabarī, *Ta'rīkh*, II 1196.
35 Al-Ṭabarī, *Ta'rīkh*, II 1195-96; Ibn al-Athīr, *al-Kāmil*, IV 533.
36 Al-Ṭabarī, *Ta'rīkh*, II 1196; Ibn al-Athīr, *al-Kāmil*, IV 533; al-Dhahabī, *Ta'rīkh*, III 238.
37 Al-Ṭabarī, *Ta'rīkh*, II 1196-97; Ibn al-Athīr, *al-Kāmil*, IV 534; al-Fāsī, *Akhbār Makkah*, II 301-02.
38 Al-Ṭabarī, *Ta'rīkh*, II 1199; Hawting, *First Dynasty*, 82.
39 Al-Ya'qūbī, *Ta'rīkh*, II 206; al-Dīnawarī, *Akhbār*, 235-236.

them. Al-Walīd, on the other hand, had no need to do so. The political circumstances 'Abd al-Malik left him meant he could afford to make a more subtle point about his power. His acts of patronage were therefore designed to demonstrate his ongoing commitment to the Holy Cities and their inhabitants; the vast building programme in Medina and its environs acting as a form of reconciliation with the city's residents, a constructive counterweight to the political damage caused by the Umayyad sieges of the Holy Cities and the fallout from the *fitnah*. A building project on such an imperial scale would also have stimulated the local economy. That it occurred within the context of a wider programme of mosque building, including the construction of the Great Mosque in Damascus and the renovations to al-Aqṣā in Jerusalem, linked these cities in an imperial chain which simultaneously underscored the caliph's political legitimacy and proclaimed his pious credentials.[40]

Al-Walīd's *ḥajj* of 91/710 was thus the concluding act in a policy of patronage which brought many tangible benefits to the people of the Holy Cities as well as to the pilgrims who visited them. Such a policy was designed to allow al-Walīd to show his authority in a non-threatening way, to tap into his "soft" power with the aim of generating support and goodwill for his leadership.

FOLLOWING IN HIS PREDECESSORS' FOOTSTEPS: AL-WALĪD'S SUCCESSION POLICY AND LEADERSHIP OF THE *ḤAJJ*

As heir apparent, al-Walīd accepted his father's wish that the caliphate rotate through those of his sons who were born to Arab mothers. Once caliph, however, al-Walīd was no different from his father or his grandfather in wanting to keep power within his own family. And just as his father had done, al-Walīd made full use of the political weapons at his disposal to try to achieve his goal.

At first, he did nothing to arouse the suspicions of his heir apparent, his brother Sulaymān, and confirmed him in his position as governor of

40 For the construction of the Great Mosque in Damascus, see Ibn Khayyāṭ, *Ta'rīkh*, I 304; al-Balādhurī, *Futūḥ*, 125-126; al-Ya'qūbī, *Ta'rīkh*, II 205-206; al-Mas'ūdī, *Murūj*, 2115; Ibn Kathīr, *Bidāyah*, IX 142-153 & 160; Quṭb al-Dīn, *Akhbār Makkah*, III 86. For the mosques in Damascus and Medina and their similarities, (particularly in decoration) see Brisch, "Observations on the Iconography of the Mosaics in the Great Mosque of Damascus" in Soucek, ed., *Content and Context of Visual Arts in the Islamic World:* 13-20 (in particular 16, 17 & 18); Ettinghausen, & Grabar, *Art and Architecture of Islam*, 37-45; Flood, *The Great Mosque of Damascus*, 188, 189, 195, 205, 215, 239 & 244.

Palestine.[41] But he also started the process of building up the profile of his preferred successor, his son ʿAbd al-ʿAzīz.[42] He appointed him governor of the Umayyad capital, Damascus; a position which kept ʿAbd al-ʿAzīz close to the caliph and the centre of political events.[43]

ʿAbd al-ʿAzīz was also appointed to lead the *ṣāʾifah* against the Byzantines. Ibn Khayyāṭ has him raiding in 94/713;[44] al-Ṭabarī in 91/710 and 94/713;[45] al-Yaʿqūbī in 90/709 and 91/710.[46]

And in 93/712, al-Walīd asked ʿAbd al-ʿAzīz to lead the *ḥajj* for him.

Thus, according to Ibn Khayyāṭ, al-Walīd's successor son led the two most high-profile mobile representations of caliphal authority, the *ḥajj* and the *ṣāʾifah*, in consecutive years: the *ḥajj* in 93/712 and the *ṣāʾifah* in 94/713.[47] Such sequencing corresponds to the pattern recorded by Ibn Khayyāṭ for al-Walīd's leadership of these events when he was being groomed for the succession.

The caliph's promotion of his son did not occur in a vacuum but fell within the wider context of his efforts to strengthen the political power of his own family. Several of his sons were given governorships close to the Umayyad base in Syria. ʿUmar, for example, was in charge of Jordan and al-ʿAbbās of Ḥimṣ.[48] Al-ʿAbbās was also a frequent campaigner against the Byzantines, often in the company of his uncle, Maslamah, while the caliph's sons ʿUmar, Bishr, and Marwān likewise saw military action on the western border.[49]

Al-Walīd's immediate family was also seen in the Holy City of Mecca: ʿAbd al-ʿAzīz, as we have seen, led the *ḥajj* in 93/712 and at least one, possibly two, of the caliph's other sons also led it: Bishr in 95/714 and possibly ʿUmar in 88/707. Bishr and ʿUmar were out of the running for the caliphate because they, unlike ʿAbd al-ʿAzīz, were not born of an Arab mother but

41 Ibn Khayyāṭ, *Taʾrīkh*, I 316; Crone, *Slaves on Horses*, 126.

42 Al-Ṭabarī, *Taʾrīkh*, II 1274. For details of his mother's descent, see al-Zubayrī, *Nasab Quraish*, 165.

43 Ibn Khayyāṭ, *Taʾrīkh*, I 316; Ibn ʿAsākir, *TMD*, Vol. 36, 369 & 373; al-Dhahabī, *Taʾrīkh*, IV 146; Crone, *Slaves on Horses*, 126.

44 Ibn Khayyāṭ, *Taʾrīkh*, I 310; Ibn ʿAsākir, *TMD*, Vol. 36, 372; al-Dhahabī, *Taʾrīkh*, III 327.

45 Al-Ṭabarī, *Taʾrīkh*, II 1217 & 1256; Ibn al-Athīr, *al-Kāmil*, IV 555; Ibn Kathīr, *Bidāyah*, IX 81 & 95.

46 Al-Yaʿqūbī, *Taʾrīkh*, II 216.

47 Ibn Khayyāṭ, *Taʾrīkh*, I 309 & 310. Al-Dhahabī agrees: *Taʾrīkh*, III 326 for the pilgrimage; III 327 for the summer campaign.

48 Ibn Khayyāṭ, *Taʾrīkh*, I 316; Crone, *Slaves on Horses*, 126.

49 Ibn Khayyāṭ, *Taʾrīkh*, I 306, 309, 310 & 317; al-Yaʿqūbī, *Taʾrīkh*, II 215-216; al-Ṭabarī, *Taʾrīkh*, II 1181, 1185, 1191, 1194, 1197-98, 1200, 1235, 1236, 1255, 1266-67 & 1269; Ibn ʿAsākir, *TMD*, Vol. 10, 268 & 269; Ibn al-Athīr, *al-Kāmil*, IV 535, 547, 578, 582 & 591; al-Dhahabī, *Taʾrīkh*, III 237, 240, 326 & 327; Ibn Kathīr, *Bidāyah*, IX 74, 76, 77, 83, 84, 95, 116 & 142.

were sons of an *umm walad*, a concubine.[50] Al-Walīd's decision to appoint them to lead the *ḥajj* broke with his father's policy of keeping leadership of the ritual for his sons who were eligible to lead the community. But al-Walīd, like his father before him, was not averse to manipulating the politics of descent to his own advantage; he merely chose to do so in a different way.

By keeping leadership of the *ḥajj* within his family, al-Walīd could keep others off the platform it offered at no political cost to himself. He did not, for example, invite his brother Sulaymān, the heir he was trying to sideline, to lead the *ḥajj*. Nor did he invite any of his brothers in line for the caliphate – Yazīd, Marwān, Hishām – to lead it. The only brother who, according to a number of sources, al-Walīd did invite to lead the *ḥajj* was Maslamah, the veteran campaigner on the eastern and western borders. He, as the son of an *umm walad*, was out of contention for the caliphate and could therefore be trusted to lead the ritual without using the occasion for his own advantage.[51]

As well as senior members of the ruling family, there were other groups al-Walīd overlooked when choosing a leader for the *ḥajj*. No descendant of the early Islamic elite, no *Anṣārī*s, and no member of the ʿAlid family was called upon by this caliph to lead this ritual. Nor was any religious figure asked to lead the community on their pilgrimage; an absence which showed that al-Walīd, like all of his predecessors, saw the *ḥajj* as a religious ritual which required political leadership.

Al-Walīd's policy of keeping leadership of the *ḥajj* restricted to a small core of people within his immediate family mirrored his intention of keeping leadership of the community within that same family. When, however, he had to look beyond his family for a leader the pilgrimage, he followed the path taken by so many of his predecessors and looked no further than his governor in Medina.

FOLLOWING IN HIS PREDECESSORS' FOOTSTEPS II: AL-WALĪD'S GOVERNORS OF MEDINA AND LEADERSHIP OF THE *ḤAJJ*

Al-Walīd confirmed his father's governor of Medina, Hishām b. Ismāʿīl, in his position and authorized him to lead the first *ḥajj* of his caliphate.[52]

50 Al-Zubayrī, *Nasab Quraish*, 165; Ibn Kathīr, *Bidāyah*, IX 166.

51 Al-Zubayrī, *Nasab Quraish*, 165; al-Ṭabarī, *Taʾrīkh*, II 1174; Wellhausen, *Arab Kingdom*, 312 note 1; Biddle, *Development of the Bureaucracy of the Islamic Empire*, 161-162.

52 Ibn Khayyāṭ, *Taʾrīkh*, I 315.

But the new caliph was said to have a poor opinion of Hishām because of his behaviour during the period of his governorship of Medina for 'Abd al-Malik. Hishām had been instructed at the time to have the *bay'ah* taken for al-Walīd and Sulaymān as the caliph's successors.[53] Only the well-known *faqīh* Sa'īd b. al-Musayyab reportedly refused to give it, claiming that he would not acknowledge any future caliph while the current one was still alive.[54]

Hishām b. Ismā'īl's response to Sa'īd's disobedience was to have him flogged and publicly humiliated to the extent that the *faqīh* feared for his life.[55] That Hishām had been working in al-Walīd's interests did nothing to sway the new caliph: he considered Hishām's treatment of Sa'īd excessive. As a result, he did not keep Hishām in the governorship of Medina for long.[56]

Beneath al-Walīd's sense of righteous indignation over Sa'īd's treatment lay the thorny issue of dynastic politics. Hishām b. Ismā'īl was the maternal grandfather of the caliph's brother, Hishām, but as Hishām and al-Walīd were sons of different mothers, Hishām b. Ismā'īl was not related to the caliph. The caliph's brother was a son of an Arab woman of status and was in line to become caliph at a future date. It was therefore unlikely that al-Walīd, with his plans of his own for the future of the caliphate, would wish to keep the grandfather of a potential rival in the prestigious governorship of the Holy City of Medina.

Al-Walīd sacked Hishām in 87/706 and replaced him with 'Umar b. 'Abd al-'Azīz b. Marwān.[57] A senior member of the Umayyad family, 'Umar was the caliph's cousin and (double) brother-in-law: he was married to al-Walīd's sister, Fāṭimah,[58] and 'Umar's sister, Umm Banīn, was al-Walīd's wife and the mother of al-Walīd's preferred successor, his son 'Abd al-'Azīz.[59] 'Umar's family connections were thus more in line with al-Walīd's hopes for the future direction of the caliphate than Hishām b. Ismā'īl's were ever likely to have been. He was given the governorships of both Holy Cities.

'Umar made a good first impression in Medina by meeting with the

---

53 Ibn Khayyāṭ, *Ta'rīkh*, I 290; al-Ṭabarī, *Ta'rīkh*, II 1169-70.

54 Al-Ṭabarī, *Ta'rīkh*, II 1169.

55 Ibn Khayyāṭ, *Ta'rīkh*, I 290-291; al-Ṭabarī, *Ta'rīkh*, II 1169-71. For the caliph's view of this, see Ibn Khayyāṭ, *Ta'rīkh*, I 291; al-Ya'qūbī, *Ta'rīkh*, II 202; al-Dhahabī, *Ta'rīkh*, III 310.

56 Wellhausen, *Arab Kingdom*, 224.

57 Al-Zubayrī, *Nasab Quraish*, 328-329; Ibn Khayyāṭ, *Ta'rīkh*, I 315; al-Ya'qūbī, *Ta'rīkh*, II 205; al-Ṭabarī, *Ta'rīkh*, II 1182-84.

58 Al-Zubayrī, *Nasab Quraish*, 165; Ibn Kathīr, *Bidāyah*, IX 71.

59 Al-Zubayrī, *Nasab Quraish*, 165 & 168; al-Ṭabarī, *Ta'rīkh*, II 1270; al-Dhahabī, *Ta'rīkh*, IV 146.

religious scholars, the *fuqahāʾ*, upon his arrival and assuring them that he would not make decisions without consulting them.[60] His predecessor, meanwhile, was not to be allowed to pass quietly into political retirement. Al-Walīd wrote to ʿUmar, instructing him to have Hishām b. Ismāʿīl stand before the people: in other words, to humiliate him before the people of the Holy City.[61] Such a step was a departure from the previous Umayyad practice in Medina and would turn out to be a dangerous precedent with de-stabilizing consequences in the future.

As governor, ʿUmar led the *ḥajj* in the year of his appointment, 87/706, and went on to lead at least three more. The two *ḥajj* seasons of his governorship when he seems not to have led the ritual, 88/707 and 91/710, were led by the most senior Umayyads of all: the caliph in 91/710 (and possibly 88/707 as well) and, according to some sources, one of the caliph's sons, ʿUmar, in 88/707. As we have seen, this policy of the governor of Medina making way for the caliphal family to lead the *ḥajj* started with Muʿāwiyah and was adopted by ʿAbd al-Malik.

Another feature common to the caliphates of both Muʿāwiyah and ʿAbd al-Malik was political dissent in the Ḥijāz. And al-Walīd, for all his good works in Mecca and Medina, was not to be untroubled by political events there. This time, however, the problems stemmed from an altogether different source and showed how the nature of political discourse was changing: it came from within the Umayyad house itself.

Two years after al-Walīd made his *ḥajj*, he felt obliged to sack his cousin from the governorship of Medina in an incident which showed where his political priorities lay. ʿUmar had written to al-Walīd to draw his attention to the harsh treatment which al-Ḥajjāj, the governor of Iraq, meted out to the people there. In response, al-Ḥajjāj claimed that rebels from his area were seeking refuge in Mecca and Medina.[62]

Al-Ḥajjāj knew from past experience what happened when the Ḥijāz became a centre of dissidence and the caliph, it seemed, knew it too. In this dispute, he sided with his governor of Iraq and ʿUmar was sacked.[63] To compound the insult, al-Walīd then turned to al-Ḥajjāj to suggest a new

60 Al-Dīnawarī, *Akhbār*, 234; al-Ṭabarī, *Taʾrīkh*, II 1183.
61 Al-Dhahabī, *Taʾrīkh*, III 236 & 310. According to III 310, the caliph's brother, the heir apparent Sulaymān, had to intervene to stop what was happening. See also al-Yaʿqūbī, *Taʾrīkh*, II 205, & al-Ṭabarī, *Taʾrīkh*, II 1183-84.
62 Al-Ṭabarī, *Taʾrīkh*, II 1254. For a slightly different version, see Ibn Kathīr, *Bidāyah*, IX 88, & see also IX 96 for the political impact of these events; Wellhausen, *Arab Kingdom*, 251; Kennedy, *Prophet*, 103.
63 Ibn Khayyāṭ, *Taʾrīkh*, I 315; al-Ṭabarī, *Taʾrīkh*, II 1254; Wellhausen, *Arab Kingdom*, 251, 267-268.

governor.[64] He recommended 'Uthmān b. Ḥayyān al-Murrī for Medina and Khālid b. 'Abd Allāh al-Qasrī for Mecca.[65]

'Uthmān, like al-Ḥajjāj, belonged to the Qaysī tribal grouping and was a man without an independent power base and therefore entirely reliant upon his political sponsor, al-Ḥajjāj, and the caliph for his position. He remained governor until al-Walīd's death in 96/715.[66]

But not once during his governorship was he invited to lead the *ḥajj*. Al-Walīd, like his Umayyad predecessors, maintained the policy of keeping leadership of the *ḥajj* within the Umayyad clan. The pilgrimages of 'Uthmān's governorship – 93/712 to 95/714 – were therefore led by members of the caliph's family: his (successor) son 'Abd al-'Azīz in 93/712; his brother Maslamah in 94/713; and his son Bishr in 95/714. Outsiders, it seemed, could find themselves appointed to the governorship of Medina or Mecca but they would soon discover that leadership of the *ḥajj* was not a privilege of the position they were destined to enjoy.

For all the similarities with the past, al-Walīd's *ḥajj* policy differed from that of his predecessors 'Abd al-Malik and Mu'āwiyah in one highly significant way: he did not rely upon the family of the murdered caliph 'Uthmān to occupy the governorship of Medina and, by extension, to proclaim his moral legitimacy at the *ḥajj*.

Al-Walīd's caliphate was the first of the post-*fitnah* era and it saw the Umayyads become more self-confident about their power. It also saw the nature of the political debate change. Al-Walīd's main political preoccupation was not to entrench Umayyad rule against external enemies but to try and entrench his own line of the family against his brother Sulaymān. With the political discourse shifting focus in this way, al-Walīd had less need to demonstrate his connection to 'Uthmān than had been the case for some of his Umayyad predecessors.

In 96/714-715 al-Walīd asked Sulaymān to step aside from the succession in favour of 'Abd al-'Azīz.[67] The caliph was supported in this by two of his most important governors: the conqueror of Bukhārā, Qutaybah b. Muslim, and the governor of Iraq, al-Ḥajjāj.[68]

Sulaymān was offered various incentives to give up his position for his

64 Al-Ṭabarī, *Ta'rīkh*, II 1254; Ibn al-Athīr, *al-Kāmil*, IV 577.
65 Ibn Khayyāṭ, *Ta'rīkh*, I 315; al-Ṭabarī, *Ta'rīkh*, II 1254. For a different version, see al-Ya'qūbī, *Ta'rīkh*, II 213.
66 Ibn Khayyāṭ, *Ta'rīkh*, I 315; Zambaur, *Généalogie*, 24.
67 Chejne, *Succession*, 47.
68 Al-Ṭabarī, *Ta'rīkh*, II 1274-75; Ibn al-Athīr, *al-Kāmil*, V 10.

nephew, including the chance to become 'Abd al-'Azīz's heir. It was a strategy the caliph's father had deployed when trying to sideline his brother from the succession. It had not worked then and it did not work now.[69]

And so, al-Walīd, so successful a caliph in so many ways, became the first of the Marwānid caliphs to fail in his efforts to remove an unwanted heir from the succession. The caliphate he left behind covered more ground than it had ever done and Umayyad control of it had rarely been stronger. But the fallout from the succession dispute between the two brothers was to linger and would come to influence Sulaymān's approach to governing in general and to his *ḥajj* policy in particular.

THE CALIPHAL PILGRIMAGE OF 97 AH: *ḤAJJ* AND *JIHĀD* IN THE SAME YEAR

Sulaymān received the oath of allegiance as caliph at his home in al-Ramlah in Palestine on the day al-Walīd died.[70] In the Umayyad political centre of Damascus, it was Sulaymān's cousin, 'Umar, the governor of Medina so unceremoniously sacked by al-Walīd, who received the oath on his behalf.[71]

The new caliph and his predecessor were full brothers: sons of the same mother, al-Wallādah bt. al-'Abbās from the Qays, but any sense of fraternity between them stopped there.[72] Al-Walīd's key lieutenant had been al-Ḥajjāj b. Yūsuf, a man who at times seemed only marginally less powerful than the caliph himself.[73] During al-Walīd's caliphate, Sulaymān found himself on the wrong side of al-Ḥajjāj when he granted shelter to the former governor of Khurāsān, Yazīd b. al-Muhallab, who was fleeing torture and almost certain death at al-Ḥajjāj's hands.[74] This series of events, together with al-Walīd's wish to remove Sulaymān from the succession, helped seal the breach between them.[75]

---

69 Al-Ṭabarī, *Ta'rīkh*, II 1274.

70 Al-Ṭabarī, *Ta'rīkh*, II 1281; Ibn al-Athīr, *al-Kāmil*, V 11.

71 Al-Ya'qūbī, *Ta'rīkh*, II 217.

72 Al-Zubayrī, *Nasab Quraish*, 162; Ibn Khayyāṭ, *Ta'rīkh*, I 302 & 314; al-Balādhurī, *Futūḥ*, 146; al-Ya'qūbī, *Ta'rīkh*, II 204 & 216; al-Mas'ūdī, *Murūj*, 2131-32 (for the bad feeling between the two brothers); al-Dhahabī, *Ta'rīkh*, III 281; Amabe, *Emergence of 'Abbasid Autocracy*, 15.

73 Wellhausen, *Arab Kingdom*, 251.

74 Ibn A'tham, *Futūḥ*, VII 209-214; al-Ṭabarī, *Ta'rīkh*, II 1209-17; Wellhausen, *Arab Kingdom*, 257-258; Crone, *Slaves on Horses*, 45; Hawting, *First Dynasty*, 74; Amabe, *Emergence of 'Abbasid Autocracy*, 15.

75 Wellhausen, *Arab Kingdom*, 258; Hawting, *First Dynasty*, 74.

Once caliph, Sulaymān had to assert his political authority. To achieve this, he broke with every Umayyad political precedent and instituted a purge of al-Walīd's key supporters. Al-Ḥajjāj had died in 95/714[76] and it was members of his family who were made to bear the brunt of the new caliph's avenging wrath.[77] Sulaymān ordered their torture and execution. Another key supporter of al-Walīd's policies, especially with regard to the succession, was Qutaybah b. Muslim. He, unlike al-Ḥajjāj, survived the caliph he served. But not for long: he was killed in the year of Sulaymān's accession.[78] In the course of this purge, Sulaymān also removed al-Walīd's governor of the strategically vital province of Iraq, Yazīd b. Abī Muslim, and replaced him with the man to whom he had so controversially given asylum during al-Walīd's caliphate: Yazīd b. al-Muhallab.[79]

These dramatic events set the political tone for Sulaymān's caliphate and provided the backdrop for the policy he adopted for the *ḥajj*. According to al-Ya'qūbī,[80] Sulaymān intended to lead the first *ḥajj* of his caliphate and he relates an account in which the caliph ordered his governor of Mecca, Khālid b. 'Abd Allāh, to carve out a stream between Zamzam and the Black Stone; the aim of which was to provide sweet water for the pilgrims instead of the salty bitter water of the Zamzam well.[81] Sulaymān's first *ḥajj* fell in the heat of summer, in August 715, which may explain his concern about water supplies in the Holy Cities. Performing the pilgrimage was a difficult undertaking at the best of times but to do it in the heat of a desert summer made it a test of endurance as well as a test of faith.

What is interesting about al-Ya'qūbī's account is that it mirrors, almost identically, al-Ṭabarī's account of a new sweet water well excavated to provide an alternative to the bitter water in the Zamzam well. The difference between the two accounts is that al-Ṭabarī has these events occurring at the request of Sulaymān's predecessor, al-Walīd.[82] Which account is more reliable is not clear; al-Ya'qūbī's continues in the same vein as al-Ṭabarī's:

76 Al-Dīnawarī, *Akhbār*, 236; al-Ya'qūbī, *Ta'rīkh*, II 214; al-Jahshiyārī, *Kitāb al-wuzarā'*, 43; al-Mas'ūdī, *Murūj*, 2137; Ibn Kathīr, *Bidāyah*, IX 117.

77 Al-Ṭabarī, *Ta'rīkh*, II 1282; Wellhausen, *Arab Kingdom*, 258; Amabe, *Emergence of 'Abbasid Autocracy*, 15-16.

78 Ibn Khayyāṭ, *Ta'rīkh*, I 318; Ibn A'tham, *Futūḥ*, VII 265-280; al-Ya'qūbī, *Ta'rīkh*, II 219-220; al-Ṭabarī, *Ta'rīkh*, II 1283-1304; Wellhausen, *Arab Kingdom*, 258.

79 Ibn A'tham, *Futūḥ*, VII 252; al-Ṭabarī, *Ta'rīkh*, II 1282; Wellhausen, *Arab Kingdom*, 259; Hawting, *First Dynasty*, 75.

80 Al-Ya'qūbī, *Ta'rīkh*, II 217.

81 Al-Ya'qūbī, *Ta'rīkh*, II 217-218; Hawting, *First Dynasty*, 82.

82 Al-Ṭabarī, *Ta'rīkh*, II 1199-1200.

when the work on the new well was successfully completed, Khālid called the people to prayer and commended the new water supply to them but the people of the Holy City ignored the new supply and drank even more from Zamzam than they had previously. Al-Yaʿqūbī records that Sulaymān decided not to lead the first *ḥajj* of his caliphate and asked his governor of Medina to do so instead.

The following year Sulaymān placed himself directly in the footsteps of many of his caliphal predecessors by taking personal charge of the pilgrimage. He was the third successive Umayyad caliph to lead his community in the performance of this religious ritual but the first to do it so early in his caliphate. For Sulaymān, the year in which he chose to do so was significant for another reason: it was the year he launched *jihād*. 97/716 saw him equip and dispatch armies against the jewel in the Byzantine crown, Constantinople.[83] And it was in the Ḥijāz, on his way back from leading the *ḥajj*, where Sulaymān's troops presented him with hundreds of Byzantine prisoners.[84]

The timing of Sulaymān's *ḥajj* with the *jihād* suggests he wanted to present an image of himself as a caliph keen to satisfy all his obligations to God. It also showed he was no less committed to extending the borders of the territories of Islam than al-Walīd had been.[85]

On his *ḥajj*, Sulaymān adopted a policy of caliphal generosity similar to that of his predecessor and doled out large sums of money to the people of the Holy Cities.[86] The impression of caliphal pomp and power was enhanced by the vast entourage of family members and courtiers Sulaymān brought with him. Mentioned as present were the propagandists and court reporters of their day: the poets,[87] including the renowned al-Farazdaq who, more than forty years earlier, had sought temporary refuge in the Ḥijāz after offending the governor of Iraq.[88] The caliph's maternal uncles, the Banū ʿAbs, were also in attendance;[89] as was the former governor of Medina, ʿUmar b. ʿAbd al-ʿAzīz.[90]

83 Ibn Khayyāṭ, *Ta'rīkh*, I 321 (listed under 98/716-717); al-Yaʿqūbī, *Ta'rīkh*, II 224 & 225; al-Ṭabarī, *Ta'rīkh*, II 1305-06; Hawting, *First Dynasty*, 73; Blankinship, *Jihad*, 31.

84 Al-Ṭabarī, *Ta'rīkh*, II 1338.

85 He was no less committed to mosque construction: he had the congregational mosque in Aleppo built, Blankinship, *Jihad*, 95.

86 Al-Yaʿqūbī, *Ta'rīkh*, II 223.

87 Al-Ṭabarī, *Ta'rīkh*, II 1338-39; Ibn al-Athīr, *al-Kāmil*, V 38.

88 Al-Ṭabarī, *Ta'rīkh*, II 1338. For details of his flight, see al-Ṭabarī, *Ta'rīkh*, II 94-108; Ibn al-Athīr, *al-Kāmil*, III 467-470; Ibn Kathīr, *Bidāyah*, VIII 45.

89 Al-Ṭabarī, *Ta'rīkh*, II 1338.

90 Ibn Kathīr, *Bidāyah*, IX 179, where the caliph comments on the number of pilgrims: "Only God

En route to Mecca, Sulaymān stopped in Medina. There, he consulted the religious jurists, the *fuqahā'*, in a manner which is open to more than one interpretation. He was said to have asked them how best to perform the *ḥajj*. Unfortunately for him, none of the scholars could agree and Sulaymān had to resort to asking how his father, 'Abd al-Malik, had performed his *ḥajj* and then proceed to do as he had done.[91]

This incident has been interpreted as significant in that it may suggest the rites of the *ḥajj* were not yet fixed.[92] In terms of the present discussion, the caliph's actions could also be interpreted as an attempt to place him in a positive light with the Ḥijāzī elite: they show him as a ruler who respected the religious establishment of the Prophet's City and who was willing to take their advice.

There was also an underlying political dimension to Sulaymān's actions: the men he consulted included descendants of former caliphs as well as the current governor of Medina: al-Qāsim b. Muḥammad b. Abī Bakr; Sālim b. 'Abd Allāh; 'Abd Allāh b. 'Umar; Khārijah b. Zayd; and Abū Bakr b. Ḥazm.[93] In view of the Umayyads' difficult history with the Ḥijāzī elite, it was in Sulaymān's interests to be seen showing these men respect especially when doing so came at no political cost.

It was reportedly after this pilgrimage that Sulaymān resolved to change the succession in favour of his son Ayyūb. His decision to do so was prompted by the death in early 98/716 of his designated heir, his brother Marwān.[94] Thus, when it came to the future of the caliphate, Sulaymān was no different from his brother, father and grandfather in wanting to keep power within his own family.[95]

According to a number of sources, he succeeded in having the *bay'ah*, the oath of allegiance, given to Ayyūb that same year.[96] Ayyūb was the son of an Arab mother and was therefore eligible for the caliphate.[97] He already enjoyed a certain profile: he had been his father's representative to al-Walīd when members of the Muhallab family sought refuge with Sulaymān in his

---

could count them," he tells 'Umar.

91 Al-Ya'qūbī, *Ta'rīkh*, II 223-224; Ibn Kathīr, *Bidāyah*, IX 237.

92 Hawting, "The Hajj in the Second Civil War", 36-37; Peters, *Hajj*, 69.

93 Al-Ya'qūbī, *Ta'rīkh*, II 223-224.

94 Al-Ṭabarī, *Ta'rīkh*, II 1317; Ibn Kathīr, *Bidāyah*, IX 175.

95 Hawting, *First Dynasty*, 72.

96 Al-Zubayrī, *Nasab Quraish*, 165; al-Ya'qūbī, *Ta'rīkh*, II 223 (who links the nomination of Ayyūb with his father's pilgrimage); al-Ṭabarī, *Ta'rīkh*, II 1317; Ibn 'Asākir, *TMD*, Vol. 10, 102; Ibn Kathīr, *Bidāyah*, IX 175; Wellhausen, *Arab Kingdom*, 264; Lassner, *Islamic Revolution*, 68.

97 Al-Zubayrī, *Nasab Quraish*, 165.

governorate of Palestine.[98] He had also led the *ṣā'ifah*.[99] Whether Sulaymān would have appointed him to lead the *ḥajj* in 98/717, the year after he led it, is impossible to know for Ayyūb died that year.[100]

Sulaymān then turned his attention to other sons as possible heirs: Dāwūd, for example.[101] He, like Ayyūb, had led the *ṣā'ifah*.[102] But as Dāwūd was the son of an *umm walad*, the plan went nowhere.[103] Another son said to have been considered was a minor and therefore also ineligible.[104] Whether as a direct result of this situation, none of Sulaymān's sons was appointed to lead the *ḥajj*.

That Sulaymān had no wish to leave the caliphate to his designated heir may be seen in his decision not to invite that heir, his brother Yazīd, to lead the *ḥajj*; an omission thrown into sharper relief by the fact that Yazīd actually performed the pilgrimage during Sulaymān's caliphate.[105]

With no heir to lead the *ḥajj* for him, Sulaymān therefore did as so many of his predecessors had done and turned to his governors of the Holy Cities to command the faithful in Mecca.

THE POLITICS OF PROTEST: SULAYMĀN'S GOVERNORS OF THE HOLY CITIES AND LEADERSHIP OF THE *ḤAJJ*

The governors of the Holy Cities did not escape Sulaymān's purge of his predecessor's governing class: they were sacked[106] and one of them, 'Uthmān, the governor of Medina, was flogged in public.[107] The humiliation of a former governor was not, in itself, new: al-Walīd had ordered that his father's governor of the city be flogged. Nor was the public humiliation of former enemies new: see, for example, al-Ḥajjāj's treatment of some of the *Ṣaḥābah* in Medina when Umayyad power had been restored after the *fitnah*.

98 Ibn A'tham, *Futūḥ*, VII 214; al-Ṭabarī, *Ta'rīkh*, II 1213-15.

99 Ibn Khayyāṭ, *Ta'rīkh*, I 325; Ibn 'Asākir, *TMD*, Vol. 10, 102.

100 Al-Zubayrī, *Nasab Quraish*, 165; al-Ṭabarī, *Ta'rīkh*, II 1335; al-Mas'ūdī, *Murūj*, 2167 (for the caliph's grief at his son's grave); Ibn 'Asākir, *TMD*, Vol. 10, 103; Chejne, *Succession*, 47.

101 Al-Ṭabarī, *Ta'rīkh*, II 1341; Ibn 'Asākir, *TMD*, Vol. 17, 154; Wellhausen, *Arab Kingdom*, 264; Lassner, *Islamic Revolution*, 68.

102 Al-Ya'qūbī, *Ta'rīkh*, II 226; al-Ṭabarī, *Ta'rīkh*, II 1306 & 1335; Ibn 'Asākir, *TMD*, Vol. 17, 155.

103 Al-Zubayrī, *Nasab Quraish*, 166; Ibn 'Asākir, *TMD*, Vol. 17, 154 & 155.

104 Al-Ṭabarī, *Ta'rīkh*, II 1341; Ibn al-Athīr, *al-Kāmil*, V 39.

105 Al-Ṭabarī, *Ta'rīkh*, II 1341 & 1464; Ibn al-Athīr, *al-Kāmil*, V 39 & 121-122.

106 Ibn Khayyāṭ, *Ta'rīkh*, I 323; al-Ya'qūbī, *Ta'rīkh*, II 218; al-Ṭabarī, *Ta'rīkh*, II 1281-82 & 1305; al-Fākihī, *Akhbār Makkah*, II 36-37, where Khālid initially keeps his job only to find himself in a compromised position: the new caliph orders that al-Ḥajjāj be cursed from the pulpits; a difficult task for Khālid as he had previously praised him in public; Ibn 'Asākir, *TMD*, Vol. 66, 46; Wellhausen, *Arab Kingdom*, 258.

107 Al-Ṭabarī, *Ta'rīkh*, II 1282.

Sulaymān's actions against 'Uthmān, like those of al-Ḥajjāj against the *Ṣaḥābah*, were meant to assert his authority: in humiliating the former governor in public, the new caliph wanted to proclaim his power and discredit the ruling order 'Uthmān had served. But there was a major difference between the actions of al-Ḥajjāj and those of Sulaymān: when al-Ḥajjāj moved against his opponents in the Ḥijāz, his ire had been directed at men who railed against Umayyad power; Sulaymān aimed his at men who had governed on behalf of that power.

The new caliph undoubtedly felt justified in his actions as al-Walīd and his supporters had tried to deny him his right to rule. But these two processes taken together – al-Walīd's efforts to oust Sulaymān and Sulaymān's response to it – indicated that all was not well within the Umayyad ruling elite.

The differences between Sulaymān and al-Walīd were political rather than tribal in nature – Sulaymān was, after all, as genetically Qaysī as his brother – but as they drew their support from different tribal groupings (al-Walīd from the Qays, Sulaymān from the Yaman),[108] Sulaymān's treatment of 'Uthmān b. Ḥayyān and his wider purge in reaction to al-Walīd's attempts to oust him showed a fault line emerging in the Umayyad power structure. And if caliphs continued to try and circumvent the succession arrangements they inherited and used rival tribal groups to back their respective points of view, tribal strife risked becoming institutionalized into the political structure. The changeover in power from one caliph to another might then see more of these acts of reprisal as the new order sought publicly to avenge itself on the old. The problem for the Umayyads as a ruling elite was how best to manage these rivalries and so preserve their power.

Sulaymān's gubernatorial appointments for Mecca and Medina were part of his strategy to deal with this issue. His replacement for 'Uthmān b. Ḥayyān in Medina was the former chief *qāḍī* of the Holy City, Abū Bakr b. Muḥammad b. 'Amr b. Ḥazm.[109] Abū Bakr and 'Uthmān were known not to have seen eye to eye in the past; a factor which may have played a role in Sulaymān's selection of him.[110]

108 Wellhausen, *Arab Kingdom*, 260-261.

109 Ibn Khayyāṭ, *Ta'rīkh*, I 323; al-Ya'qūbī, *Ta'rīkh*, II 218; al-Ṭabarī, *Ta'rīkh*, II 1282; Ibn al-Athīr, *al-Kāmil*, V 11; al-Dhahabī, *Ta'rīkh*, V 22, remarks that he was the only *Anṣārī* ever to be appointed to govern the Holy City; Ibn 'Asākir, *TMD*, Vol. 66, 45 & 46; Ibn Kathīr, *Bidāyah*, IX 166; Wellhausen, *Arab Kingdom*, 264.

110 Al-Ṭabarī, *Ta'rīkh*, II 1282.

The appointment of a local man to the governorship was an unusual move for an Umayyad caliph but it became an unprecedented one when Sulaymān asked him to lead the first *ḥajj* of his caliphate in 96/715. Sulaymān thus became the first Umayyad caliph ruling in a time of political stability to look beyond the Umayyad family for a leader of the pilgrimage.[111] He was also the first caliph – Umayyad or *Rāshidūn* – to appoint a member of the religious establishment in Medina to lead the ritual.

The appointment of Abū Bakr, however, owed as much to politics as religion. Sulaymān drew his support mainly from the Yaman but it was a neutral *Anṣārī* he appointed to govern Medina and to whom he gave the privilege of leading his inaugural pilgrimage. Abū Bakr was the equivalent of a compromise candidate and an attempt to keep the governorship of Medina and leadership of the pilgrimage free of the tribal affiliations which influenced gubernatorial appointments in other provinces of the Muslim world.

The caliph returned to standard Umayyad practice for the *ḥajj* the following year, 97/716, by leading it himself. For a leader of the *ḥajj* in 98/717, he again deviated from customary Umayyad practice by appointing his governor of Mecca, 'Abd al-'Azīz b. 'Abd Allāh b. Khālid b. Asīd,[112] rather than his governor of Medina, to lead it.

As with Sulaymān's appointment of Abū Bakr to Medina, the appointment of 'Abd al-'Azīz to Mecca owed much to the caliph's political agenda. 'Abd al-'Azīz was an Umayyad (albeit one distant from the centre of power)[113] and as such, his governorship and leadership of the pilgrimage continued to keep the Holy City and the *ḥajj* free from the toxin of tribal politics. 'Abd al-'Azīz was useful to the caliph in another way: his leadership of the *ḥajj* in 98/717 acted as a counterweight to Abū Bakr's in 96/715. If members of the ruling family had been concerned by Sulaymān's decision to appoint an outsider like Abū Bakr to lead the ritual, then 'Abd al-'Azīz's leadership of it in 98/717 would have gone some way to reassure them.

Thus, Sulaymān's brief caliphate saw him adopt a *ḥajj* policy which, at times, echoed those of his Umayyad predecessors but, at other times, turned Umayyad practices on their head. Whether he would have continued to innovate is simply impossible to know given the brevity of his caliphate.

One of the acts for which Sulaymān is most remembered came right at the end of his caliphate. Unsure who to nominate as his successor, he left

111 Crone, *Medieval Islamic Political Thought*, 97.
112 Ibn Khayyāṭ, *Ta'rīkh*, I 323; al-Ṭabarī, *Ta'rīkh*, II 1335-36.
113 Al-Zubayrī, *Nasab Quraish*, 187-191 (in particular 190).

it until he was on his deathbed to decide the next caliph. With the help of his advisor, Rajā' b. Ḥaywah, he altered the succession, taking the caliphate away from the Banū 'Abd al-Malik and giving it to his cousin 'Umar b. 'Abd al-'Azīz.[114]

'Umar had received the oath of allegiance on Sulaymān's behalf when he became caliph; he had been with him in Medina during his *ḥajj*, and he would lead the prayers over his bier. 'Umar, like Sulaymān, had opposed some of al-Walīd's policies and, like Sulaymān, he had given refuge to those fleeing the severity of al-Ḥajjāj's governorship in the east. That opposition had cost him his job as governor of Medina for al-Walīd but in *Ṣafar* 99/ September 717, it may have helped him assume the highest position of all.

114 Wellhausen, *Arab Kingdom*, 265; Bosworth, "Rajā' ibn Ḥaywa al-Kindī and the Umayyad Caliphs", 36-80; Hawting, *First Dynasty*, 72; Kennedy, *Prophet*, 106; Amabe, *Emergence of 'Abbasid Autocracy*, 16.

SEVEN

'Umar II and Yazīd II: A Different Approach to the *Ḥajj*

'Umar became caliph in 99/717; a position he occupied until his death in 101/720.[1] His caliphate included two *ḥajj* seasons: 99/718 and 100/719. He was succeeded by Yazīd b. 'Abd al-Malik who remained caliph until his death in 105/724.[2] His caliphate covered four *ḥajj* seasons: 101/720 to 104/723 inclusive. Table 6 shows 'Umar's and Yazīd's choice of *ḥajj* leaders for their respective caliphates.

Table 6

Year	*Ḥajj leader*	*Relationship to caliph*	*Governor of Medina?*
'Umar II			
99/718	Abū Bakr b. Muḥammmad b. 'Amr b. Ḥazm[3]	x	yes
100/719	Abū Bakr b. Muḥammad b. 'Amr b. Ḥazm[4]	x	yes

1 *EI* 2nd edition, s.v. 'Umar b. 'Abd al-'Azīz.
2 *EI* 2nd edition, s.v. Yazīd b. 'Abd al-Malik.
3 Ibn Khayyāṭ, *Ta'rīkh*, I 326 & 331; al-Ya'qūbī, *Ta'rīkh*, II 235; al-Ṭabarī, *Ta'rīkh*, II 1346; al-Mas'ūdī, *Murūj*, 3637; Ibn 'Asākir, *TMD*, Vol. 66, 45.
4 Ibn Khayyāṭ, *Ta'rīkh*, I 327 & 331; al-Ya'qūbī, *Ta'rīkh*, II 235; al-Ṭabarī, *Ta'rīkh*, II 1358-59; al-Mas'ūdī, *Murūj*, 3637; Ibn 'Asākir, *TMD*, Vol. 66, 45.

Yazīd II			
101/720	ʿAbd al-Raḥmān b. al-Ḍaḥḥāk b. Qays al-Fihrī[5] *or* ʿAbd ʿAzīz b. ʿAbd Allāh[6]	x distant relative	yes x
102/721	ʿAbd al-Raḥmān b. al-Ḍaḥḥāk[7]	x	yes
103/722	ʿAbd al-Raḥmān b. al-Ḍaḥḥāk[8] *or* ʿAbd al-Wāḥid b. ʿAbd Allāh al-Naṣrī (or al-Naḍrī)[9]	x x	yes x
104/723	ʿAbd al-Wāḥid b. ʿAbd Allāh al-Naṣrī (or al-Naḍrī)[10]	x	yes

ʿUMAR II: A *ḤAJJ* POLICY BASED IN THE ḤIJĀZ

ʿUmar's nomination to the highest office in Islam was not welcomed by everyone in the Umayyad house. Hishām b. ʿAbd al-Malik, for one, was less than happy when he heard the caliphate had been taken away from the sons of ʿAbd al-Malik.[11] Another caliphal son went further than merely voicing his opinions: al-Walīd's son ʿAbd al-ʿAzīz took the opportunity of Sulaymān's passing to stake his own claim for power.

The new caliph faced another difficulty: neither of the major tribal groupings, the Qays or the Yaman, saw him as their caliph of choice. Once

5 Ibn Khayyāṭ, *Taʾrīkh*, I 332 & 343; al-Yaʿqūbī, *Taʾrīkh*, II 242; al-Ṭabarī, *Taʾrīkh*, II 1394; Ibn ʿAsākir, *TMD*, Vol. 34, 440 & 441.

6 Al-Masʿūdī, *Murūj*, 3638.

7 Ibn Khayyāṭ, *Taʾrīkh*, I 335 & 343; al-Yaʿqūbī, *Taʾrīkh*, II 242; al-Ṭabarī, *Taʾrīkh*, II 1436; al-Masʿūdī, *Murūj*, 3638; Ibn ʿAsākir, *TMD*, Vol. 34, 440 & 441.

8 Ibn Khayyāṭ, *Taʾrīkh*, I 336 & 343; al-Yaʿqūbī, *Taʾrīkh*, II 242; al-Ṭabarī, *Taʾrīkh*, II 1437; Ibn ʿAsākir, *TMD*, Vol. 34, 440 & 441.

9 Al-Masʿūdī, *Murūj*, 3638.

10 Ibn Khayyāṭ, *Taʾrīkh*, I 338 & 343; al-Yaʿqūbī, *Taʾrīkh*, II 243; al-Ṭabarī, *Taʾrīkh*, II 1461; al-Masʿūdī, *Murūj*, 3638; Ibn ʿAsākir, *TMD*, Vol. 37, 249 & 250.

11 Al-Ṭabarī, *Taʾrīkh*, II 1344 & 1345; al-Masʿūdī, *Murūj*, 2170.

caliph, ʿUmar worked to turn this situation to his advantage and tried to plot a more independent course than some of his predecessors had done. In the first year of his caliphate, he recalled the expedition Sulaymān had sent to Constantinople.[12] This mission had become increasingly costly in terms of men and material and ʿUmar judged the time had come for his armies to cut their losses and return home. He would later take a similar approach to the campaigns in the east.[13]

ʿUmar's policy shifts were not limited to foreign affairs. He made major changes at home, the best known of which was his attempt to reform taxation policy.[14] Another radical departure from standard Umayyad practice was his effort to stop the public cursing of the ʿAlids from the pulpit during Friday prayer.[15] Al-Masʿūdī records that he even ordered stipends to be made available for ʿAlī's descendants.[16]

On the delicate issue of the political influence wielded by the different tribal blocs, ʿUmar tried to steer a less partisan course than his predecessors, al-Walīd or Sulaymān, had done. He patronized neither the Qays nor the Yaman when it came to gubernatorial appointments and broke up the vast governorate of the east into smaller units, thus preventing it turning into the personal fiefdom of a governor aligned to one tribal grouping or the other.[17]

Nor did ʿUmar patronize the main political tribe of the day – the Umayyad family – in the way his predecessors had done. According to al-Masʿūdī, the opposite was the case and ʿUmar was said to have been reluctant to give his family governorships.[18]

The caliph's new approach was immediately apparent in the Holy Cities where ʿUmar showed how different he was from his predecessors by doing nothing at all. He did not implement a policy of reprisal which saw the representative of the old order humiliated in public but chose, instead, to

12 Al-Ṭabarī, *Taʾrīkh*, II 1346; Ibn Kathīr, *Bidāyah*, IX 184; Kennedy, *Prophet*, 107; Blankinship, *Jihad*, 19, 32-33, & 38; Hoyland, *Seeing Islam*, 653; Hitti, *History*, 203.

13 Al-Ṭabarī, *Taʾrīkh*, II 1365; Wellhausen, *Arab Kingdom*, 268-269.

14 Al-Ṭabarī, *Taʾrīkh*, II 1354 & 1366-67; Wellhausen, *Arab Kingdom*, 271-299; Gibb, "The Fiscal Rescript of ʿUmar II", 1; Barthold, "The Caliph ʿUmar and the Conflicting Reports about His Personality", 69-95; Hodgson, *The Venture of Islam*, vol.1, 268-271; Hawting, *First Dynasty*, 76-81; Kennedy, *Prophet*, 107; Blankinship, *Jihad*, 85; Hoyland, *Seeing Islam*, 340, 490 & 596; Hitti, *History*, 209, 219 & 234.

15 Al-Yaʿqūbī, *Taʾrīkh*, II 231; al-Masʿūdī, *Murūj*, 2171; Ibn al-Athīr, *al-Kāmil*, V 42-43; Wellhausen, *Arab Kingdom*, 309-310; Blankinship, *Jihad*, 32.

16 Al-Masʿūdī, *Murūj*, 2174.

17 For the caliph's treatment of Yazīd b. al-Muhallab, for example, see al-Ṭabarī, *Taʾrīkh*, II 1350-52 & 1359-61; al-Jahshiyārī, *Kitāb al-wuzarāʾ*, 50. For his choice of governors, see al-Ṭabarī, *Taʾrīkh*, II 1346-47 & 1352-57; Wellhausen, *Arab Kingdom*, 269-270; Kennedy, *Prophet*, 106; Blankinship, *Jihad*, 21 & 31-32.

18 Al-Masʿūdī, *Murūj*, 2171.

ensure administrative continuity by confirming Sulaymān's governors of the Holy Cities in their positions: Abū Bakr b. Muḥammad b. 'Amr b. Ḥazm remained governor of Medina and 'Abd al-'Azīz b. 'Abd Allāh b. Khālid b. Asīd remained governor of Mecca.[19]

In purely political terms, 'Umar had no need to indulge in a purge of Sulaymān's governors in the Holy Cities, as the governors he inherited served his political agenda. Abū Bakr, as an *Anṣārī*, was a neutral in the political tug-of-war between the Qays and the Yaman and 'Abd al-'Azīz, as an Umayyad, maintained the ruling family's presence in Islam's Holiest City.

A former governor of Medina himself, 'Umar appointed his own governor of that city to lead the *ḥajj*. The two men knew each other personally: Abū Bakr had become chief *qāḍī* of Medina during 'Umar's governorship[20] and when 'Umar was sacked, it was Abū Bakr he nominated as his replacement until the new governor arrived.[21]

Abū Bakr led both *ḥajj* seasons of 'Umar's caliphate, making 'Umar the first Umayyad caliph since Yazīd I to give leadership of all his *ḥajj* seasons to his governor of Medina. But that is where the similarity between the two caliphs ends: Yazīd's governors of the Holy City were Umayyads; 'Umar's governor was not. 'Umar was not the first Umayyad caliph to appoint an *Anṣārī* to lead the *ḥajj*; Sulaymān broke that precedent but even he, trailblazer that he was, only did so once. 'Umar, however, was trying to initiate a different political narrative during his caliphate and Abū Bakr's leadership of the *ḥajj* allowed him to achieve two political objectives at once. First, it maintained the *ḥajj*'s neutrality in the competition for power between the Banū 'Abd al-Malik and their tribal supporters and, second, it formed part of 'Umar's broader strategy of trying to facilitate access to power for people who were not traditionally part of the political elite. We have seen that he did not hesitate to overlook high-ranking Umayyads when making gubernatorial appointments and he may have sought to make a similar statement about leadership of the *ḥajj*.

In this, the caliph practised what he preached for the highest ranking Umayyad he overlooked when it came to leadership of the *ḥajj* was himself. 'Umar was the eighth Umayyad caliph but the first who had the time – his caliphate, brief though it was, included two *ḥajj* seasons – and the

19 Ibn Khayyāṭ, *Ta'rīkh*, I 329; al-Ṭabarī, *Ta'rīkh*, II 1346; Ibn 'Asākir, *TMD*, Vol. 36, 297 & Vol. 66, 45-46; Zambaur, *Généalogie*, 19 & 24.

20 Ibn Khayyāṭ, *Ta'rīkh*, I 317; al-Ṭabarī, *Ta'rīkh*, II 1191; Ibn al-Athīr, *al-Kāmil*, IV 530; Ibn Kathīr, *Bidāyah*, IX 72-73.

21 Al-Ṭabarī, *Ta'rīkh*, II 1255.

permissive political environment – he controlled the Holy Cities and the routes to them – who did not lead the *ḥajj* in person. One historian felt the need to offer an explanation for this state of affairs: according to Ibn Kathīr, 'Umar was so involved with matters relating to the government (*li'shughlihi bi'l-umūri*) he did not have time to lead the *ḥajj* in person.[22]

There may have been other reasons why 'Umar did not travel to the Ḥijāz. Before he became caliph, he had already led the *ḥajj* several times and may not therefore have felt any urgency to lead it at the beginning of his caliphate. A similar set of circumstances was true of Yazīd I. He led the *ḥajj* during his father's caliphate and did not hurry to do so when he became caliph. The matter was soon taken out of his hands when he lost political control of the Holy Cities. Like Yazīd I, 'Umar's caliphate turned out to be brief – he died before he reached his forties[23] – and it is impossible to know whether he would have gone to the Ḥijāz to lead the *ḥajj* in person had he ruled for longer.

Nevertheless, 'Umar clearly understood what the performance of this religious duty meant for his fellow Muslims. He wrote to his governor of Iraq, 'Abd al-Ḥamīd b. 'Abd al-Raḥmān, and instructed him to make available allowances of one hundred *dirhams* for any woman or child who wished to make the *ḥajj*.[24]

'Umar came to be so widely respected that people were said to pray for Sulaymān out of gratitude for making him caliph.[25] And he was truly unique in Umayyad politics in at least one way: he alone of the Umayyad caliphs did not interfere with the succession arrangements left to him by his predecessor. When he died in *Rajab* 101/February 720, he was therefore succeeded by Yazīd b. 'Abd al-Malik.[26]

YAZĪD II: ANOTHER *ḤAJJ* POLICY BASED IN THE ḤIJĀZ

The death of 'Umar II signalled an end to attempts at systematic fiscal reform.[27] Gone, too, were any efforts to neutralize the political toxin between the Qays and the Yaman. With the accession of Yazīd II, the political order

22 Ibn Kathīr, *Bidāyah*, IX 189.
23 Al-Ya'qūbī, *Ta'rīkh*, II 235; al-Ṭabarī, *Ta'rīkh*, II 1361; al-Mas'ūdī, *Murūj*, 2169.
24 Al-Ṭabarī, *Ta'rīkh*, II 1367. See also al-Ya'qūbī, *Ta'rīkh*, II 231.
25 Al-Ṭabarī, *Ta'rīkh*, II 1345. See also Ibn al-Athīr, *al-Kāmil*, V 37.
26 Al-Zubayrī, *Nasab Quraish*, 163; Ibn Khayyāṭ, *Ta'rīkh*, I 328; al-Ya'qūbī, *Ta'rīkh*, II 236.
27 Blankinship, *Jihad*, 87-89 & 125.

last seen in the days of al-Walīd returned with a vengeance. The interests of the Qays were once again at the heart of the caliphate and the new state of affairs was soon evident in the Ḥijāz.[28]

One of Yazīd's first acts as caliph was to sack his predecessor's representative in Medina, Abū Bakr the *Anṣārī*, and replace him with a Qaysī, 'Abd al-Raḥmān b. al-Ḍaḥḥāk al-Fihrī.[29] This appointment signalled an abrupt change in policy in the governance of the Ḥijāz: Yazīd, unlike 'Umar or Sulaymān, was making no attempt at compromise in his choice of a governor for the Holy City but declaring his tribal affiliations openly with the appointment of a well-known Qaysī. And when Yazīd appointed 'Abd al-Raḥmān to lead the first *ḥajj* of his caliphate in 101/720, he became the first Umayyad caliph to bring tribal politics overtly into leadership of the *ḥajj*.

The Umayyad governor of Mecca, 'Abd al-'Azīz b. 'Abd Allāh, initially fared batter in the changeover of power – as might be expected of a member, however marginal, of the ruling family – and kept his job for the first few years of Yazīd's caliphate. In 103/721-722, however, he was sacked and the governorship of Mecca was added to 'Abd al-Raḥmān's responsibilities.[30]

'Abd al-Raḥmān went on to lead the *ḥajj* again in 102/721 and, according to a number of sources, in 103/722 as well. His governorship came to a sudden end when he was sacked in 104/722 for his rather too persistent wooing of Fāṭimah bt. al-Ḥusayn.[31] Yazīd was said to have been so displeased with him that he refused to allow him to slip quietly into a comfortable retirement: 'Abd al-Raḥmān's money was confiscated[32] and the caliph ordered the former governor to be given such a severe beating that the sound of his screams should reach Yazīd as he reclined on his bed in Damascus.[33]

Yazīd appointed 'Abd al-Wāḥid b. 'Abd Allāh al-Naṣrī (or al-Naḍrī) to replace 'Abd al-Raḥmān.[34] The new governor, like the old one, was not a

28 As a demonstration of the changes in the ruling order, al-Ya'qūbī, *Ta'rīkh*, II 237, records that the caliph sacked all of his predecessor's governors; al-Ṭabarī, *Ta'rīkh*, II 1394; Wellhausen, *Arab Kingdom*, 312-313, 320 & 323; Hawting, *First Dynasty*, 75; Kennedy, *Prophet*, 107; Blankinship, *Jihad*, 88 & 136-137.

29 Ibn Khayyāṭ, *Ta'rīkh*, I 340; al-Ya'qūbī, *Ta'rīkh*, II 237 & 240; al-Ṭabarī, *Ta'rīkh*, II 1372; Ibn 'Asākir, *TMD*, Vol. 34, 440, & Vol. 66, 46; Zambaur, *Généalogie*, 24. He was a Qurashī: al-Zubayrī, *Nasab Quraish*, 447.

30 Ibn Khayyāṭ, *Ta'rīkh*, I 340; al-Ṭabarī, *Ta'rīkh*, II 1437; Ibn 'Asākir, *TMD*, Vol. 36, 297; al-Fāsī, *Akhbār Makkah*, II 177-178; Zambaur, *Généalogie*, 19.

31 Ibn Khayyāṭ, *Ta'rīkh*, I 340; al-Ya'qūbī, *Ta'rīkh*, II 240; al-Ṭabarī, *Ta'rīkh*, II 1449-1452; Ibn 'Asākir, *TMD*, Vol. 34, 441-443; Ibn Kathīr, *Bidāyah*, IX 229.

32 Ibn 'Asākir, *TMD*, Vol. 34, 443; Ibn Kathīr, *Bidāyah*, IX 229.

33 Ibn 'Asākir, *TMD*, Vol. 34, 443; Ibn Kathīr, *Bidāyah*, IX 229.

34 Ibn Khayyāṭ, *Ta'rīkh*, I 340; al-Ya'qūbī, *Ta'rīkh*, II 240; al-Ṭabarī, *Ta'rīkh*, II 1452; Ibn 'Asākir, *TMD*, Vol. 34, 441, & Vol. 37, 249; al-Fāsī, *Akhbār Makkah*, II 178.

member of the Umayyad family. But unlike the old governor, 'Abd al-Wāḥid set out to establish an entirely different relationship with the people of the Holy City he governed. For all the colourful reasons given to explain 'Abd al-Raḥmān's sacking, there had been murmurings of discontent within the Prophet's City over the direction of his governorship. He was said to have put his own interests first[35] and rejected well-meaning advice that he should consult with eminent members of the local community like al-Qāsim b. Muḥammad, the grandson of the first caliph Abū Bakr, and Sālim b. 'Abd Allāh, the grandson of the second caliph 'Umar.[36] These were men of considerable standing in Medina and the city's governor should at least have given the impression that he took their opinions into consideration. When, for example, 'Umar II arrived in Medina to serve as governor, one of his first acts was to receive the *fuqahā'* and assure them of his willingness to take on board their points of view. In the City of the Prophet, it was politically unwise to adopt any other course.

'Abd al-Raḥmān, however, rejected the advice he was given and decided instead to treat the *Anṣār* with contempt. He even had the former governor Abū Bakr flogged.[37] The result was that no one had a good word to say about him. His replacement, by contrast, was said to have been one of the most popular governors ever to serve in the Holy City.[38] One of the reasons for his enduring popularity was that he never failed to consult al-Qāsim and Sālim before deciding on a matter.[39] 'Abd al-Wāḥid led the *ḥajj* in 104/724 in what would turn out to be the last pilgrimage season of Yazīd's caliphate.

Thus, throughout his caliphate Yazīd looked no further than his governor of Medina for a leader of the *ḥajj*. Of the eight Umayyad caliphs who came before him, only Yazīd I and 'Umar II adopted the same policy. But, as we have seen, Yazīd I's governors belonged to the Umayyad family; 'Umar II's and Yazīd II's did not.

This was not the only area of common ground between Yazīd's *ḥajj* policy and 'Umar II's: Yazīd, like 'Umar, did not take advantage of the opportunity to lead the *ḥajj* in person. In Yazīd's case, this omission is particularly glaring. His caliphate, covering four *ḥajj* seasons, was twice as long

35 Al-Ṭabarī, *Ta'rīkh*, II 1452.

36 For details of al-Qāsim, see al-Dhahabī, *Ta'rīkh*, IV 182-185. For Sālim, see al-Dhahabī, *Ta'rīkh*, IV 115-117. See also al-Zubayrī, *Nasab Quraish*: 350 & 357 for Sālim; 279 for al-Qāsim.

37 Al-Ṭabarī, *Ta'rīkh*, II 1452. See also Ibn al-Athīr, *al-Kāmil*, V 114, for the governor's treatment of the *Anṣār*.

38 Al-Ṭabarī, *Ta'rīkh*, II 1452.

39 Al-Ṭabarī, *Ta'rīkh*, II 1452; Ibn al-Athīr, *al-Kāmil*, V 114.

as 'Umar II's and there was no political reason to prevent him from going to the Ḥijāz as he enjoyed full control of the Holy Cities and the routes to them. Furthermore, Yazīd, unlike his predecessor 'Umar, had not led the *ḥajj* before he became caliph.[40]

In this, he was almost unique. Of his eight Umayyad predecessors, four of them led the *ḥajj* as caliph: Mu'āwiyah I, 'Abd al-Malik, al-Walīd and Sulaymān; and five of them did so prior to becoming caliph either as successor-in-waiting or as governor of Medina: Yazīd I, al-Walīd and Sulaymān as the former; Marwān and 'Umar as the latter. Of the Umayyad caliphs prior to Yazīd II, only Mu'āwiyah II did not lead the *ḥajj* and the circumstances facing him were vastly different from those facing Yazīd II. As caliph, Mu'āwiyah II did not control the Ḥijāz; nor did his caliphate include a *ḥajj* season, and as heir apparent, a number of factors combined to prevent him from venturing to the Ḥijāz.

Why, then, Yazīd II did not lead the *ḥajj* during his caliphate is not entirely clear. He became caliph at a relatively young age and, like 'Umar before him, he died before he reached his forties.[41] Whether he would have led the pilgrimage had he lived longer and ruled for as long as the likes of Mu'āwiyah, 'Abd al-Malik or al-Walīd is simply impossible to know.

As a caliph, Yazīd II is often portrayed as a dissolute character, more interested in the affairs of his heart than in the affairs of government; his devotion to his singing girl Ḥabābah more worthy of a love-struck poet than a ruling caliph.[42] When Ḥabābah died, Yazīd was so wracked with grief that his brother Maslamah had to advise him to stay secluded for a week for fear of the public's reaction to the caliph's distressed emotional state.[43] It mattered little. Yazīd's grief was of truly epic proportions. So inconsolable was he over Ḥabābah's loss that he died soon afterwards, aged in his thirties.

Even though Yazīd was one of the few Umayyad caliphs who never led the *ḥajj*, Islam's fifth pillar did nevertheless play a defining role in his personal, if not his political, life. For it was in Medina on the way back from the pilgrimage he performed during Sulaymān's reign that he first met his beloved Ḥabābah.[44]

40 For his pilgrimages, see al-Ṭabarī, *Ta'rīkh*, II 1341 & 1464; Ibn al-Athīr, *al-Kāmil*, V 39 & 121-122; Hamilton, *Walid and His Friends*, 64.

41 Ibn Khayyāṭ, *Ta'rīkh* I 340; al-Ya'qūbī, *Ta'rīkh*, II 242; al-Ṭabarī, *Ta'rīkh*, II 1463; al-Mas'ūdī, *Murūj*, 2196; al-Dhahabī, *Ta'rīkh*, IV 88.

42 Wellhausen, *Arab Kingdom*, 324; Hamilton, *Walid and His Friends*, 63.

43 Al-Ṭabarī, *Ta'rīkh*, II 1466. Al-Mas'ūdī, *Murūj*, 2203 & 2204, is more diplomatic: he does not name names but relies upon the impersonal "*fa-qīla lahu*"; Ibn al-Athīr, *al-Kāmil*, V 120; Wellhausen, *Arab Kingdom*, 324.

44 Al-Ṭabarī, *Ta'rīkh*, II 1464-65; Ibn al-Athīr, *al-Kāmil*, V 121-122.

ʿUMAR II, YAZĪD II AND LEADERSHIP OF THE *ḤAJJ*: SOME UNANSWERED QUESTIONS

ʿUmar II and Yazīd II had very different visions for the caliphate they governed. ʿUmar II tried to adopt a more inclusive approach to government, facilitating entry into the political system for people who were not usually the first in line to receive caliphal favours. Yazīd II, by contrast, reverted to the old system of bestowing favours upon his own tribal supporters.

These differences notwithstanding, ʿUmar II and Yazīd II adopted *ḥajj* policies which were remarkably similar and which differed noticeably from standard Umayyad practice. The fact that they are not usually seen as caliphs with much in common makes their overlapping *ḥajj* policies all the more worthy of note, suggesting that a different political narrative for the pilgrimage was unfolding during their caliphates.

From Muʿāwiyah I to al-Walīd, it had become the norm for caliphs to lead the *ḥajj* in person; to use it as a platform for promoting their preferred successors (usually their sons); to rely heavily on their immediate family to lead it (often brothers and sons who were out of contention for the caliphate and therefore no threat to the caliph's future plans); and, to rely equally heavily on the governor of Medina to lead it, as long as he was an Umayyad. Furthermore, no one with an independent power base was allowed near the ritual, for fear they would use it to promote their own profile. Particularly noticeable by their absence from leadership of the *ḥajj* were the heirs which caliphs had inherited from their predecessors and whom they were encouraging, by every method available, to exit the political stage.

It was Sulaymān who, in politically settled circumstances, first broke with this model when he appointed an *Anṣārī* to govern Medina then gave him leadership of the *ḥajj* as part of his gubernatorial responsibilities. But he only did so once. ʿUmar II and Yazīd II, by contrast, gave leadership of all their *ḥajj* seasons to their governors in Medina and left the Umayyad family out in the political cold. Such repeated reliance on the governor of Medina to lead the *ḥajj* at the expense of the first family seems to suggest, upon first examination, a level of caliphal disengagement from the ritual and a subsequent lessening of its political significance.

What, however, these two caliphs had in common which set them apart from their Umayyad predecessors is the issue of succession. ʿUmar II, uniquely amongst Umayyad caliphs, made no attempt to interfere with the succession arrangements he had been given. As a result, there was no need for him to manipulate the stage provided by the *ḥajj* to promote the successor of his choosing.

Yazīd II also had the succession issue settled. He was expected to pass the caliphate to one of his father's sons and his half-brother Hishām was next in line. But when it came to the succession, Yazīd was no different from his Umayyad predecessors in wanting to pass power to one of his own sons. His preferred heir, his son al-Walīd, was only eleven years old when Yazīd became caliph.[45] At that age, he was too young to lead the Friday prayer or the *ḥajj*, both key functions of state, and was not therefore a credible candidate to become his father's heir. It was the caliph's half-brother Maslamah who came up with what seemed to be a compromise solution when he suggested that Yazīd comply with their father's wishes and confirm Hishām as heir apparent, with al-Walīd as successor-in-waiting.[46] Yazīd consented to this arrangement, perhaps because of al-Walīd's youth and the potential complications if he himself were to die suddenly. He may also have agreed because, given Maslamah's standing in the family, he believed he had no choice.

By doing so, he became the first of the Marwānid caliphs to have the succession resolved largely to his satisfaction early in his caliphate. As such, there was no need for him to expend considerable efforts preparing the ground for his son's nomination as heir because al-Walīd's place in the succession was secure. The connection between the *ḥajj* and the high politics of the day, so apparent in the caliphates of Mu'āwiyah I through to al-Walīd, was therefore less obvious during the caliphates of 'Umar II and Yazīd II.

Whether it would have stayed that way is impossible to know. Yazīd was a relatively young man when he became caliph and he may have mistakenly assumed there would be many opportunities for him, and for his son, to lead the *ḥajj* at a later date. Al-Walīd was too young at this time to lead it but if Yazīd had ruled for as long as his own father had, he may have sent his successor son to make an appearance in the Ḥijāz. 'Umar II, as a pious Muslim, may also have wished to avail himself of the opportunity to lead the *ḥajj* as caliph, had he too ruled longer.

---

45 For al-Walīd's birth, see al-Ṭabarī, *Ta'rīkh*, II 1192 (where it is in 88/707) & II 1740-41; al-Dhahabī, *Ta'rīkh*, V 173 (who places his birth in 90/708-709 or 92/710-711). For his nomination, see al-Ya'qūbī, *Ta'rīkh*, II 241; Ibn al-Athīr, *al-Kāmil*, V 91.

46 Wellhausen, *Arab Kingdom*, 325; Chejne, *Succession*, 48; Hawting, *First Dynasty*, 81; Hamilton, *Walid and His Friends*, 73; Hillenbrand, tr. *Waning of the Umayyad Caliphate*, 87 note 439; Blankinship, *Jihad*, 79.

The decisions of ʿUmar II and Yazīd II not to lead the *ḥajj* in person undoubtedly had an impact on the political profile of the ritual during their respective caliphates. Even so, the pilgrimage did not lose its political significance entirely; the means of expressing it merely changed. The fact that ʿUmar II and Yazīd II accepted the succession arrangements they inherited did not mean they were happy to do so. Had ʿUmar been free to choose his own successor, it is unlikely he would have chosen Yazīd II.[47] And had Yazīd II been free to do the same, it is likely he would have bypassed Hishām altogether and opted for al-Walīd, regardless of his age. During his caliphate, ʿUmar did not appoint Yazīd to lead the *ḥajj*; during his, Yazīd did not appoint Hishām to do so either. Their absence from the Holy Cities proved just how political the pilgrimage still was, even when appearances suggested otherwise.

47 Chejne, *Succession*, 48.

EIGHT

The Last of a Line: Hishām b. ʿAbd al-Malik

Hishām b. ʿAbd al-Malik became caliph in 105/724 and remained in the position until his death in 125/743.[1] His caliphate spanned twenty *ḥajj* seasons: from 105/724 to 124/742. Table 7 shows his choice of *ḥajj* leaders for the two decades of his caliphate.

Table 7

Year	***Ḥajj leader***	***Relationship to caliph***	***Governor of Medina?***
105/724	Ibrāhīm b. Hishām al-Makhzūmī[2]	maternal uncle	x
	or Hishām b. Ismāʿīl al-Makhzūmī[3]	maternal grandfather	x
106/725	CALIPH[4]	-	-
107/726	Ibrāhīm b. Hishām al-Makhzūmī[5]	maternal uncle	yes (& Mecca)

1 *EI* 2nd edition, s.v. Hishām b. ʿAbd al-Malik. For his caliphate in general, see Gabrieli, *Il califfatto di Hisham*, & Blankinship, *Jihad*.

2 Al-Yaʿqūbī, *Taʾrīkh*, II 259; al-Ṭabarī, *Taʾrīkh*, II 1467; al-Masʿūdī, *Murūj*, 3638; Ibn ʿAsākir, *TMD*, Vol. 7, 259 & 260, & Vol. 37, 249.

3 Ibn Khayyāṭ, *Taʾrīkh*, II 376.

4 Ibn Khayyāṭ, *Taʾrīkh*, II 349 & 376; al-Balādhurī, *Ansāb*, VI B 30 & 42; al-Yaʿqūbī, *Taʾrīkh*, II 259; al-Ṭabarī, *Taʾrīkh*, II 1482; al-Masʿūdī, *Murūj*, 3638; Ibn ʿAsākir, *TMD*, Vol. 7, 260; al-Fāsī, *Akhbār Makkah*, II 236.

5 Ibn Khayyāṭ, *Taʾrīkh*, II 351 & 376; al-Yaʿqūbī, *Taʾrīkh*, II 259; al-Ṭabarī, *Taʾrīkh*, II 1491; al-Masʿūdī, *Murūj*, 3638; Ibn ʿAsākir, *TMD*, Vol. 7, 259, 260 & 261.

108/727	Ibrāhīm b. Hishām al-Makhzūmī[6]	maternal uncle	yes (& Mecca)
109/728	Ibrāhīm b. Hishām al-Makhzūmī[7]	maternal uncle	yes (& Mecca)
110/729	Ibrāhīm b. Hishām al-Makhzūmī[8] *or* Ibrāhīm b. Ismā'īl[9]	maternal uncle x	yes (& Mecca) x
111/730	Ibrāhīm b. Hishām al-Makhzūmī[10]	maternal uncle	yes (& Mecca)
112/731	Ibrāhīm b. Hishām al-Makhzūmī[11] *or* Sulaymān b. Hishām[12]	maternal uncle caliph's son	yes (& Mecca) x
113/732	Sulaymān b. Hishām[13] *or* Ibrāhīm b. Hishām al-Makhzūmī[14]	caliph's son maternal uncle	x yes (& Mecca)
114/733	Khālid b. 'Abd al-Malik b. al-Ḥārith b. al-Ḥakam[15] *or* Muḥammad b. Hishām al-Makhzūmī[16]	cousin maternal uncle	yes Mecca

6 Ibn Khayyāṭ, *Ta'rīkh*, II 351 & 376; al-Ya'qūbī, *Ta'rīkh*, II 259; al-Ṭabarī, *Ta'rīkh*, II 1494; al-Mas'ūdī, *Murūj*, 3638; Ibn 'Asākir, *TMD*, Vol. 7, 259, 260 & 261.

7 Ibn Khayyāṭ, *Ta'rīkh*, II 353 & 376; al-Ya'qūbī, *Ta'rīkh*, II 259; al-Ṭabarī, *Ta'rīkh*, II 1505; al-Mas'ūdī, *Murūj*, 3638; Ibn 'Asākir, *TMD*, Vol. 7, 260 & 261.

8 Ibn Khayyāṭ, *Ta'rīkh*, II 354 & 376; al-Ya'qūbī, *Ta'rīkh*, II 259; al-Ṭabarī, *Ta'rīkh*, II 1526; al-Mas'ūdī, *Murūj*, 3638; Ibn 'Asākir, *TMD*, Vol. 7, 260 & 261; Ibn Kathīr, *Bidāyah*, IX 260.

9 Ibn al-Athīr, *al-Kāmil*, V 155.

10 Ibn Khayyāṭ, *Ta'rīkh*, II 355 & 376; al-Ya'qūbī, *Ta'rīkh*, II 259; al-Ṭabarī, *Ta'rīkh*, II 1530; al-Mas'ūdī, *Murūj*, 3638; Ibn 'Asākir, *TMD*, Vol. 7, 260 & 261.

11 Ibn Khayyāṭ, *Ta'rīkh*, II 357 & 376; al-Ya'qūbī, *Ta'rīkh*, II 259; al-Ṭabarī, *Ta'rīkh*, II 1559; al-Mas'ūdī, *Murūj*, 3638; Ibn al-Athīr, *al-Kāmil*, V 171; Ibn 'Asākir, *TMD*, Vol. 7, 260 & 261.

12 Al-Ṭabarī, *Ta'rīkh*, II 1559; Ibn al-Athīr, *al-Kāmil*, V 171.

13 Ibn Khayyāṭ, *Ta'rīkh*, II 359 & 376; al-Ya'qūbī, *Ta'rīkh*, II 259; al-Ṭabarī, *Ta'rīkh*, II 1560-61; Ibn 'Asākir, *TMD*, Vol. 22, 399.

14 Al-Ṭabarī, *Ta'rīkh*, II 1561; al-Mas'ūdī, *Murūj*, 3638; Ibn Kathīr, *Bidāyah*, IX 304.

15 Ibn Khayyāṭ, *Ta'rīkh*, II 360 & 376; al-Ya'qūbī, *Ta'rīkh*, II 259; al-Mas'ūdī, *Murūj*, 3639; al-Ṭabarī, *Ta'rīkh*, II 1562; Ibn 'Asākir, *TMD*, Vol. 16, 171-172.

16 Al-Ṭabarī, *Ta'rīkh*, II 1562.

114/733 (cont.)	*or* Sulaymān b. Hishām[17]	caliph's son	x
115/734	Muḥammad b. Hishām al-Makhzūmī[18]	maternal uncle	Mecca
116/735	al-Walīd b. Yazīd II[19]	caliph's nephew & heir apparent	x
117/735-736	Khālid b. ʿAbd al-Malik b. al-Ḥārith b. al-Ḥakam[20]	cousin	yes
	or Maslamah b. ʿAbd al-Malik[21]	half-brother	x
118/736	Muḥammad b. Hishām al-Makhzūmī[22]	maternal uncle	possibly Mecca
	or Khālid b. ʿAbd al-Malik b. al-Ḥārith b. al-Ḥakam[23]	cousin	possibly
119/737	Abū Shākir Maslamah b. Hishām[24]	caliph's son	x
120/738	Muḥammad b. Hishām al-Makhzūmī[25]	maternal uncle	yes (& Mecca)

17 Ibn ʿAsākir, *TMD*, Vol. 22, 399.

18 Ibn Khayyāṭ, *Taʾrīkh*, II 361 & 377; al-Yaʿqūbī, *Taʾrīkh*, II 259; al-Ṭabarī, *Taʾrīkh*, II 1563; al-Masʿūdī, *Murūj*, 3639.

19 Ibn Khayyāṭ, *Taʾrīkh*, II 362 & 377; Ibn Aʿtham, *Futūḥ*, VIII 137; al-Yaʿqūbī, *Taʾrīkh*, II 259; al-Ṭabarī, *Taʾrīkh*, II 1572 & 1741; al-Masʿūdī, *Murūj*, 3639; Ibn ʿAsākir, *TMD*, Vol. 63, 326.

20 Ibn Khayyāṭ, *Taʾrīkh*, II 363 & 377; al-Yaʿqūbī, *Taʾrīkh*, II 259; al-Ṭabarī, *Taʾrīkh*, II 1586; al-Masʿūdī, *Murūj*, 3639.

21 Al-Masʿūdī, *Murūj*, 3639.

22 Ibn Khayyāṭ, *Taʾrīkh*, II 363 (yet, at II 377, he has Muḥammad, the son of the caliph); al-Ṭabarī, *Taʾrīkh*, II 1592; al-Masʿūdī, *Murūj*, 3639; Ibn Kathīr, *Bidāyah*, IX 320.

23 Ibn Kathīr, *Bidāyah*, IX 320.

24 Ibn Khayyāṭ, *Taʾrīkh*, II 364 & 377; Ibn Aʿtham, *Futūḥ*, VIII 138; al-Yaʿqūbī, *Taʾrīkh*, II 259; al-Ṭabarī, *Taʾrīkh*, II 1634-35 & 1742; al-Masʿūdī, *Murūj*, 3639; Ibn ʿAsākir, *TMD*, Vol. 58, 66 & 67; al-Fāsī, *Akhbār Makkah*, II 302.

25 Ibn Khayyāṭ, *Taʾrīkh*, II 365 & 377; al-Yaʿqūbī, *Taʾrīkh*, II 259; al-Ṭabarī, *Taʾrīkh*, II 1666; al-Masʿūdī, *Murūj*, 3640.

120/738 (cont.)	*or* Sulaymān b. Hishām[26] *or* Yazīd b. Hishām[27]	caliph's son caliph's son	x x
121/739	Muḥammad b. Hishām al-Makhzūmī[28]	maternal uncle	yes (& Mecca)
122/740	Muḥammad b. Hishām al-Makhzūmī[29]	maternal uncle	yes (& Mecca)
123/741	Yazīd b. Hishām[30] *or* Muḥammad b. Hishām al-Makhzūmī[31]	caliph's son maternal uncle	x yes (& Mecca)
124/742	Muḥammad b. Hishām al-Makhzūmī[32] *or* 'Abd al-'Azīz b. al-Ḥajjāj b. 'Abd al-Malik[33]	maternal uncle caliph's nephew	yes (& Mecca) x

RESTORING PRECEDENT: THE CALIPHAL *ḤAJJ* OF 106 AH

Hishām b. 'Abd al-Malik received the insignia of the caliphal office at his home in al-Zaytūnah in the Syrian desert in *Sha'bān* 105/January 724.[34] He was the fourth and final of 'Abd al-Malik's sons to become caliph. His caliphate was to last for nearly two decades; a length of time matched only by the first Umayyad caliph, Mu'āwiyah b. Abī Sufyān.

26 Al-Ṭabarī, *Ta'rīkh*, II 1666.

27 Al-Ṭabarī, *Ta'rīkh*, II 1666.

28 Ibn Khayyāṭ, *Ta'rīkh*, II 367 & 377; al-Ya'qūbī, *Ta'rīkh*, II 259; al-Ṭabarī, *Ta'rīkh*, II 1697-98; al-Mas'ūdī, *Murūj*, 3640.

29 Ibn Khayyāṭ, *Ta'rīkh*, II 369 & 377; al-Ya'qūbī, *Ta'rīkh*, II 259; al-Ṭabarī, *Ta'rīkh*, II 1717; al-Mas'ūdī, *Murūj*, 3640.

30 Ibn Khayyāṭ, *Ta'rīkh*, II 370 & 377; al-Ya'qūbī, *Ta'rīkh*, II 259; al-Ṭabarī, *Ta'rīkh*, II 1725.

31 Al-Mas'ūdī, *Murūj*, 3640.

32 Ibn Khayyāṭ, *Ta'rīkh*, II 372 & 377; al-Ya'qūbī, *Ta'rīkh*, II 259; al-Ṭabarī, *Ta'rīkh*, II 1727; al-Mas'ūdī, *Murūj*, 3640; Ibn Kathīr, *Bidāyah*, IX 340.

33 Ibn Kathīr, *Bidāyah*, IX 340.

34 Ibn Khayyāṭ, *Ta'rīkh*, II 340; al-Balādhurī, *Ansāb*, VI B 3; al-Ya'qūbī, *Ta'rīkh*, II 244; al-Ṭabarī, *Ta'rīkh*, II 1466-67.

In only the second year of his caliphate, Hishām gave a clear indication of the course his *ḥajj* policy was to take: that year, 106/725, he set out for the Ḥijāz to lead the ritual in person. In doing so, he broke with the practice of his two immediate predecessors, 'Umar II and Yazīd II, who had not led the ritual, and aligned himself with the likes of Mu'āwiyah, 'Abd al-Malik, al-Walīd and Sulaymān, who had. Thus, at this early stage of his caliphate, Hishām appeared to favour the Sufyānid model for leadership the *ḥajj*.

The caliph knew that travelling to Mecca was no easy undertaking for pilgrims. The intense heat, scarcity of water and the fear of attack by Bedouin tribesmen were just some of the dangers they faced. The twenty *ḥajj* seasons of Hishām's caliphate fell in early spring and rotated back into the winter months. The year he set out for Mecca, 106/725, saw the *ḥajj* fall in April/May when temperatures in the Ḥijāz were not as high as they would become in summer. Even so, Hishām adopted a policy of patronage similar to that implemented by his predecessors and had aqueducts and water tanks built along the route from Syria to Mecca to ease the way for the travelling pilgrims.[35] For his own *ḥajj*, Hishām went to great lengths to make sure he was adequately equipped: reportedly travelling with six hundred camels to carry his luggage, he seemed to have prepared for every eventuality.[36] It was a far cry from the days of the *Rāshidūn* when the caliph 'Umar had claimed two riding animals from the spoils of conquest to meet his needs for the *ḥajj*.[37]

Hishām's preparations were not limited to his material needs: he made considerable efforts to familiarize himself with the details of the ritual which brought him to the Ḥijāz. Before he reached Medina, he was in contact with the traditionist and jurist, Abū al-Zinād 'Abd Allāh b. Dhakwān, about the recommended rituals, *sunan*, of the pilgrimage.[38] Such a degree of preparation on the caliph's part may seem wise or even obvious. The *ḥajj*, as the fifth and final pillar of the faith, would be the last place a caliph would want to slip up while commanding the faithful. The added pressure of so many religious scholars and experts in attendance – not all of whom were wholehearted in their support for Umayyad rule – made it even more imperative for the caliph to make sure he knew what he was doing when he set out to follow in the footsteps of the Prophet.

---

35 Al-Mas'ūdī, *Murūj*, 2219; al-Rasheed, *Darb Zubaydah*, 9 & 11; Hamilton, *Walid and His Friends*, 75; Bacharach, "Marwanid Umayyad Building Activities: Speculations on Patronage", 31.

36 Hamilton, *Walid and His Friends*, 75.

37 Al-Ṭabarī, *Ta'rīkh*, I 2415-16.

38 Al-Ṭabarī, *Ta'rīkh*, II 1482; Ibn al-Athīr, *al-Kāmil*, V 130; Ibn Kathīr, *Bidāyah*, IX 234.

Hishām was not the first Umayyad caliph to ask for guidance in this matter; his father, 'Abd al-Malik, and his brother, Sulaymān, had also consulted religious scholars before performing their pilgrimages; a fact which, as mentioned above, has contributed to the debate about the timing of the development of the rites of the *ḥajj*. As was the case with his predecessors, Hishām's decision to ask Abū al-Zinād for guidance could be interpreted as more than a caliph seeking to perfect his knowledge of what made a *ḥajj* valid: it may have demonstrated his awareness of the influence wielded by the religious figures of the Holy Cities and of the legitimacy conferred upon him, as Commander of the Faithful, of acknowledging that influence. According to Blankinship, Hishām "specifically made a point of cultivating the rising class of religious scholars".[39] The caliph applied the same principle to his son Maslamah's pilgrimage when, as we shall see below, he arranged for him to be accompanied on his *ḥajj* by one of the foremost religious scholars in Medina.

There were several occasions during Hishām's *ḥajj* when he took the opportunity of demonstrating this duality, the religious and the political, of his position as Commander of the Faithful. In Medina, he was reported to have led the prayers at the funeral of a scholar, Sālim b. 'Abd Allāh b. 'Umar, a grandson of the second caliph.[40] The usual practice at funerals was for a city's governor to lead prayers over the eminent dead. However, if the caliph happened to be present, he took precedence and performed the rite. In Mecca, Hishām continued this practice of leading the prayers over well-known figures: there, he prayed over Ṭā'ūs b. Kaysān, the authority on Qur'ānic *tafsīr*, exegesis.[41] But even at a funeral, Hishām could not, it seems, forget his responsibilities as caliph: according to al-Dhahabī, he was so struck by the vast numbers of people attending Sālim b. 'Abd Allāh b. 'Umar's funeral that he decided to levy a number of them for the army.[42]

Being drafted into military service was probably not what the residents of Medina had anticipated from a caliphal *ḥajj*. Nor would it have been what the pilgrims passing through the city had in mind when they left their homes to set out for Mecca. The year of Hishām's *ḥajj* came to be known as "the Year of the Four Thousand"[43] and the drafted men saw action the following year as part of the summer campaigns.[44]

---

39 Blankinship, *Jihad*, 78 & 96.
40 Al-Balādhurī, *Ansāb*, VI B 34-35; al-Ṭabarī, *Ta'rīkh*, II 1472; al-Dhahabī, *Ta'rīkh*, IV 117.
41 Ibn Khayyāṭ, *Ta'rīkh*, II 349; al-Ṭabarī, *Ta'rīkh*, II 1472; al-Mas'ūdī, *Murūj*, 2214; Blankinship, *Jihad*, 96.
42 Al-Dhahabī, *Ta'rīkh*, IV 117.
43 Al-Ṭabarī, *Ta'rīkh*, II 1472.
44 Al-Ṭabarī, *Ta'rīkh*, II 1487-88.

In the past, Umayyad caliphs had used the occasion of their pilgrimages to harangue the opponents of ʿUthmān but an incident occurred during Hishām's *ḥajj* which showed he was seeking a different course. The caliph was in a procession which came upon Saʿīd b. ʿAbd Allāh b. al-Walīd b. ʿUthmān, a great-grandson of the murdered third caliph. Hishām dismounted to greet Saʿīd who, in the course of their brief conversation, commended the caliph's family and praised the people of "these good lands *(al-mawāṭin al-ṣāliḥah)*"[45] for their cursing of ʿAlī, the fourth caliph. Saʿīd did nor refer to ʿAlī by name, preferring instead the pejorative term "*Abū Turāb*" used by ʿAlī's opponents. Saʿīd then proceeded to advise the Commander of the Faithful that he ought "to curse him (ʿAlī) in these good lands".[46]

Yet Hishām, whose family based their political and moral legitimacy on the right to avenge ʿUthmān's murder, did not agree with the martyr's son. Instead, he responded by saying:

> "We did not come to revile (*shatm*) anyone nor to curse (*laʿn*) him; we have come as pilgrims."[47]

The significance of this apparently minor incident lay in what it revealed about how far the Umayyad political discourse had travelled from its original legitimizing dynamic and how the dynasty's political priorities had changed: just as caliphs no longer considered it politically imperative to appoint members of ʿUthmān's family to the governorship of Medina and to leadership of the *ḥajj* in order to proclaim their right to rule, so too Hishām declined to engage in the politics of recrimination while on his *ḥajj*. The main rivals to Umayyad authority were no longer in the Ḥijāz or the ʿAlid centre of al-Kūfah. Hishām's immediate political concerns were centred elsewhere: on securing the succession for his sons and securing the borders of his territories.[48]

The *ḥajj* of 106/725 was the only one of the twenty pilgrimage seasons of Hishām's caliphate he led in person. His pattern of leadership of the ritual largely chimed with that of previous Umayyad caliphs whose rule lasted ten years or more. Political circumstances permitting, Umayyad caliphs

45 Al-Ṭabarī, *Taʾrīkh*, II 1482-83; Blankinship, tr. *The End of Expansion*, 19.
46 Al-Ṭabarī, *Taʾrīkh*, II 1483; Blankinship, tr. *The End of Expansion*, 19; Ibn al-Athīr, *al-Kāmil*, V 130-131; Ibn Kathīr, *Bidāyah*, IX 234.
47 Al-Ṭabarī, *Taʾrīkh*, II 1483; Blankinship, tr. *The End of Expansion*, 19; Blankinship, *Jihad*, 96.
48 Hawting, *First Dynasty*, 83-88; Kennedy, *Prophet*, 108-111; Blankinship, *Jihad*, 97-116, 117-143, 145-165, 167-197, & 199-222.

favoured a policy of leading the *ḥajj* once, or at the most twice, during their caliphates. Hishām's caliphate arguably provides the clearest indication that Umayyad caliphs considered leading the *ḥajj* a religious and political duty they had to perform only once. Hishām had the joint highest number of *ḥajj* seasons of any Umayyad caliph; he also enjoyed the political security to travel back and forth to the Ḥijāz as often as he wished, and his *ḥajj* seasons fell in the friendlier conditions of early spring and winter than the heat of summer. There was no obstacle to his fulfilling this religious on a regular basis, if he so chose. The *ḥajj* is a religious duty which Muslims are required to perform once in a lifetime; this once-in-a-lifetime nature of the requirement may, in some way, explain why the Umayyad caliphs adopted the once-in-a-caliphate policy.

THE *ḤAJJ* OF THE HEIR APPARENT IN 116 AH

Hishām's policy for the pilgrimage was truly unique in one respect: he alone of the Umayyad caliphs invited his unwanted heir to go to Mecca and lead the *ḥajj* for him. In 116/735, a year which saw Syria and Iraq hit by the plague,[49] Hishām appointed his nephew al-Walīd to leave the caliphal centre and make the journey to the Ḥijāz to lead this most solemn of religious rituals.[50] Al-Walīd did not depart alone:

> Al-Walīd also acquired drinking companions ... Al-Walīd took with him some dogs in boxes (*ṣanādīq*), one of which ... fell from the camel. In the box was a dog. People trained whips on the man who had hired out the camel and they beat him hard. Al-Walīd also took with him a domed canopy (*qubbah*), which had been made to the exact size of the Ka'bah so that he could place it over the Ka'bah. He also took wine with him. He wanted to erect the domed canopy over the Ka'bah and to sit in it.[51]

Al-Walīd's friends managed to talk him out of placing the canopy over the Ka'bah.[52] Nevertheless:

49 Ibn al-Athīr, *al-Kāmil*, V 182; Ibn Kathīr, *Bidāyah*, IX 309 & 312.

50 *EI* 2nd edition, s.v. al-Walīd b. Yazīd b. 'Abd al-Malik.

51 Al-Ṭabarī, *Ta'rīkh*, II 1741; Hillenbrand, tr. *The Waning of the Umayyad Caliphate*, 88. See also Ibn A'tham, *Futūḥ*, VIII 137; Ibn al-Athīr, *al-Kāmil*, V 264; Ibn Kathīr, *Bidāyah*, X 2; Hamilton, *Walid and His Friends*, 95. Al-Mas'ūdī, *Murūj*, 2238, provides a list of his shortcomings.

52 Ibn A'tham, *Futūḥ*, VIII 137; al-Ṭabarī, *Ta'rīkh*, II 1741; Ibn al-Athīr, *al-Kāmil*, V 264.

> ... people saw him behaving in a contemptuous and flippant way towards religion and Hishām came to hear about it.[53]

The caliph, suitably outraged on behalf of Muslims everywhere, deemed al-Walīd unfit for the highest office in Islam and took advantage of the situation to try and insert his son Maslamah into the succession.[54]

For all Hishām's reported dismay over al-Walīd's behaviour, none of it should have come as any surprise to him. Al-Walīd was one of the most colourful characters in the Umayyad dynasty and stories of his hedonism have passed into historical legend.[55] This was the man who filled his swimming pool with wine and tried, quite literally, to drink it dry.

It may very well have been these tales of over-indulgence which prompted the caliph to ask his heir to lead the *ḥajj* in the first place. Hishām had to proceed with caution in his quest to oust al-Walīd from the succession for he could not risk jeopardizing the unity of the ruling house by overtly overturning the decision of his predecessor.[56] Nor, as Commander of the Faithful, could he risk compromising the *bay'ah*, the oath of allegiance, given to him and his heir. To do so would have left him open to allegations that as someone who had broken an oath given to God, he was unfit for the office he held. And there was a political calculation to be made: the *bay'ah*, once broken, lost much of its value and became a debased political currency. Any caliph who broke it could not be sure that the *bay'ah* he would then seek for his successors would be honoured.[57]

By inviting al-Walīd onto the biggest stage in Islam, Hishām may have been hoping the playboy prince would live up to his hedonistic reputation, discredit himself in the eyes of the assembled pilgrims and be obliged to step aside from the succession.[58]

The plan did not work. The *faux*-Ka'bah, the wine, the singers he paid to perform for him, and the ritually unclean dogs were not enough to undo the

53 Al-Ṭabarī, *Ta'rīkh*, II 1741; Hillenbrand, tr. *The Waning of the Umayyad Caliphate*, 89. See also Ibn A'tham, *Futūḥ*, VIII 137; Ibn al-Athīr, *al-Kāmil*, V 264.

54 Al-Ṭabarī, *Ta'rīkh*, II 1742; Ibn al-Athīr, *al-Kāmil*, V 264; Wellhausen, *Arab Kingdom*, 351; Chejne, *Succession*, 48; Hawting, *First Dynasty*, 91; Hamilton, *Walid and His Friends*, 96; Amabe, *Emergence of the 'Abbasid Autocracy*, 19-20.

55 Hawting, *First Dynasty*, 91; Kennedy, *Prophet*, 111.

56 The only Umayyad caliph who managed to break the oath was Marwān and he did so against the backdrop of the *fitnah* when the Umayyads were effectively out of power.

57 For the importance of the oath to the legitimacy to the succession process, see Sourdel, *Medieval Islam*, 112-113.

58 For the caliph's wish to depose his nephew, see al-Balādhurī, *Ansāb*, VI B 23, 28 & 36; al-Dhahabī, *Ta'rīkh*, V 31 & 174; Hamilton, *Walid and His Friends*, 95. For an insight into the relationship between the caliph and the heir apparent, see al-Ya'qūbī, *Ta'rīkh*, II 258.

religious oath underpinning the *bay'ah* which bound al-Walīd to Hishām as his heir.[59] None other than Maslamah, the very man who encouraged Yazīd to appoint Hishām his successor, chose to remind the caliph of his obligations. And Hishām, however reluctantly, had to stand by the succession plans he had been given.[60] But he did not abandon his own plans for the succession altogether. While he waited and hoped for a change in circumstances, this caliph did as so many of his predecessors had done and prepared the groundwork for his preferred successor, his son Maslamah, to be elevated into the succession and he made full use of the *ḥajj* to raise Maslamah's profile.

THE *ḤAJJ* OF THE WOULD-BE HEIR APPARENT IN 119 AH

After Hishām's strategy of reverse psychology failed at the *ḥajj* of 116/735, he resorted to the precedent set by so many of his predecessors of appointing his successor of choice, his son Maslamah, to lead the ritual in 119/737. Maslamah was the first of Hishām's sons eligible for the caliphate to be appointed to lead the *ḥajj*:[61] his half-brother Sulaymān may have already done so on several occasions but as the son of an *umm walad*, Sulaymān was out of the running to be caliph.[62]

Maslamah, like the heir apparent al-Walīd, did not perform his pilgrimage alone and his choice of travelling companion, the Medinan scholar Ibn Shihāb al-Zuhrī, said much about the purpose of this pilgrimage.[63] Having a scholar like al-Zuhrī by his side lent Maslamah's *ḥajj* a religious legitimacy which al-Walīd's had clearly lacked. And it seems the caliph intended it this way: Hishām was reported to have been less than pleased to learn that Maslamah had struck up a friendship with al-Walīd and had, on occasion, joined his social gatherings:

> "Al-Walīd is using you to mock me," Hishām told his son. "To think I was rearing you for the caliphate! Behave in a civilized way and attend the collective prayer."[64]

59 Hamilton, *Walid and His Friends*, 95.

60 Hamilton, *Walid and His Friends*, 97; Bacharach, "Marwanid Umayyad Building Activities: Speculations on Patronage", 31.

61 Al-Zubayrī, *Nasab Quraish*, 167 (where Maslamah is mistakenly referred to as Marwān); al-Balādhurī, *Ansāb*, VI B 2 & 104; Ibn 'Asākir, *TMD*, Vol. 58, 65.

62 Al-Zubayrī, *Nasab Quraish*, 168; al-Balādhurī, *Ansāb*, VI B 104.

63 Al-Ṭabarī, *Ta'rīkh*, II 1635; Ibn al-Athīr, *al-Kāmil*, V 214; Ibn Kathīr, *Bidāyah*, IX 324.

64 Al-Ṭabarī, *Ta'rīkh*, II 1742; Hillenbrand, tr. *The Waning of the Umayyad Caliphate*, 89-90; Hamilton,

As a way of halting this politically dangerous liaison, the caliph decided to send Maslamah to the Ḥijāz to lead the *ḥajj*. He hoped that by placing some distance – geographical and spiritual – between his son and al-Walīd, he would be able to show Maslamah in a good light and accrue goodwill for him amongst the people of the Holy Cities and the travelling pilgrims.

This propaganda exercise was enhanced by the presence of al-Zuhrī who not only considered al-Walīd unsuitable for the office of caliph but was amongst those who encouraged Hishām to divest him.[65] His appearance by Maslamah's side as the young prince led the *ḥajj* was therefore as much about politics as it was about religion. In the heart of Islam, at the holiest time of year, al-Zuhrī was throwing the weight of his immense religious learning behind the caliph's choice of heir apparent.

By all accounts, Maslamah acquitted himself well on his *ḥajj* and his generosity was even celebrated in verse.[66] During his time in the Ḥijāz:

> Maslamah devoted himself to acts of religious devotion (*al-nask; al-waqār*) and behaved in a steady gentle manner. He distributed money in Mecca and Medina ...[67]

The caliph also appointed Maslamah to lead the *ṣā'ifah*: Ibn Khayyāṭ records him leading it the year after his *ḥajj*.[68] His account of the caliph's preferred heir leading these events in successive years corresponds to his record of 'Abd al-Malik and al-Walīd's pattern of appointments when they were trying to insert their sons into the succession.

Hishām also followed al-Walīd's policy of strengthening his own line by appointing another potential heir to lead the *ḥajj*: his son Yazīd is believed to have led it in 120/738 or 123/741. Yazīd, like his brother Maslamah, was the son of an Arab mother and therefore a contender for the caliphate.[69] And like his brother Maslamah, Yazīd's pilgrimage(s) also took place after the eventful *ḥajj* of the heir apparent in 116/735. Hishām may have been preparing both of them to go forward as his heirs in the event that circumstances changed.

Walid and His Friends, 91-92.

65 Ibn 'Asākir, *TMD*, Vol. 63, 327; Ibn Kathīr, *Bidāyah*, X 3.

66 Al-Balādhurī, *Ansāb*, VI B 36; al-Ṭabarī, *Ta'rīkh*, II 1742.

67 Al-Ṭabarī, *Ta'rīkh*, II 1742; Hillenbrand, tr. *The Waning of the Umayyad Caliphate*, 90. See also Ibn A'tham, *Futūḥ*, VIII 138; al-Balādhurī, *Ansāb*, VI B 36; Ibn 'Asākir, *TMD*, Vol. 58, 67.

68 Ibn Khayyāṭ, *Ta'rīkh*, II 365; Blankinship, *Jihad*, 169. Al-Ya'qūbī, *Ta'rīkh*, II 260; Ibn 'Asākir, *TMD*, Vol. 58, 67; al-Dhahabī, *Ta'rīkh*, V 26, give the following year.

69 Al-Zubayrī, *Nasab Quraish*, 167; al-Balādhurī, *Ansāb*, VI B 104.

The caliph further consolidated the political profile of his immediate family by appointing several of his sons to lead the *ṣā'ifah* on a regular basis. Mu'āwiyah, Sa'īd and Sulaymān became seasoned campaigners against the Byzantines.[70] By contrast, the heir apparent al-Walīd was not invited to lead the *ṣā'ifah*.

The most seasoned campaigner of all in the Umayyad family was the caliph's half-brother, Maslamah,[71] the man who played the critical role in bringing Hishām to the caliphate by encouraging Yazīd II to nominate him as his heir. Maslamah was the only senior member of his generation in the Umayyad family whom Hishām is believed to have honoured with leadership of the *ḥajj*: reportedly doing so in 117/735-736. According to some accounts, Maslamah may also have led it during al-Walīd's caliphate in 94/713. Maslamah was in fact the only (half) brother of a ruling caliph believed to have led the *ḥajj* since the days of the dynasty's founding-father Mu'āwiyah. He was also the last. During Mu'āwiyah's caliphate, the caliph's brothers were among his closest allies. By the time of al-Walīd, Sulaymān, Yazīd and Hishām, the caliph's brothers were often his main rivals. Consequently, they were not given the privilege of leading the *ḥajj*. That Maslamah was different owed much to his unusual combination of military prowess, personal influence and lack of political power. For, influential though Maslamah was within the Umayyad family, often playing the role of kingmaker, as the son of an *umm walad* he could not translate that personal power into political authority and posed no threat to either al-Walīd's or Hishām's ambitions for the future of the caliphate.

Hishām, like so many of his predecessors, used the *ḥajj* to further the interests of his own family. They did not, however, lead all the *ḥajj* seasons of his caliphate and for those occasions when they were absent from the Ḥijāz, the caliph turned to a group of men who served him loyally and upon whom he could rely totally: his governors of the Holy Cities.

---

70 This list is not comprehensive but for some instances of the caliph's sons in action, see the following references. For Maslamah, Ibn Khayyāṭ, *Ta'rīkh*, II 365. For Mu'āwiyah, see Ibn Khayyāṭ, *Ta'rīkh*, II 349, 350, 351, 352, 353, 355, 357, 360, 361, 362, 363, 364, 369 & 377; al-Ya'qūbī, *Ta'rīkh*, II 259-260; al-Ṭabarī, *Ta'rīkh*, II 1487, 1495, 1506, 1560, 1561, 1562-63, 1564, 1573 & 1588; Ibn 'Asākir, *TMD*, Vol. 22, 398, & Vol. 59, 280-282; Ibn al-Athīr, *al-Kāmil*, V 145, 155, 158, 171, 176, 179, 181, 182, 186, 195, 196; Wellhausen, *Arab Kingdom*, 339; Blankinship, *Jihad*, 168-169; Hoyland, *Seeing Islam*, 656-657. For Muḥammad, see Ibn Khayyāṭ, *Ta'rīkh*, II 369; al-Balādhurī, *Ansāb*, VI B 64; Blankinship, *Jihad*, 169. For Sa'īd, see Ibn Khayyāṭ, *Ta'rīkh*, II 355; al-Ya'qūbī, *Ta'rīkh*, II 259-260; al-Ṭabarī, *Ta'rīkh*, II 1526. For Sulaymān, see Ibn Khayyāṭ, *Ta'rīkh*, II 360, 364, 365, 369, 370 & 377; al-Ya'qūbī, *Ta'rīkh*, II 260; al-Ṭabarī, *Ta'rīkh*, II 1561, 1573, 1588, 1635; 1727; Ibn 'Asākir, *TMD*, Vol. 22, 398-399; Ibn al-Athīr, *al-Kāmil*, V 179, 186, 195, 196, 228 & 259; Wellhausen, *Arab Kingdom*, 339; Blankinship, *Jihad*, 168-169.

71 This list is also not exhaustive: for some details of Maslamah's campaigns during Hishām's caliphate, see Ibn Khayyāṭ, *Ta'rīkh*, II 353 & 377; al-Ya'qūbī, *Ta'rīkh*, II 259-260; al-Ṭabarī, *Ta'rīkh*, II 1488, 1491, 1506, 1531-32, 1560 & 1667.

KEEPING IT IN THE FAMILY: HISHĀM'S GOVERNORS OF THE HOLY CITIES AND LEADERSHIP OF THE *ḤAJJ*

When Hishām became caliph, he confirmed Yazīd's appointee to the Holy Cities, 'Abd al-Wāḥid, in his position as governor.[72] As Yazīd had nominated Hishām, the new caliph had no political scores to settle and no need to institute a purge of predecessor's ruling class.

He did not, however, ask his governor in the Ḥijāz to lead the first *ḥajj* of his caliphate; instead, he appointed his maternal uncle, Ibrāhīm b. Hishām al-Makhzūmī, to do so. Ibrāhīm hailed from a family with previous *ḥajj* connections: his father had served 'Abd al-Malik as governor of the Holy Cities and led the *ḥajj* for him on several occasions. In fact, the caliph owed his name to this grandfather: news of Hishām's birth first reached 'Abd al-Malik after his forces had defeated Muṣ'ab b. al-Zubayr and 'Abd al-Malik, interpreting Hishām's birth as a good omen, named him Manṣūr in celebration of his victory. Hishām's mother, 'Ā'ishah, had other ideas and named him after her father.[73]

Hishām's appointment of his maternal uncle to lead the inaugural *ḥajj* of his caliphate signalled the return of the Umayyad family to positions of influence in the Ḥijāz and a year later, when the caliph led the *ḥajj* in person, it was Ibrāhīm who occupied the governorship of the Holy Cities.[74] The changeover from one governor to another was less dramatic than previous years had often seen: there were no orders from the caliph to humiliate 'Abd al-Wāḥid and the politics of reprisal were, for the moment, on hold. Ibrāhīm went on to lead at least five more *ḥajj* seasons for his nephew: from 107/726 to 111/730; becoming the first man in the Umayyad era to lead five consecutive *ḥajj* seasons.

The caliph carried out a re-shuffle of his governors in the Ḥijāz in 114/732-733. After eight years as governor of the Holy Cities and the oasis city of al-Ṭā'if, Ibrāhīm made way for two successors, both of whom were relatives of the caliph: Khālid b. 'Abd al-Malik b. al-Ḥārith b. al-Ḥakam, the caliph's distant cousin, was appointed to Medina[75] and Muḥammad

---

72 Al-Ṭabarī, *Ta'rīkh*, II 1471.

73 Al-Balādhurī, *Ansāb*, VI B 1; al-Ṭabarī, *Ta'rīkh*, II 1466; Wellhausen, *Arab Kingdom*, 325.

74 Al-Ṭabarī, *Ta'rīkh*, II 1471; Ibn 'Asākir, *TMD*, Vol. 7, 260, & Vol. 37, 250; al-Fāsī, *Akhbār Makkah*, II 178. Ibn Khayyāṭ, *Ta'rīkh*, II 373, makes no mention of Ibrāhīm: instead he records Muḥammad b. Hishām as governor of Mecca from 106/724-725 to the end of Hishām's caliphate and as governor of Medina until 114/732-733. However, elsewhere, II 378, he does cite Ibrāhīm as governor of Medina until 114/732-733.

75 They shared a great-grandfather in al-Ḥakam.

b. Hishām, the brother of the former governor, to Mecca and al-Ṭā'if.[76] Leadership of the *ḥajj* then largely rotated between Khālid and Muḥammad until the governorship of Medina was added to Muḥammad's portfolio of gubernatorial responsibilities in 118/736 or 119/737.

Hishām did not, however, give Muḥammad leadership of all the *ḥajj* seasons of his governorship. On those occasions when he does not seem to have appointed his uncle to lead the *ḥajj*, he appointed members of his immediate family: his son Maslamah in 119/737; his sons Yazīd or Sulaymān in 120/738 and his son Yazīd in 123/741. By doing so, Hishām conformed to the policies of his predecessors Muʿāwiyah, ʿAbd al-Malik and al-Walīd who kept leadership of the ritual restricted to a very tight core of people, made up of the caliph's sons and governors of the Holy Cities – but only if the latter were members of the ruling family.

Hishām's adherence to this political model showed that his reinstatement of members of the ruling family to governorships in the Ḥijāz was no accident. The presence of the caliph's relatives, whether by birth or marriage, in gubernatorial positions in the Holy Cities maintained the neutrality of Mecca and Medina in the battle for political influence between Qays and the Yaman. And Hishām, like his predecessors, had to try and balance the distribution of key governorships between these two groups. One way to keep the Holy Cities out of this power struggle was to place its governance in the hands of the ruling family. That Hishām had such a low turnover of governors in the Ḥijāz during his twenty-year caliphate reflects the degree of stability he managed to achieve there.

Hishām's reliance on his maternal family, in particular, to provide him with governors for the Holy Cities and leaders of the *ḥajj* harked back to his father's decision to appoint his father-in-law to fulfil the same function. Both decisions were based on the need to find someone within the ruling structure who was loyal only to the caliph; someone who owed his appointment solely to his personal relationship with him rather than to his position within the ruling family. In-laws and maternal relatives fitted the bill perfectly. They also proved particularly useful when it came to the caliph's plans for the future of the caliphate. As the only way they could maintain their position was for the caliphate to remain in the hands of their relatives, they tended to be vocal supporters of the caliph's plans to divert the succession to

76 Al-Zubayrī, *Nasab Quraish*, 170 & 328-329; Ibn Khayyāṭ, *Ta'rīkh*, II 373 (where Khālid replaces Muḥammad as governor) & 378 (where Khālid replaces Ibrāhīm); al-Ṭabarī, *Ta'rīkh*, II 1561; Ibn ʿAsākir, *TMD*, Vol. 7, 260 (where the changeover happens a year earlier); Ibn Kathīr, *Bidāyah*, IX 306 (where Muḥammad, not Khālid, replaces Ibrāhīm as governor of both cities).

his sons. Ibrāhīm and Muḥammad, for example, were two of Hishām's main supporters for his plan to change the succession in favour of their great-nephew Maslamah.[77]

The succession was only one of Hishām's political headaches. The latter part of his caliphate saw a number of rebellious movements seeking to overthrow the ruling regime. And as happened so often in the past, they made use of the *ḥajj* to try to achieve it.

ALL ROADS LEAD TO MECCA: THE *ḤAJJ* AS A PLATFORM FOR REBELLION

As time passed, Hishām was faced with an increasing number of internal challenges. The Umayyads' old foes, the *Khawārij*, were still active and, as they had done in the past, they made use of the *ḥajj* as a way to meet and share information. In 119/717, the *Khārijī* rebel Bahlūl b. Bishr set off for Mecca where he met like-minded people *(man kāna 'alā mithli ra'yihi)*[78] and they arranged to meet in al-Mawṣil.[79]

Bahlūl's rebellion ultimately failed. For the caliph, the problem was less the *Khawārij* themselves than the tenacity of their doctrine of resistance to the central government and their ability to make use of the *ḥajj* as a means of communication to spread that message.

Another equally tenacious ideology re-emerged in rebellious form towards the end of Hishām's caliphate: support for the family of the Prophet. Their leader this time was Zayd b. 'Alī, a grandson of the 'Alid martyr *par excellence*, al-Ḥusayn.[80] Unfortunately for Zayd, the passing of two generations had done nothing to alter the political fortunes of his family. Hishām, on the other hand, had learnt from the past and was wary of the consequences of putting down an 'Alid revolt. His correspondence with his governor of Iraq, Yūsuf b. 'Umar,[81] shows that before the revolt began, he considered the option of sending Zayd into exile in the Ḥijāz.[82] Zayd,

---

77 Al-Balādhurī, *Ansāb*, VI B 36; al-Ṭabarī, *Ta'rīkh*, II 1741-42; Ibn al-Athīr, *al-Kāmil*, V 264; Hamilton, *Walid and His Friends*, 136.

78 Al-Ṭabarī, *Ta'rīkh*, II 1622. See also al-Balādhurī, *Ansāb*, VI B 96; Ibn al-Athīr, *al-Kāmil*, V 209-212 (in particular 210); Ibn Kathīr, *Bidāyah*, IX 323-324.

79 Al-Ṭabarī, *Ta'rīkh*, II 1622.

80 Al-Dīnawarī, *Akhbār*, 244; al-Ya'qūbī, *Ta'rīkh*, II 255-256; al-Ṭabarī, *Ta'rīkh*, II 1667-88; al-Mas'ūdī, *Murūj*, 2220-22 & 2224; Wellhausen, *Arab Kingdom*, 337-339; Kennedy, *Prophet*, 111-112.

81 *EI* 2nd edition s.v. Yūsuf b.'Umar.

82 Al-Ṭabarī, *Ta'rīkh*, II 1682.

however, went ahead with his revolt in 121/739 and history duly repeated itself: the Kūfans deserted him and another 'Alid rebellion was put down by another zealous governor working on behalf of the Umayyads.[83]

But the idea lived on to inspire others.[84] Members of the family of the Prophet's uncle, 'Abbās, were working secretly to build up a network of supporters.[85] The family itself was based in southern Jordan but their key supporters were in the province of Khurāsān. To avoid detection by the Umayyad authorities, these men used the *ḥajj* as cover for their travels between their various centres of support. While en route to Mecca, a group of them arrived in al-Kūfah in 124/742 to meet with activists there.[86] The group from Khurāsān included Sulaymān b. Kathīr, the head of 'Abbāsid propaganda and the personal appointee of the 'Abbāsid *Imām* Muḥammad.

The flexibility and mobility offered by the *ḥajj* allowed these undercover rebels to travel and meet supporters without arousing undue suspicion.[87] Posing as pious pilgrims on the way to perform the most solemn of religious acts, these revolutionaries plotted the caliph's overthrow under the very eyes of the central authority and there was little the caliph could do to stop them.

83 Ibn A'tham, *Futūḥ*, VIII 110-126; al-Ṭabarī, *Ta'rīkh*, II 1698-1716.

84 Omar, *'Abbasid Caliphate*, 88.

85 Al-Ya'qūbī, *Ta'rīkh*, II 247; al-Ṭabarī, *Ta'rīkh*, II 1639-40.

86 Al-Dīnawarī, *Akhbār*, 241-242, 243 & 244; al-Ya'qūbī, *Ta'rīkh*, II 257 (where the events are not, however, dated); al-Ṭabarī, *Ta'rīkh*, II 1726-27; Ibn al-Athīr, *al-Kāmil*, V 254-255 (where the *Imām* is Ibrāhīm not Muḥammad); Omar, *'Abbasid Caliphate*, 74.

87 Lassner, *Islamic Revolution*, 82.

NINE

The Third and Final Generation: Al-Walīd II to Marwān II

Al-Walīd became caliph in 125/743; a position he held until he was murdered the following year. His brief caliphate spanned only one *ḥajj* season: 125/743. He was succeeded by Yazīd III, a son of al-Walīd I, whose caliphate turned out to be even briefer than that of his predecessor. It lasted barely six months but did include a *ḥajj* season: 126/744. Following Yazīd's death, his brother Ibrāhīm became caliph. But Ibrāhīm's authority was not universally recognized and his time in power was even shorter than his brother's and did not include a *ḥajj* season. Marwān II, a grandson of the founder of the Marwānid dynasty, took power after him. His caliphate covered five *ḥajj* seasons, from 127/745 to 131/749. Table 8 shows who these caliphs appointed to lead the *ḥajj*.

Table 8

Year	*Ḥajj leader*	*Relationship to caliph*	*Governor of Medina?*
al-Walīd II			
125/743	Yūsuf b. Muḥammad b. Yūsuf al-Thaqafī[1]	maternal uncle	yes (& Mecca)

1 Ibn Khayyāṭ, *Ta'rīkh*, II 385; al-Ṭabarī, *Ta'rīkh*, II 1769; al-Mas'ūdī, *Murūj*, 3640.

125/743 (cont.)	*or* Muḥammad b. Mūsā al-Thaqafī[2]	x	x
	or Yūsuf b. 'Umar[3]	x	x
Yazīd III			
126/744	'Umar b. 'Abd Allāh b. 'Abd al-Malik[4]	cousin	x
	or 'Abd al-'Azīz b. 'Umar II[5]	cousin	yes (& Mecca)
Marwān II			
127/745	'Abd al-'Azīz b. 'Umar II[6]	cousin	yes (& Mecca)
128/746	'Abd al-'Azīz b. 'Umar II[7]	cousin	yes (& Mecca)
129/747	'Abd al-Wāḥid b. Sulaymān[8]	cousin	yes (& Mecca)
	or Abū Ḥamzah *al-Khārijī*[9]	x	claiming leadership
130/748	Muḥammad b. 'Abd al-Malik b. Marwān[10]	cousin	yes (& Mecca)
	or 'Abd al-Malik b. Muḥammad b. Marwān I[11]	half-brother	x

2 Al-Ya'qūbī, *Ta'rīkh*, II 265.

3 Ibn Khayyāṭ, *Ta'rīkh*, II 380.

4 Al-Ya'qūbī, *Ta'rīkh*, II 267; al-Ṭabarī, *Ta'rīkh*, II 1875; al-Mas'ūdī, *Murūj*, 3640.

5 Al-Ṭabarī, *Ta'rīkh*, II 1874-75; Ibn al-Athīr, *al-Kāmil*, V 319; Ibn Kathīr, *Bidāyah*, X 17.

6 Ibn Khayyāṭ, *Ta'rīkh*, II 398 & 433; al-Ya'qūbī, *Ta'rīkh*, II 281; al-Ṭabarī, *Ta'rīkh*, II 1917; al-Mas'ūdī, *Murūj*, 3640; Ibn 'Asākir, *TMD*, Vol. 36, 328.

7 Ibn Khayyāṭ, *Ta'rīkh*, II 403 & 433; al-Ya'qūbī, *Ta'rīkh*, II 281; al-Ṭabarī, *Ta'rīkh*, II 1941-42; al-Mas'ūdī, *Murūj*, 3640; Ibn 'Asākir, *TMD*, Vol. 36, 328; al-Fāsī, *Akhbār Makkah*, II 179.

8 Ibn Khayyāṭ, *Ta'rīkh*, II 411 & 433; al-Ya'qūbī, *Ta'rīkh*, II 281; al-Ṭabarī, *Ta'rīkh*, II 1983-84; al-Mas'ūdī, *Murūj*, 3640; Ibn 'Asākir, *TMD*, Vol. 37, 239 & 240; Ibn al-Athīr, *al-Kāmil*, V 376; Ibn Kathīr, *Bidāyah*, X 34.

9 Ibn Kathīr, *Bidāyah*, X 34. See also al-Mas'ūdī, *Murūj*, 3640; al-Ya'qūbī, *Ta'rīkh*, II 281.

10 Al-Ṭabarī, *Ta'rīkh*, II 2017; al-Mas'ūdī, *Murūj*, 3640; Ibn 'Asākir, *TMD*, Vol. 54, 148; Ibn al-Athīr, *al-Kāmil*, V 393; Ibn Kathīr, *Bidāyah*, X 37.

11 Al-Ya'qūbī, *Ta'rīkh*, II 281.

130/748 (cont.)	*or* 'Abd al-Malik b. Muḥammad b. 'Aṭiyyah[12]	x	x
	or Muḥammad b. 'Abd al-Malik b. Muḥammad b. 'Aṭiyyah al-Sa'dī[13]	x	x
131/749	al-Walīd b. 'Urwah b. Muḥammad b. 'Aṭiyyah al-Sa'dī[14]	x	yes (& Mecca)
	or Muḥammad b. 'Abd al-Malik b. 'Aṭiyyah al-Sa'dī[15]	x	x

THE *ḤAJJ* OF 125 AH: THE POLITICS OF REPRISAL REVISITED

Once caliph, al-Walīd moved against everyone who had tried to oust him from the succession. Such a course of action was not without precedent: his uncle, the caliph Sulaymān, had done the same but what distinguished al-Walīd's reprisal strategy from his uncle's was *who* he turned against. Sulaymān had sacked, detained and tortured employees of the state he controlled. Al-Walīd's victims, by contrast, were some of the most well connected members of the Umayyad ruling house including sons of his predecessor Hishām,[16] particularly Sulaymān.[17]

Al-Walīd's actions may seem nothing more than the satisfaction of a personal vendetta but beneath his desire for revenge was the issue of the future distribution of power. His immediate predecessors, with the exception of

12 Ibn Khayyāṭ, *Ta'rīkh*, II 433.

13 Ibn Khayyāṭ, *Ta'rīkh*, II 417; Ibn 'Asākir, *TMD*, Vol. 54, 144.

14 Ibn Khayyāṭ, *Ta'rīkh*, II 421 & 433; al-Ṭabarī, *Ta'rīkh*, III 11; al-Mas'ūdī, *Murūj*, 3641; Ibn 'Asākir, *TMD*, Vol. 63, 217; Ibn al-Athīr, *al-Kāmil*, V 402.

15 Al-Ya'qūbī, *Ta'rīkh*, II 281.

16 Al-Ya'qūbī, *Ta'rīkh*, II 261; al-Ṭabarī, *Ta'rīkh*, II 1751; Wellhausen, *Arab Kingdom*, 353; Hamilton, *Walid and His Friends*, 136.

17 Ibn Khayyāṭ, *Ta'rīkh*, II 379; al-Ṭabarī, *Ta'rīkh*, II 1776; Ibn al-Athīr, *al-Kāmil*, V 280; Hawting *First Dynasty*, 91; Kennedy, *Prophet*, 112; Hamilton, *Walid and His Friends*, 136; Amabe, *Emergence of the 'Abbasid Autocracy*, 20.

'Umar II, were sons of the great restorer of Umayyad fortunes 'Abd al-Malik. Al-Walīd II was the first of the next generation to become caliph but he did so without the support of many of his peers in the ruling family. Al-Walīd I and Hishām had sons aplenty, many of whom believed they were more competent than the flamboyant new caliph.

Al-Walīd inflamed the situation by nominating two of his young sons, 'Uthmān and al-Ḥakam, as his heirs;[18] one of whom, al-Ḥakam, was the son of a slave woman, an *umm walad*.[19] Thus far, the Umayyads had only considered sons of free-born Arab women, usually women of status, eligible for the highest office in Islam.[20] Al-Walīd's decision to nominate his sons helped solidify the opposition against him, especially among the sons of al-Walīd I and Hishām who interpreted al-Walīd's plans for the succession as meaning political oblivion for them.[21] If they were to maintain any kind of influence, then al-Walīd had to go.

The most immediate problem they faced was how to secure his removal without threatening the unity of the Umayyad family for the caliph was not without powerful royal supporters of his own.[22] As time passed, the Umayyad house became ever more divided with its members lining up in rival camps behind the ruling caliph or the dissident princes.

All of these tensions fed through into al-Walīd's *ḥajj* policy. His initial preference was to assert his authority by leading his inaugural *ḥajj* himself.[23] He had, as we have seen, led the ritual as heir apparent, an event which was not an unqualified success. He may therefore have viewed his first *ḥajj* as caliph as an opportunity to shape the pilgrims' perceptions of him by presenting himself in a positive light.[24]

That al-Walīd understood the latent political, as well as the social, potential of the *ḥajj* was not in doubt: as heir apparent he had often provided food for pilgrims at Zīzā', a staging post on the way from Syria to Mecca, and had made fodder available for their animals.[25] His generosity was such that he

18 Al-Ya'qūbī, *Ta'rīkh*, II 262; al-Ṭabarī, *Ta'rīkh*, II 1755 & 1763; Ibn al-Athīr, *al-Kāmil*, V 269; Ibn Kathīr, *Bidāyah*, X 4; Chejne, *Succession*, 49; Crone, *Slaves on Horses*, 129; Hawting, *First Dynasty*, 91-92; Kennedy, *Prophet*, 112; Hamilton, *Walid and His Friends*, 140-141; Amabe, *Emergence of the 'Abbasid Autocracy*, 20.

19 Al-Zubayrī, *Nasab Quraish*, 167.

20 Bligh-Abramski, *From Damascus to Baghdad*, 77-78.

21 Wellhausen, *Arab Kingdom*, 361.

22 Al-Ṭabarī, *Ta'rīkh*, II 1752-54.

23 Al-Ṭabarī, *Ta'rīkh*, II 1778.

24 Al-Ṭabarī, *Ta'rīkh*, II 1741-42; Ibn al-Athīr, *al-Kāmil*, V 264.

25 Ibn A'tham, *Futūḥ*, VIII 139; al-Ṭabarī, *Ta'rīkh*, II 1754; King, "The Umayyad *Qusur* and Related Settlements in Jordan", 77, & King, "Settlement Patterns in Islamic Jordan: The Umayyads and Their Use of Land", 371; Hamilton, *Walid and His Friends*, 49; Bacharach, "Marwanid Umayyad Building Activities: Speculations on Patronage", 37.

was said to have refused no request for assistance that was put before him.[26] Once caliph, he again showed his generosity: this time to the people of the Holy Cities when he reinstated the pensions Hishām revoked in the aftermath of Zayd b. ʿAlī's revolt.[27]

But it was to be al-Walīd's political allegiances which prevented him realizing his wish to lead the *ḥajj* as caliph. His favouritism towards the Qays tribal grouping alienated the Yaman to the point that a group of them in Damascus decided to kill him.[28] They approached the former governor of Iraq, Khālid b. ʿAbd Allāh al-Qasrī, and asked him to join them.[29] Khālid was non-committal but promised not to reveal their plans.[30] When al-Walīd announced he was going on the *ḥajj*, Khālid advised him against it but refused to explain why.[31] The caliph interpreted his silence as disobedience; he had him thrown in prison then handed him over to the Qaysī governor of Iraq, Yūsuf b. ʿUmar, who tortured him to death.[32]

The circumstances of Khālid's death would soon come back to haunt al-Walīd but in the meantime, he had to appoint someone to govern the Holy Cities and lead the first *ḥajj* of his reign. He looked no further than his family and appointed his maternal uncle, Yūsuf b. Muḥammad b. Yūsuf al-Thaqafī, nephew of the legendary governor of the east al-Ḥajjāj, governor of the Holy Cities and al-Ṭā'if.[33]

When the new governor arrived in Medina to take up his position, he did not do so alone. Under instructions from the caliph, Yūsuf had with him two of the men who had governed the Holy Cities for Hishām: Ibrāhīm and Muḥammad.[34] Their family had political ties with this Holy City dating back to the time of ʿAbd al-Malik when their father was governor and led the *ḥajj* several times. Ibrāhīm and Muḥammad, like Yūsuf, were maternal

26 Al-Ṭabarī, *Ta'rīkh*, II 1754. There is debate whether the Umayyads built their *quṣūr* along the pilgrimage routes in order to provide food and water for the travelling pilgrims. See King, "The Umayyad *Qusur* and Related Settlements in Jordan", 71-80 (in particular 74, 75 & 77) & "Settlement Patterns in Islamic Jordan: The Umayyads and Their Use of Land", 369-375 (in particular 371); Bacharach, "Marwanid Umayyad Building Activities: Speculations on Patronage", 27-44 (in particular 27, 28, 30, 31, 33, 34, 37 & 39); Kennedy & Petersen, "Guardians of the Pilgrim Wells: Damascus to Aqaba", 12-19.

27 Wellhausen, *Arab Kingdom*, 353.

28 Al-Ṭabarī, *Ta'rīkh*, II 1778.

29 *EI* 2nd edition, s.v. Khālid b. ʿAbd Allāh al-Qasrī.

30 Al-Ṭabarī, *Ta'rīkh*, II 1778; al-Dhahabī, *Ta'rīkh*, V 175.

31 Al-Ṭabarī, *Ta'rīkh*, II 1778; Ibn al-Athīr, *al-Kāmil*, V 281; al-Dhahabī, *Ta'rīkh*, V 175; Hamilton, *Walid and His Friends*, 144; Amabe, *Emergence of the ʿAbbasid Autocracy*, 19-20.

32 Al-Ṭabarī, *Ta'rīkh*, II 1779-80; Hawting, *First Dynasty*, 93.

33 Al-Zubayrī, *Nasab Quraish*, 166-167; Ibn Khayyāṭ, *Ta'rīkh*, II 384; al-Yaʿqūbī, *Ta'rīkh*, II 262; al-Ṭabarī, *Ta'rīkh*, II 1768; al-Jahshiyārī, *Kitāb al-wuzarā'*, 65; Wellhausen, *Arab Kingdom*, 354-355.

34 Al-Ṭabarī, *Ta'rīkh*, II 1768; Ibn al-Athīr, *al-Kāmil*, V 273; Ibn Kathīr, *Bidāyah*, X 4-5.

uncles of the caliph they served. And they, like Yūsuf, were loyal to their caliph's interests. As such, they backed Hishām's plans to oust al-Walīd from the succession in favour of Hishām's son, Maslamah.[35] Now, with the accession of al-Walīd, they would suffer for it. The newly installed governor paraded them before the people of the City of the Prophet. Not content with this public humiliation, Yūsuf went on to have them flogged.[36] Then, on the orders of the caliph, he handed them over to the governor of Iraq, Yūsuf b. 'Umar, who tortured them to death.[37]

There had been acts of political reprisal before but never on this scale. The treatment meted out to these two men by Yūsuf b. Muḥammad at the behest of the caliph was not just as assault on them personally; it was an attack on the political establishment to which they belonged. Their public degradation at the hands of the new governor of Medina was not merely intended to signify that the old order had made way for the new; it implied that the old order was being destroyed. The humiliation of Ibrāhīm and Muḥammad was cruel and harsh but it was no rash act of revenge. It was politically motivated and when the caliph ordered the man complicit in it to lead the most prestigious religious event of all, the *ḥajj*, al-Walīd's rivals could not have failed to understand the message he was sending them. If the caliph so wished, he could use the occasion of the *ḥajj* to promote social unity and effect reconciliation. By contrast, al-Walīd's choice of leader for the *ḥajj* suggested an escalation of the tensions at the very centre of the political elite.

To inflict such punishments, and so publicly, was dangerous for the stability of the Umayyad ruling system, because one of the pillars supporting that system was the unity of the ruling family. When one caliph set out to purge his predecessor's representatives – who also happened to be members, however marginal, of that ruling family – in so brutal a manner, the only conclusion to be drawn was that Umayyad unity no longer existed. And if the Umayyads themselves could no longer invest in their own myths, their political enemies would see no reason to do so either.

At the very time the Umayyads locked themselves ever more tightly into their internal political dialogue, the 'Abbāsids continued their efforts to overthrow them and they used the *ḥajj* as the channel of communication to

35 Al-Balādhurī, *Ansāb*, VI B 230; al-Ṭabarī, *Ta'rīkh*, II 1741-42; Ibn al-Athīr, *al-Kāmil*, V 264.

36 Al-Ṭabarī, *Ta'rīkh*, II 1768; Ibn al-Athīr, *al-Kāmil*, V 273 & 274; Wellhausen, *Arab Kingdom*, 354; Hamilton, *Walid and His Friends*, 137.

37 Al-Zubayrī, *Nasab Quraish*, 329; Ibn Khayyāṭ, *Ta'rīkh*, II 379; al-Balādhurī, *Ansāb*, VI B 230-231; al-Ya'qūbī, *Ta'rīkh*, II 264; al-Ṭabarī, *Ta'rīkh*, II 1768; Ibn 'Asākir, *TMD*, Vol. 7, 259, & Vol. 63, 328; al-Dhahabī, *Ta'rīkh*, V 29; Wellhausen, *Arab Kingdom*, 354; Hamilton, *Walid and His Friends*, 137.

do it. In 125/743, a group of their senior leaders, including their chief of propaganda, Sulaymān b. Kathīr, arrived in Mecca.[38] They met with their *Imām*, Muḥammad b. 'Alī, and gave him the money they had collected, around two hundred thousand *dirhams*, as well as clothes to the value of thirty thousand *dirhams*. Amongst other matters, they discussed Muḥammad's designation of a future leader for the movement and the purchase of a certain slave by the name of Abū Muslim.[39]

Well organized though the 'Abbāsid revolutionaries were, they were not the most pressing political problem for al-Walīd. For that, he had to look closer to home. The torture and murder of Ibrāhīm and Muḥammad, along with that of Khālid al-Qasrī, fed into the fury already felt by many of the sons of al-Walīd I and Hishām.[40] Their opposition found its focus in Yazīd, a son of the caliph al-Walīd I.[41] Backed by no fewer than thirteen of his brothers, a large number of cousins, and the Yaman tribal grouping,[42] Yazīd's men set off to confront the caliph.[43] In *Jumadā* II 126/April 743, they found and killed him at the desert fortress of al-Bakhrā'.[44]

With al-Walīd's passing, Yazīd b. al-Walīd b. 'Abd al-Malik became caliph.[45] He was not the first of his dynasty to win power by force of arms – his grandfather had done so against Ibn al-Zubayr fifty years previously – but he was the first to do so against another member of the Umayyad family and some within that family, most notably the governor of Armenia and Ādharbayjān, Marwān b. Muḥammad b. Marwān I, would not forgive him for it.[46]

THE *ḤAJJ* OF 126 AH: THE SEARCH FOR UMAYYAD UNITY

The campaign which Yazīd III and his supporters launched against al-Walīd had focused on the politics of the caliph's impiety and, therefore, of his

38 Al-Ṭabarī, *Ta'rīkh*, II 1769; Ibn al-Athīr, *al-Kāmil*, V 274; Lassner, *Islamic Revolution*, 82-83.

39 Al-Ṭabarī, *Ta'rīkh*, II 1769.

40 Al-Ya'qūbī, *Ta'rīkh*, II 264; al-Ṭabarī, *Ta'rīkh*, II 1780 & 1784.

41 Al-Zubayrī, *Nasab Quraish*, 166; Ibn Khayyāṭ, *Ta'rīkh*, II 380-383; al-Ya'qūbī, *Ta'rīkh*, II 264-265; al-Ṭabarī, *Ta'rīkh*, II 1784; Ibn al-Athīr, *al-Kāmil*, V 283; al-Dhahabī, *Ta'rīkh*, V 31; Wellhausen, *Arab Kingdom*, 362; Hawting, *First Dynasty*, 93.

42 Hawting, *First Dynasty*, 93.

43 Al-Dīnawarī, *Akhbār*, 247; al-Ṭabarī, *Ta'rīkh*, II 1794; al-Dhahabī, *Ta'rīkh*, V 176-178.

44 Ibn A'tham, *Futūḥ*, VIII 141; al-Ya'qūbī, *Ta'rīkh*, II 265; al-Ṭabarī, *Ta'rīkh*, II 1810; al-Mas'ūdī, *Murūj*, 2236; Ibn al-Athīr, *al-Kāmil*, V 280-289 (in particular 280 & 288); Ibn Kathīr, *Bidāyah*, X 6-11.

45 Ibn Khayyāṭ, *Ta'rīkh*, II 386; Ibn A'tham, *Futūḥ*, VIII 141; al-Ya'qūbī, *Ta'rīkh*, II 265; al-Ṭabarī, *Ta'rīkh*, II 1825; Ibn al-Athīr, *al-Kāmil*, V 291; Ibn Kathīr, *Bidāyah*, X 12.

46 Al-Ṭabarī, *Ta'rīkh*, II 1850-51; Ibn al-Athīr, *al-Kāmil*, V 284 & 309-310; Amabe, *Emergence of the 'Abbasid Autocracy*, 21.

unsuitability for the highest office in Islam.[47] But, in reality, their actions had more to do with staking their own claim for power. One of the (many) charges they laid against al-Walīd was his decision to disregard Umayyad precedent and nominate the son of an *umm walad* as his heir. Yet Yazīd's assumption of the caliphate showed the extent to which this had merely served as cover for their real concerns: Yazīd was himself the son of an *umm walad*[48] and the heir he designated to be his immediate successor, his brother Ibrāhīm,[49] was another son of an *umm walad*.[50] In the aftermath of al-Walīd's murder, contradictions such as these did nothing to help ease tensions within the Umayyad family.

Once caliph, Yazīd III had to address several seemingly impossible tasks at once: he had to establish his own authority as quickly as possible; he had to try and be more representative of the community as a whole than his predecessor had been, yet he also had to reward that particular section of it – the Yaman – which backed his bid for power. Most crucially of all, the divisive circumstances of his accession made unity within the Umayyad ruling family his most urgent political priority.

The quickest way for a new caliph to assert his authority was to remove the governors appointed by his predecessor and install an entirely new governing class, one which more accurately reflected his political agenda. And so, one by one, Yazīd ousted al-Walīd's Qaysī governors to make way for his own protégés. Two governorships in particular served as political bellwethers: Iraq for its power, Medina for its prestige. Yazīd III moved swiftly to sack al-Walīd's appointees to both.[51]

The Qaysī governor of Iraq, Yūsuf b. ʻUmar, a zealous enthusiast for the tribal grouping to which he belonged, and the man responsible for the torture and death of Khālid al-Qasrī, Ibrāhīm and Muḥammad, was initially replaced by a Yamanī of equal enthusiasm for the tribal grouping to which he belonged: Manṣūr b. Jumhūr.[52] He, however, soon made way for ʻAbd Allāh, a son of the caliph ʻUmar II.[53]

---

47 *EI* 2nd edition, s.v. Yazīd b. al-Walīd b. ʻAbd al-Malik. For a summary of the changes taking place at this time, see Crone, *Slaves on Horses*, 46-48.

48 Al-Zubayrī, *Nasab Quraish*, 165; Ibn Khayyāṭ, *Ta'rīkh*, II 386-387; al-Yaʻqūbī, *Ta'rīkh*, II 265; al-Masʻūdī, *Murūj*, 2262, highlights this fact; al-Dhahabī, *Ta'rīkh*, V 188; Wellhausen, *Arab Kingdom*, 362.

49 *EI* 2nd edition, s.v. Ibrāhīm b. al-Walīd b. ʻAbd al-Malik.

50 Al-Zubayrī, *Nasab Quraish*, 165; al-Yaʻqūbī, *Ta'rīkh*, II 267.

51 Ibn Khayyāṭ, *Ta'rīkh*, II 388.

52 Ibn Khayyāṭ, *Ta'rīkh*, II 388; al-Ṭabarī, *Ta'rīkh*, II 1836-50; Crone, *Slaves on Horses*, 158-159; Hawting, *First Dynasty*, 96; Kennedy, *Prophet*, 113.

53 Ibn Khayyāṭ, *Ta'rīkh*, II 388; al-Ṭabarī, *Ta'rīkh*, II 1854-55; Wellhausen, *Arab Kingdom*, 383; Hawting, *First Dynasty*, 96; Kennedy, *Prophet*, 113.

In Medina, Yūsuf b. Muḥammad al-Thaqafī was removed and, as with Iraq, this governorship was also given to a scion of a former caliph: to the great-grandson of the third caliph ʿUthmān, ʿAbd al-ʿAzīz b. ʿAbd Allāh b. ʿAmr b. ʿUthmān.[54]

With these actions, Yazīd seemed to have achieved the politically impossible: he banished the Qaysī old order from positions of power and prestige and replaced them, not with their Yamanī rivals, but with descendants of caliphs highly regarded within the Umayyad establishment and beyond: ʿUthmān and ʿUmar II. The appointment of ʿAbd al-ʿAzīz to govern Medina was particularly significant: not since ʿAbd al-Malik made Abān b. ʿUthmān governor of Medina in the wake of the *fitnah* against Ibn al-Zubayr had a descendant of the murdered third caliph governed this Holy City. Now Yazīd, faced with his own crisis of legitimacy, returned to the talismanic figure of the third caliph to help restore Umayyad political fortunes. His appointment of ʿAbd al-ʿAzīz as governor of the Prophet's City tapped into the wellspring of Umayyad political legitimacy and sought to remind the ruling family of what was at stake if they failed to unite. ʿAbd al-ʿAzīz was later replaced by another man of the same name who was the son of another well-respected caliph with connections of his own to the Holy Cities, ʿUmar II.[55]

That the Umayyad ruling elite needed to pull together was not in any doubt. Their caliphate had long rested on the seemingly unassailable twin pillars of the unity of the Umayyad family and the strength of the Syrian army.[56] During this turbulent period it could count on neither. The internecine struggle for power within the Umayyad elite often negated the effectiveness of both and as time passed, positions became more entrenched.

Yazīd did not always help matters. His imprisonment of al-Ḥakam and ʿUthmān, the sons al-Walīd II nominated as his heirs, did nothing to foster reconciliation within the ruling family but seemed to suggest that if unity were to be achieved, it was to be on the caliph's terms and no one else's.[57] But even that began to look increasingly unlikely: standing up for al-Walīd's legacy was the influential governor of Armenia and Ādharbayjān, Marwān

54 For the appointment, see Ibn Khayyāṭ, *Taʾrīkh*, II 388; al-Ṭabarī, *Taʾrīkh*, II 1870; Ibn ʿAsākir, *TMD*, Vol. 36, 329; Ibn al-Athīr, *al-Kāmil*, V 319. For his descent, see al-Zubayrī, *Nasab Quraish*, 113-114.

55 Ibn Khayyāṭ, *Taʾrīkh,* II 388; al-Ṭabarī, *Taʾrīkh*, II 1875.

56 Kennedy, *Armies of the Caliphs*, 47.

57 Al-Ṭabarī, *Taʾrīkh*, II 1830. See also Ibn Khayyāṭ, *Taʾrīkh*, II 392: in this account, they are imprisoned by Ibrāhīm.

b. Muḥammad b. Marwān,[58] who wrote to al-Walīd's brother and offered to avenge the murdered caliph personally.[59]

These splits in the ruling family came to be reflected in the wider community. In Ḥimṣ, people attacked the family of the caliph's brother, al-'Abbās, in revenge for al-Walīd's murder.[60] In Jordan and Palestine, local people drove out their governors and appointed their own as a sign of protest against Yazīd.[61] The words of al-Ṭabarī, "In this year the unity of the Banū Marwān was disturbed and discord prevailed," seem almost an understatement.[62]

In the midst of so much political turmoil, Yazīd needed someone reliable and loyal to represent his interests at the *ḥajj* in 126/744. As the son of an *umm walad*, he could not do as some of his predecessors had done and turn to a member of his maternal family to provide him with a leader for the *ḥajj*. Nor could he take charge of the *ḥajj* himself: journeying to Mecca would have entailed a prolonged period away from Syria and in such politically unsettled times, Yazīd's absence may have proven too tempting a prospect for some of his rivals to resist. In addition, the two to three months required for the round trip to the Ḥijāz would have provided ample opportunity for an assassination attempt on the open roads between Syria and the Holy Cities.

To find a suitable leader for the *ḥajj*, Yazīd looked to the ruling family. By appointing a royal prince to lead the pilgrimage, he could shore up the illusion of Umayyad unity in front of the masses of pilgrims. Thus, the *ḥajj* of 126/744, the first and last of Yazīd's caliphate, was led by a direct descendant of a former caliph. According to Ibn al-Athīr and Ibn Kathīr, it was 'Abd al-'Azīz, the son of 'Umar II, and the incumbent governor of Medina, who led it; according to al-Mas'ūdī and al-Ya'qūbī, it was 'Umar, a grandson of 'Abd al-Malik, who did so.

It was during the month of the *ḥajj* that Yazīd fell seriously ill.[63] His illness did not last long and it was reportedly during the *ḥajj* itself that he died, aged in his mid-thirties.[64] The succession was secured. His brother

58 Ibn Khayyāṭ, *Ta'rīkh*, II 391-392; Ibn A'tham, *Futūḥ*, VIII 141; al-Ṭabarī, *Ta'rīkh*, II 1877; al-Mas'ūdī, *Murūj*, 2263; Ibn Kathīr, *Bidāyah*, X 16.

59 Al-Ṭabarī, *Ta'rīkh*, II 1850-51; Ibn al-Athīr, *al-Kāmil*, V 309.

60 Al-Ṭabarī, *Ta'rīkh*, II 1826; Ibn al-Athīr, *al-Kāmil*, V 292-294; Wellhausen, *Arab Kingdom*, 365.

61 Al-Ṭabarī, *Ta'rīkh*, II 1831-36; Ibn al-Athīr, *al-Kāmil*, V 294-295.

62 Al-Ṭabarī, *Ta'rīkh*, II 1825; Hillenbrand, tr. *The Waning of the Umayyad Caliphate*, 183. See also al-Ya'qūbī, *Ta'rīkh*, II 266; al-Mas'ūdī, *Murūj*, 2253; Ibn al-Athīr, *al-Kāmil*, V 292; al-Dhahabī, *Ta'rīkh*, V 32 (for similar comments about the following year).

63 Al-Ṭabarī, *Ta'rīkh*, II 1870 & 1873-74.

64 According to al-Dhahabī, *Ta'rīkh*, V 189, Yazīd actually died on *Dhū al-Ḥijjah* 7, the day before the pilgrimage began. If so, it would have fallen within his successor's caliphate. As the pilgrimage was

Ibrāhīm was to succeed him and his cousin ʿAbd al-ʿAzīz b. al-Ḥajjāj b. ʿAbd al-Malik was successor-in-waiting.[65]

Upon Yazīd's death, Ibrāhīm duly succeeded his brother but his rule was not universally recognized. Barely a few months later, Marwān deposed him and supporters of al-Walīd II killed Ibrāhīm's heir apparent.[66] Ibrāhīm's caliphate was brief; reports vary as to how brief: from seventy days to four months.[67] It did not last long enough to include a *ḥajj* season.

Marwān did not become caliph immediately after Ibrāhīm's deposition. Just as Muʿāwiyah had done in his battles against ʿAlī, Marwān shrewdly claimed that he was not acting to further his own interests but was motivated by nothing more than the right to avenge his murdered relative and return the caliphate to al-Walīd's sons and heirs.[68] But when they were killed by supporters of Yazīd III, the caliphate was Marwān's.[69] The grandson of another Marwān who came to power at a time of political division, it was now the responsibility of this Marwān to repair the unity of the community which had been so badly fractured by the events of the past two years.

THE ONGOING SEARCH FOR UMAYYAD UNITY: THE *ḤAJJ* SEASONS OF 127 AH AND 128 AH

Marwān II faced an even greater struggle to consolidate his power and restore the political fortunes of the Umayyads than his predecessors had done.[70] Political differences within the Umayyad establishment had been internalized to such a degree that the Umayyads had effectively become their own opposition and by the time Marwān II became caliph, he could

a prestigious event, a leader would have been appointed well in advance. According to Ibn Khayyāṭ, *Taʾrīkh*, II 387, the caliph was 35 or 36 when he died; al-Ṭabarī, *Taʾrīkh*, II 1874, has him aged either in his mid-30s or 46.

65 Al-Dīnawarī, *Akhbār*, 248. For the nomination of the caliph's brother as heir apparent, see Ibn Khayyāṭ, *Taʾrīkh*, II 387; al-Ṭabarī, *Taʾrīkh*, II 1870; al-Dhahabī, *Taʾrīkh*, V 31, 190 & 224.

66 The caliph is said to have deposed himself "*khalaʿa nafsahu*": Ibn Khayyāṭ, *Taʾrīkh*, II 393; Ibn Aʿtham, *Futūḥ*, VIII 141; al-Yaʿqūbī, *Taʾrīkh*, II 268.

67 Ibn Khayyāṭ, *Taʾrīkh*, II 393, has his caliphate lasting a month; al-Yaʿqūbī, *Taʾrīkh*, II 267, & al-Ṭabarī, *Taʾrīkh*, II 1875, four months; Ibn al-Athīr, *al-Kāmil*, V 311, four months or seventy days; and al-Dhahabī, *Taʾrīkh*, V 42 & 224, seventy days.

68 Al-Ṭabarī, *Taʾrīkh*, II 1878; al-Dhahabī, *Taʾrīkh*, V 299; Wellhausen, *Arab Kingdom*, 375-376; Omar, *ʿAbbasid Caliphate*, 87; Hawting, *First Dynasty*, 97.

69 Al-Yaʿqūbī, *Taʾrīkh*, II 268-269; al-Ṭabarī, *Taʾrīkh*, II 1890-91; Ibn al-Athīr, *al-Kāmil*, V 323; Ibn Kathīr, *Bidāyah*, X 23; Wellhausen, *Arab Kingdom*, 376.

70 *EI* 2nd edition, s.v. Marwān b. Muḥammad b. Marwān.

not seek to establish his personal authority without some cost to the already disintegrating unity of the Umayyad ruling family.

In spite of these seemingly insurmountable difficulties, Marwān made a concerted effort to unite the ruling family. Not long after he was acknowledged caliph, he moved to secure the succession and named two of his sons, ʿUbayd Allāh and ʿAbd Allāh, his heirs.[71] In a bid to heal some of the wounds caused by the *fitnah*, he married his heirs to two daughters of the caliph Hishām and invited the entire Umayyad elite and their supporters to witness these most political of marriages.[72]

Marwān's efforts to unite the ruling family also formed the basis for the policy he adopted towards the *ḥajj*. Upon becoming caliph, he did not aggravate tensions by instituting a purge of the governors in the Ḥijāz he inherited from his predecessor. Instead, he kept ʿAbd al-ʿAzīz b. ʿUmar II in place as the governor of both Holy Cities.[73] By doing so, he maintained a degree of stability in the governance of the Ḥijāz at a time when other parts of the caliphate were less secure.

This sense of continuity in the Holy Cities was reinforced by Marwān's decision to appoint ʿAbd al-ʿAzīz to lead the *ḥajj* in 127/745. ʿAbd al-ʿAzīz was a safe choice to lead the inaugural *ḥajj* of the new caliphate; he was experienced in the politics of the area and his father, who had governed the city before he became caliph, was well regarded by the people of Medina.

The caliph's decision to follow Yazīd III's example and appoint a caliphal son to the prestigious governorships of the Holy Cities and, by extension, to leadership of the *ḥajj*, owed much to the political circumstances both men were obliged to confront in the aftermath of the *fitnah*. Thus far, it had not been standard Umayyad practice to appoint caliphal sons to these governorships. When royal princes led the *ḥajj* in the past, they had done so at the specific request of the caliph and not as part of their duties as governor of either Mecca or Medina. There were exceptions, Muʿāwiyah's brother and ʿUmar, to name two, but usually, the royal family stayed closer to the caliphal centre in Syria and the governorships in the Ḥijāz were given to more marginal figures in the Umayyad power structure.

But Marwān, like Yazīd III before him, had to bring the ruling family together and the appointment of one of their princes to the governorships of Mecca and Medina and leadership of the *ḥajj* was one way to achieve it.

71 Al-Ṭabarī, *Taʾrīkh*, II 1895; Ibn Kathīr, *Bidāyah*, X 24.
72 Al-Ṭabarī, *Taʾrīkh*, II 1895; Ibn Kathīr, *Bidāyah*, X 24; Wellhausen, *Arab Kingdom*, 380-381.
73 Ibn Khayyāṭ, *Taʾrīkh*, II 388 & 431; al-Ṭabarī, *Taʾrīkh*, II 1917; al-Fāsī, *Akhbār Makkah*, II 179.

And as the Umayyad era neared a century in power, there were more princes who could be appointed to these positions. The Umayyad family as a political unit, especially the Marwānid branch of it, was now well into its third generation. As their numbers grew, it became more likely they would be appointed to positions which had not previously been associated with the ruling family.

Furthermore Marwān, like Yazīd III and Ibrāhīm, was the son of an *umm walad*, and certain options for leadership of the *ḥajj* were not open to him.[74] He could not, for example, do as some of his predecessors had done and rely upon a member of his maternal family to provide him with someone reliable to safeguard his interests in Islam's Holiest Cities.

Marwān appointed 'Abd al-'Azīz to lead the *ḥajj* in 128/746. By 129/746-747, he had given the governorships in the Ḥijāz to another scion of a former caliph: 'Abd al-Wāḥid, a son of the caliph Sulaymān, and it was 'Abd al-Wāḥid who was due to lead the *ḥajj* that year.[75] The caliph, however, was not alone in making plans for the *ḥajj* of 129/747. His opponents had plans of their own for it.

THE *ḤAJJ* SEASONS 129 AH TO 131 AH: POWER SLIPS AWAY

The Umayyad governor of the Holy Cities, 'Abd al-Wāḥid, was appointed to lead the *ḥajj* in 129/747. The ritual began smoothly enough. No one suspected anything was amiss until the pilgrims saw horses coming into view on the road from al-Ṭā'if. Then:

> ... the pilgrims had not yet gone to 'Arafāt when standards appeared (in Mecca) made of black turbans of *ḥirqānī* stuff fixed to the heads of lances, carried by seven hundred men.[76]

Alarm spread through the pilgrims, not only for their own personal safety but also for the validity of their pilgrimages. If fighting were to ensue within the *Ḥaram*, they would not be able to fulfil the obligations of the *ḥajj* and their pilgrimage would be invalid.

74 Al-Zubayrī, *Nasab Quraish*, 169; Ibn Khayyāṭ, *Ta'rīkh*, II 433; al-Ya'qūbī, *Ta'rīkh*, II 268; al-Dhahabī, *Ta'rīkh*, V 298; Bligh-Abramski, *From Damascus to Baghdad*, 77-78.

75 Al-Zubayrī, *Nasab Quraish*, 114 & 166; Ibn Khayyāṭ, *Ta'rīkh*, II 431; al-Ya'qūbī, *Ta'rīkh*, II 270; al-Ṭabarī, *Ta'rīkh*, II 1981 & 1984; al-Fāsī, *Akhbār Makkah*, II 179.

76 Al-Ṭabarī, *Ta'rīkh*, II 1981; Williams, tr. *'Abbāsid Revolution*, 90. See also al-Ya'qūbī, *Ta'rīkh*, II 270-271; al-Mas'ūdī, *Murūj*, 2290; Ibn 'Asākir, *TMD*, Vol. 37, 239-240; al-Fāsī, *Akhbār Makkah*, II 179-180.

When they questioned the new arrivals, they learnt the worst: they were *Khawārij* rebels who had come to oppose the caliph and throw off their allegiance to him. The pilgrims gathered round the official leader of the *ḥajj*, ʿAbd al-Wāḥid, hoping he would take the necessary steps to enable them to perform their *ḥajj*.

He entered into negotiations with the rebels, his attempts at diplomacy going so far as to send a group of high-ranking Medinan notables to discuss the situation with the *Khārijī* leader Abū Ḥamzah. But this delegation, which included descendants of all four of the *Rāshidūn* caliphs, made no progress.[77] In the end, the Umayyad governor departed Minā and left Mecca to Abū Ḥamzah without a fight.[78]

The Umayyad governor's treaty with the *Khawārij* was a form of success as it guaranteed a peaceful end to the pilgrimage but it was also a sign of political weakness. A ruling Umayyad caliph's authority had not been contested at the *ḥajj* in this way since the days of Yazīd I over sixty years previously. It was not an encouraging sign for those seeking a full restoration of Umayyad power. ʿAbd al-Wāḥid duly suffered the same fate as a previous governor of the Holy Cities who lost control of the *ḥajj*: he was sacked.[79] Marwān would later appoint the son of another caliph, Muḥammad b. ʿAbd al-Malik, to the Ḥijāz.[80]

The following year brought even more bad news for the caliph from the Ḥijāz. Fresh from their success at the *ḥajj* the year before, Abū Ḥamzah and his supporters took over Medina and the caliph's governor departed for Syria[81] with the result that – as happened to Yazīd I towards the end of his caliphate – Marwān was obliged to send a military expedition to the Ḥijāz to reclaim control of Medina and enforce his choice of leader for the *ḥajj*.[82]

This army, led by a Qaysī, ʿAbd al-Malik b. Muḥammad b. ʿAṭiyyah,[83] was joined by people from the Holy City and the caliph's troops were able to secure victory against the *Khawārij*.[84] The *ḥajj* for that year, 130/748, was back under Umayyad control and was led by Muḥammad b. ʿAbd al-Malik.

77 Ibn Khayyāṭ, *Ta'rīkh*, II 406; al-Ṭabarī, *Ta'rīkh*, II 1982; Ibn al-Athīr, *al-Kāmil*, V 374.

78 Al-Zubayrī, *Nasab Quraish*, 114 & 166; Ibn Khayyāṭ, *Ta'rīkh*, II 406 & 431; al-Yaʿqūbī, *Ta'rīkh*, II 270; al-Ṭabarī, *Ta'rīkh*, II 1983; al-Masʿūdī, *Murūj*, 3640; al-Fāsī, *Akhbār Makkah*, II 236.

79 Ibn Khayyāṭ, *Ta'rīkh*, II 413.

80 Ibn Khayyāṭ, *Ta'rīkh*, II 431; al-Ṭabarī, *Ta'rīkh*, II 2017; Zambaur, *Généalogie*, 20 & 24.

81 Al-Ṭabarī, *Ta'rīkh*, II 2008; Ibn al-Athīr, *al-Kāmil*, V 389; al-Dhahabī, *Ta'rīkh*, V 38-39.

82 Ibn Khayyāṭ, *Ta'rīkh*, II 413-417; al-Ṭabarī, *Ta'rīkh*, II 2012-13; al-Masʿūdī, *Murūj*, 2290; Ibn ʿAsākir, *TMD*, Vol. 63, 217; Ibn al-Athīr, *al-Kāmil*, V 391-392; al-Fāsī, *Akhbār Makkah*, II 179-180.

83 Crone, *Slaves on Horses*, 164.

84 Al-Ṭabarī, *Ta'rīkh*, II 2012-15; Ibn al-Athīr, *al-Kāmil*, V 391-392; Ibn Kathīr, *Bidāyah*, X 35-37.

The caliph's success, however, was not an unqualified one. The events in Mecca in 129/747 and those in Medina a year later would have political consequences for Marwān. For the caliph's authority to be so undermined that he had to send a military expedition to fight for what was supposed to be his by right suggested that his overall grip on power was weakening. No longer was the *ḥajj* a grand spectacle of caliphal power and prestige. No longer did it involve the caliph proclaiming his authority, as 'Abd al-Malik had done, or showing his generosity, as al-Walīd I did. By the time of Marwān's caliphate, it was all about survival.

In losing control of the *ḥajj* in 129/747, Marwān II became only the third caliph in history to have his authority questioned in this way. 'Alī's authority had been contested by Mu'āwiyah b. Abī Sufyān at the *ḥajj* in 39/660. A year later, 'Alī was dead and the era of the *Rāshidūn* was over. Yazīd I was challenged at the *ḥajj* in 62/682 by Ibn al-Zubayr and by the *Khārijī* Najdah b. 'Āmir. Two years later, Yazīd was dead and the Sufyānid era was over. For Marwān, only the timing was different: it was three years after he lost control of the *ḥajj* that the Umayyads lost control of the caliphate.

This analogy also holds true in the case of the rebel turned caliph Ibn al-Zubayr. He took over Mecca in 63/683 and led the *ḥajj* uncontested until 68/688 when three groups opposed him. The events of that year's *ḥajj* were a sign of what was to come. By 72/692, Ibn al-Zubayr and his Umayyad opponent, al-Ḥajjāj, each performed some, but not all, of the rituals of the *ḥajj*. The following year, Ibn al-Zubayr was defeated and his caliphate slipped into history.

In all of these cases, opponents of whoever held power in Mecca, regardless of his political hue, took advantage of the *ḥajj* as the biggest religious and political platform in the Islamic world to inflict maximum damage on his credibility. Timing was everything: when rebels sensed that the regime's authority was in crisis and the ruling elite's grip on power was loosening, they moved to claim leadership of the community by leading their *ḥajj*. The loss of the *ḥajj* was the tipping point; the final push which facilitated the fall.

The *ḥajj* of 131/749, in what would turn out to be the last of their era, saw the Umayyad family's relationship with the *ḥajj* come full circle and end as it had begun: with a forgery. In 40/661, al-Mughīrah b. Shu'bah forged the authorization to lead the pilgrimage and rushed through the rituals in fear of the imminent arrival of the officially appointed leader. Just over ninety Islamic years later, al-Walīd b. 'Urwah b. Muḥammad b. 'Aṭiyyah al-Sa'dī, temporarily governing Medina on behalf of his uncle, forged a letter allowing him to do the same.[85]

And so it was al-Walīd, rather than the caliph's officially appointed leader, who led the last *ḥajj* season of the Umayyad era. For the final time, the *ḥajj* had slipped beyond the control of an Umayyad caliph.

The political story for the Umayyads in Syria and across the central Islamic lands was almost over. It would officially end in the Iraqi city of al-Kūfah in *Rabī'* I or II 132/November-December 749 when the 'Abbāsid Abū al-'Abbās b. Muḥammad b. 'Alī received the oath of allegiance as the new leader of the Muslim world.[86]

—

The 'Abbāsid takeover of the caliphate heralded a number of changes in the Islamic polity: Syria lost its political pole position to Iraq and the Syrian armies lost their influence to those of Khurāsān.

Yet, when it came to the *ḥajj*, the early 'Abbāsid caliphs – Abū al-'Abbās (r. 132-136/749-754), al-Manṣūr (r. 136-158/754-775), al-Mahdī (r. 158-169/775-785), al-Hādī (r. 169-170/785-786) and al-Rashīd (r. 170-193/786-809) – adopted a *ḥajj* policy that was almost identical to that of their Umayyad predecessors.

The new caliphs, like their predecessors, understood the need to lead the *ḥajj* in person. Where they differed was in the number of times they did so. Al-Manṣūr, for example, led it four times: 140/758,[87] 144/762,[88] 147/765[89] and 152/769,[90] and planned to lead another two. In 142/760, he set out for the Ḥijāz but was obliged to turn back to deal with rebellions in Yemen and Sind.[91] And in 158/775, he managed to reach the Ḥijāz but died before he arrived in the Holy Cities.[92]

His successor, his son al-Mahdī, also led the ritual as caliph, doing so in 160/777,[93] and he too planned to lead it on another occasion: 164/781. That

85 Al-Ṭabarī, *Ta'rīkh*, III 11; al-Mas'ūdī, *Murūj*, 3641. The verb used is *ifta'ala*.
86 Ibn Khayyāṭ, *Ta'rīkh*, II 434; Ibn A'tham, *Futūḥ*, VIII 178-179; al-Dīnawarī, *Akhbār*, 260; al-Ya'qūbī, *Ta'rīkh*, II 282; al-Ṭabarī, *Ta'rīkh*, III 23; al-Mas'ūdī, *Murūj*, 2308.
87 Al-Ya'qūbī, *Ta'rīkh*, II 329 & 331; al-Ṭabarī, *Ta'rīkh*, III 129; al-Mas'ūdī, *Murūj*, 3642.
88 Al-Ya'qūbī, *Ta'rīkh*, II 329 & 331; al-Ṭabarī, *Ta'rīkh*, III 143; al-Mas'ūdī, *Murūj*, 3643.
89 Al-Ya'qūbī, *Ta'rīkh*, II 329 & 331; al-Ṭabarī, *Ta'rīkh*, III 353; al-Mas'ūdī, *Murūj*, 3643.
90 Al-Ya'qūbī, *Ta'rīkh*, II 329 & 332; al-Ṭabarī, *Ta'rīkh*, III 369; al-Mas'ūdī, *Murūj*, 3644.
91 Al-Ya'qūbī, *Ta'rīkh*, II 310.
92 Al-Ya'qūbī, *Ta'rīkh*, II 329-330.
93 Al-Ya'qūbī, *Ta'rīkh*, II 346; al-Ṭabarī, *Ta'rīkh*, III 482; al-Mas'ūdī, *Murūj*, 3644.

year, the *ḥajj* fell in early August and the caliph was obliged to turn back because of a lack of water en route.[94]

It was al-Mahdī's second successor son, the caliph al-Rashīd, whose name would become synonymous with the *ḥajj*. He led the ritual no fewer than nine times: 170/787,[95] 173/790,[96] 174/791,[97] 175/792,[98] 177/794,[99] 179/796,[100] 181/798,[101] 186/802[102] and 188/804.[103]

The 'Abbāsids, like the Umayyads before them, also used the *ḥajj* as a platform to promote their chosen successors: Abū al-'Abbās appointed his heir apparent, his brother Abū Ja'far, to lead it in 136/754;[104] Abu Ja'far, once caliph, appointed his son Muḥammad al-Mahdī to lead it in 153/770,[105] and al-Mahdī did likewise and appointed his first successor, his son Mūsā al-Hādī, to do so in 161/778.[106] But yet again, it was al-Rashīd who took this practice to an entirely new level when, in 186/802, he removed his entire court to Mecca to have the oath of allegiance given to his sons al-Amīn and al-Ma'mūn during that year's *ḥajj*.[107]

The timing of these royal pilgrimages was also reminiscent of Umayyad practices: Mu'āwiyah, as we have seen, linked his son Yazīd to his authority by appointing him to lead the *ḥajj* within a year of his own pilgrimage with the aim of presenting father and son as an indivisible political unit. The early 'Abbāsid caliphs were no different: al-Mahdī's *ḥajj* in 153/770 followed his father's in 152/769. Another of al-Manṣūr's sons, Ja'far, was rumoured to be in line for the succession and he led the *ḥajj* in 148/766, a year after his father led it in 147/765.[108] But Ja'far died a few years later and al-Mahdī succeeded his father alone. Once caliph he, too, adopted the "father and son" policy and had his son/heir, al-Hādī, lead the *ḥajj* in 161/778, the year after his in 160/777.

The early 'Abbāsids, like the Umayyads before them, also adhered to the idea that leadership of the *ḥajj* should be restricted to members of the ruling

94 Al-Ṭabarī, *Ta'rīkh*, III 502-503.
95 Al-Ya'qūbī, *Ta'rīkh*, II 380; al-Ṭabarī, *Ta'rīkh*, III 605; al-Mas'ūdī, *Murūj*, 3645.
96 Al-Ya'qūbī, *Ta'rīkh*, II 380; al-Ṭabarī, *Ta'rīkh*, III 609; al-Mas'ūdī, *Murūj*, 3646.
97 Al-Ya'qūbī, *Ta'rīkh*, II 380; al-Ṭabarī, *Ta'rīkh*, III 610; al-Mas'ūdī, *Murūj*, 3646.
98 Al-Ya'qūbī, *Ta'rīkh*, II 380; al-Ṭabarī, *Ta'rīkh*, III 612; al-Mas'ūdī, *Murūj*, 3646.
99 Al-Ya'qūbī, *Ta'rīkh*, II 380-381; al-Ṭabarī, *Ta'rīkh*, III 629.
100 Al-Ya'qūbī, *Ta'rīkh*, II 381; al-Ṭabarī, *Ta'rīkh*, III 638-639.
101 Al-Ya'qūbī, *Ta'rīkh*, II 381; al-Ṭabarī, *Ta'rīkh*, III 646; al-Mas'ūdī, *Murūj*, 3647.
102 Al-Ya'qūbī, *Ta'rīkh*, II 381; al-Ṭabarī, *Ta'rīkh*, III 651; al-Mas'ūdī, *Murūj*, 3647.
103 Al-Ya'qūbī, *Ta'rīkh*, II 381; al-Ṭabarī, *Ta'rīkh*, III 701; al-Mas'ūdī, *Murūj*, 3647.
104 Al-Ya'qūbī, *Ta'rīkh*, II 331; al-Ṭabarī, *Ta'rīkh*, III 86-87; al-Mas'ūdī, *Murūj*, 3642.
105 Al-Ya'qūbī, *Ta'rīkh*, II 332; al-Ṭabarī, *Ta'rīkh*, III 371; al-Mas'ūdī, *Murūj*, 3644.
106 Al-Ya'qūbī, *Ta'rīkh*, II 346; al-Ṭabarī, *Ta'rīkh*, III 492; al-Mas'ūdī, *Murūj*, 3645.
107 Al-Ya'qūbī, *Ta'rīkh*, II 361-369; al-Ṭabarī, *Ta'rīkh*, III 651-667.
108 Al-Ya'qūbī, *Ta'rīkh*, II 331; al-Ṭabarī, *Ta'rīkh*, III 353; al-Mas'ūdī, *Murūj*, 3643.

family: the leaders of all sixty-one *ḥajj* seasons from 132/750 to 192/808 were 'Abbāsids.[109]

The 'Abbāsid caliphs also adopted a policy of patronage for the Holy Cities and the routes to them: Abū al-'Abbās had beacons and milestones built along the route to Mecca;[110] al-Manṣūr undertook renovations to the Holy Mosques in the Ḥijāz[111] and al-Mahdī used his *ḥajj* to tap into his powers of patronage: he granted an amnesty to an 'Alid political rival; gave grants to descendants of the *Anṣār*; dished out millions of *dīnār*s; and had the Mosque of the Prophet enlarged and the Ka'bah stripped of its many coverings, anointed with saffron and covered with a new silk veil.[112] Nor did he neglect the routes to Mecca. He had the caravanserai built by Abū al-'Abbās repaired and new ones constructed.[113] This caliph, whose *ḥajj* seasons fell in the intense heat of a desert summer, was particularly aware of the need to maintain a water supply for pilgrims. Cisterns were built at each halting place; tanks and milestones were restored; and an official was appointed to look after these works.[114]

His son, al-Rashīd, followed his lead and gave away vast sums of money during his many trips to Mecca.[115] His generosity was such that every time he went on pilgrimage, he took one hundred jurists with him and covered their expenses.[116]

In these respects, the early 'Abbāsid caliphs followed *ḥajj* policies which were remarkably similar to those of the dynasty they overthrew. In doing so, they showed that caliphal involvement with the *ḥajj* transcended partisan interests – whether *Rāshidūn*, Umayyad, Zubayrid or 'Abbāsid – and provided a link back to the Prophet and a sense of continuity within the Muslim community.

---

109 Crone, *Medieval Islamic Political Thought*, 97.
110 Al-Ṭabarī, *Ta'rīkh*, III 81.
111 Al-Ya'qūbī, *Ta'rīkh*, II 306-307; Peters, *Mecca*, 110-112.
112 Al-Ṭabarī, *Ta'rīkh*, III 482-483 & 486; Peters, *Mecca*, 112-117.
113 Al-Ṭabarī, *Ta'rīkh*, III 486.
114 Al-Ṭabarī, *Ta'rīkh*, III 486.
115 Al-Dīnawarī, *Akhbār*, 270 & 273; al-Ya'qūbī, *Ta'rīkh*, II 352; al-Ṭabarī, *Ta'rīkh*, III 605, 610, 741 & 762.
116 Al-Ṭabarī, *Ta'rīkh*, III 741.

TEN

Summary: The Meaning of Mecca

POWER AND PATRONAGE AT THE PILGRIMAGE

In the pre-modern world, before mobile and mass communications could beam news from one part of the planet to another in the blink of an eye, leaders had to go to great lengths to make contact with their people. Leading the *ḥajj* provided a unique opportunity for a caliph to appear before his people and to shape their perceptions of him and the regime he headed. It was also the ideal platform to introduce a successor son to the cross-section of the Muslim community gathered in Mecca.

There was, however, more to a caliphal *ḥajj* than mere show: authority is an abstract idea, made real only when it is translated into concrete acts and for a caliph, leading the *ḥajj* gave him the chance to make his power real to the pilgrims gathered in the birthplace of the faith. But the Commander of the Faithful had to do more than that; he had to persuade the pilgrims and the residents of the Holy Cities to endorse his leadership of their community.

To create the goodwill necessary to achieve this, he could tap into his considerable powers of patronage. This patronage, as we have seen, manifested itself in many ways: from money given directly to the pilgrims to massive building projects in the Holy Cities.

Those caliphs who ruled at times of political instability were less able to indulge a policy of patronage: for caliphs like ʿAlī, Yazīd III, Ibrāhīm, and Marwān II, the priority was to secure their power rather than project their patronage.

For those caliphs, however, who were fortunate enough to rule in more politically settled times, the need to show their generosity in the Holiest Cities of Islam was firmly held and deep-seated. It originated in their religious convictions as Muslims and fed into their political ambitions as caliphs. Whether they draped the Ka'bah in silk, renovated the Mosque of the Prophet or built a water well, their motivation was the same: to show their authority in the heart of Islam and to strengthen the ties between ruler and ruled, endorsing the unwritten social contract between them.

History was not kind to any caliph who did not show the respect due to the Holy Cities. The second Umayyad caliph, Yazīd I, never fully recovered from the political fallout of the attacks he launched against Mecca and Medina. Over a hundred years after these events took place, the 'Abbāsid caliph al-Ma'mūn referred derisively to Yazīd as the man who had forced the people of the Prophet's City to fight one of the most loathsome battles in Islam.[1]

In al-Ma'mūn's view, the collapse of Sufyānid power was Yazīd's just reward for such blatant disrespect of the birthplace of Islam.

GOVERNING ISLAM'S FIRST CITIES AND LEADERSHIP OF THE *ḤAJJ*

For caliphs of the Umayyad political dynasty, leadership of the *ḥajj* was a privilege they often sought for themselves and their chosen heirs. When, however, an Umayyad caliph decided not to lead the *ḥajj* in person or to delegate leadership of it to the innermost circles of his ruling elite, the honour of leading it was usually awarded to his representative in the Ḥijāz. Delegating leadership of the *ḥajj* to a governor in the Ḥijāz was such common practice that no Umayyad caliph, even if his caliphate only covered one *ḥajj* season, failed to do so.

This reliance on the governor of Mecca and/or Medina to lead the *ḥajj* went back to the days of the fourth caliph 'Alī. He, like the Umayyads who came after him, did not rule from the Ḥijāz and he therefore chose his governor of Mecca to represent him at the *ḥajj*. It was a decision which made sense politically: the governor was *in situ* and could easily perform the duty; and, as a relative of 'Alī, he could be trusted to serve his political interests.

The first three caliphs, Abū Bakr, 'Umar, 'Uthmān, had pursued a different course. By following the Prophet's example of governing from Medina, they had no need to appoint a governor of that city and their proximity to Mecca meant they were well placed to lead the *ḥajj* on a regular basis: 'Umar and 'Uthmān doing so nearly every year of their respective caliphates.

---

1 Al-Ṭabarī, *Ta'rīkh*, III 2173.

This model of *ḥajj* leadership was no longer feasible when the political centre of Islam moved beyond Arabia. Only when Ibn al-Zubayr re-centred the political axis of Islam in the Ḥijāz in the 60s/680s did such a degree of caliphal involvement in the *ḥajj* resume. But it did not survive his rebellion. With the victory of the Umayyads and the return of the caliphate to Syria, caliphs reinstated the policy of appointing the governors of the Holy Cities to lead the *ḥajj*.

The governor of any city was a crucial link in the chain of authority between rulers and ruled but the governorship of the Holy Cities held a special symbolic importance because its influence extended beyond those who lived in the immediate area to include the annual influx of travelling pilgrims. Arabia – and the Holy Cities in particular – differed from the rest of the provinces in the caliphate in the most fundamental way: they formed the only part of the Muslim world whose population was almost entirely Muslim. The Holy Cities were therefore home to the earliest adherents of the Islamic faith and their descendants and they could not be administered the way a conquered city or a garrison town in a frontier province would be.

The caliphs, for their part, had to ensure their choice of governors reflected their respect for the City of God, the City of God's Prophet, and for their inhabitants as the first citizens of the Islamic state. Umayyad caliphs invested in the prestige of these governorships by keeping them largely in the hands of the ruling family. The Umayyad governors in question were then awarded the privilege of leading the *ḥajj* more often than the caliphs themselves did.

One of the consequences of the Holy Cities becoming the preserve of the ruling family is that the changing nature of politics in the Umayyad era may be read in the selection of governors for these cities. In response to the first *fitnah*, Muʿāwiyah appointed members of the Umayyad family related to ʿUthmān to govern the Holy Cities and lead the *ḥajj* for him. In the aftermath of the second *fitnah*, ʿAbd al-Malik did the same, appointing one of ʿUthmān's sons to govern Medina and lead the *ḥajj*. But as Umayyad power became more firmly established and the *fitnah* receded into memory, so too did the need for constant reminders of ʿUthmān. New challenges emerged; primarily from within the Umayyad house itself as the sons of ʿAbd al-Malik tried to outmanoeuvre one another over the succession.

These divisions at the centre of the Umayyad power structure became all too apparent in the Ḥijāz. As the sons of ʿAbd al-Malik aligned themselves with different tribal groupings to back their choice of successor, the governorships in the Ḥijāz and, by extension, leadership of the *ḥajj*, became more politicized.

A corollary of this politicization was the increasingly brutal nature of the changeover of power from one administration to the next. As the unity of the Umayyad house splintered, it was no longer sufficient simply to dismiss the governors appointed by the previous caliph. To discredit the old regime, the men who served it had to be publicly humiliated. The extent of the damage inflicted by such reprisals was clear during the caliphate of al-Walīd II: his revenge on two of his predecessor's governors of the Holy Cities contributed to his downfall.

Later Umayyad caliphs tried to repair the fractured unity of the ruling house by adopting a policy of appointing scions of former caliphs to govern the Holy Cities. However, the aura of political unity, once shattered, is almost impossible to retrieve. Opponents of the Umayyad regime had become too emboldened to give up their struggle and it was the rebels, rather than the rulers, whose turn at power had come.

THE POLITICS OF PROTEST: ALTERNATIVE USES OF THE *ḤAJJ*

Leading the *ḥajj* was a privilege of rule; the prerogative of caliphal power. In times of political security, it offered an unrivalled platform for the ruling caliph to assert his authority and to bestow his patronage on the Holiest Cities in Islam, their inhabitants and the pilgrims visiting them as God's Guests.

The converse of this privilege was the responsibility which guardianship of the Holy Cities and the *ḥajj* placed upon the ruling caliph. The high political profile of the *ḥajj* could prove to be a double-edged sword: it was an event like no other where the ruling caliph's authority could be called into question in front of believers assembled from all parts of the Islamic world. This transformed the *ḥajj* into a barometer of the political fortunes of the ruling elite, as happened in 39/660, 62/682, and 129/747.

That leadership of the *ḥajj* was universally understood to be a metaphor of caliphal power was further illustrated by the actions of the rebel-turned-caliph ʿAbd Allāh b. al-Zubayr. During the period he ruled the Holy Cities, he led every *ḥajj* he could. But he, too, experienced what it was like to be challenged by his rivals at the *ḥajj*: it happened to him in 68/688 and it was his loss of the *ḥajj* in 72/692 to the Umayyads that signalled his imminent political demise and their imminent renaissance.

For any ruling caliph, there was another problem associated with the *ḥajj* which could, potentially, pose a threat to his authority: he could not control who went on the *ḥajj* or what they proposed to do during it. 'Uthmān learnt that to his cost at the *ḥajj* of 35/656. 'Uthmān's successor, 'Alī, had to deal with a similar problem when two of his opponents left Medina to go to Mecca to perform the *'umrah*, the lesser pilgrimage, where they met more of 'Alī's opponents and decided to challenge his leadership.

The *Rāshidūn* caliphs were not alone in facing these challenges. Towards the end of the Umayyad era, supporters of the 'Abbāsids used the *ḥajj* as a cover to meet with their leader and, in the guise of pious pilgrims, they were able to plot the overthrow of the central authority without anyone noticing.

THE POLITICS OF PILGRIMAGE

One theme emerges consistently throughout the 120 *ḥajj* seasons examined here: successive caliphs, whether *Rāshidūn* or Umayyad, considered the *ḥajj* a religious ritual which required political leadership.

Year after year, caliphs appointed their political allies, rather than men of piety, to lead the most public religious event in the Islamic calendar. 'Abd al-Malik consulted a Qur'ān reciter during his *ḥajj* as to the validity of Ibn al-Zubayr's renovations to the *Ḥarām* but he never thought to invite such a man to lead the event for him.

Similarly, al-Walīd I took care to show his respect for the renowned *faqīh*, Sa'īd b. al-Musayyab, when he came upon him in the Prophet's Mosque in Medina. But he too never thought to appoint a man of Sa'īd's religious learning to lead the *ḥajj*.

Hishām also took care to show his respect for the religious establishment of the Holy Cities during his *ḥajj*: he consulted them about the rituals of the pilgrimage and led the funeral prayers for two well-known religious figures. He even had his son, Maslamah, make his *ḥajj* in the company of one of the foremost religious authorities of his day, al-Zuhrī. But not once did Hishām consider asking al-Zuhrī or one of his colleagues in the religious establishment to lead the event for him.

Sulaymān briefly broke the mould in 96/717 when he appointed an *Anṣārī* who was a former chief judge of Medina to lead the *ḥajj* for him but it was a decision which, in the final analysis, owed more to politics than religion. 'Umar II followed Sulaymān's example but his successor, Yazīd, wasted no time in reverting to the practice of appointing a political ally to lead the *ḥajj*.

And from Hishām's caliphate to the end of the Umayyad era, the men of politics replaced the men of piety on the platform of the *ḥajj*.

Given the nature of Islamic society and political culture, it could be no other way. This was a society firmly rooted in the religion which had established it: it was Islam which gave the community its identity and defined how members related to each other and the world beyond.

Just as the community remained rooted in the faith which founded it, so too did its political leadership. Virtually every aspect of political culture in the caliphate was infused with religious significance: prayer was a form of political allegiance where the pulpit was used to curse political rivals; arrangements for the succession were underpinned by religious oaths; and success in the *ṣā'ifah* campaigns against the Byzantines was believed to come from God rather than the military strategists on the ground. Even taxation policy was inspired by the faith.

All of these factors helped to sacralize political power. Consequently, caliphs had to express their political power in overtly religious terms. Nowhere, arguably, was this more evident than in Mecca at the time of the *ḥajj*. The pilgrimage saw the lines between religion and politics blur to become the place where a caliph could quite literally command the faithful. To the pilgrims, the Holy City signified spiritual salvation. But to the caliphs who ruled over it, Mecca had more than one meaning. In the words of one historian, it was only by controlling the *Ḥaramayn* and the *ḥajj* that a caliph could truly consider himself deserving of the caliphate.

APPENDIX A

The Sources and Their Challenges

THE SOURCES

The building blocks of the Muslim historical tradition were the *ḥadīth* and the *isnād* [1] which developed out of the need to record the Prophet's sayings. The *ḥadīth* was the relevant saying of the Prophet; the *isnād* was the chain of transmission which traced it back to him along the lines of "I heard this from x who heard this from y who heard it from the Prophet". Ensuring the accuracy of the *isnād* was of paramount importance and for that reason, every effort was made to verify the continuity of the chain and the reliability of each link in it.[2]

When Muslims took up writing history in earnest, they adapted the *ḥadīth-isnād* principle and applied it to their new work: the *ḥadīth* was replaced by the *khabar*, the historical account, but the *isnād* remained as the means by which the information was verified back to the source, the eye-witness to the event in question.

As was the case for the traditionists reporting the *ḥadīth* of the Prophet, the new class of historians were equally concerned with verifying the reliability of the *isnāds* they used.[3] The earliest Muslim sources for the formative period include 'Urwa b. al-Zubayr (d. 94/712), Muḥammad b. Muslim al-Zuhrī (d. 124/741), 'Awāna b. al-Ḥakam (d. 147/764), Muḥammad b. Isḥāq (d. 151/768), Abū Mikhnaf (d. 157/774), Sayf b. 'Umar (d. 180/796), al-Haytham b. 'Adī (d. 207/822), al-Wāqidī (d. 207/823), Abū 'Ubayda (d. 210/825) and al-Madā'inī (d. 225/839); all of whom used the *isnād* technique to check their information.[4] Most of their works, however, are lost and survive only in the writings of later historians: Ibn Isḥāq's *Sīrah*, the life of the Prophet, for example, is the basis for Ibn Hishām's work on Muḥammad; al-Wāqidī's and Abū Mikhnaf's works on the history of the Islamic conquests have partially survived in the later accounts of al-Balādhurī and al-Ṭabarī.

Wellhausen classified these early historians as belonging to one of two traditions: Medina or Iraq.[5] Accordingly, Abū Mikhnaf, as a Kūfan, presented an Iraqi interpretation of events[6] whereas Ibn Isḥāq and al-Wāqidī presented a Medinan one.[7] Wellhausen gave al-Madā'inī a middle position between these two traditions,

1 Khalidi, *Arabic historical thought*, 81-82.
2 Hitti, *Origins*, 2-3.
3 Hitti, *Origins*, 7.
4 Kennedy, *Prophet*, 358.
5 Wellhausen, *Arab Kingdom*, xi-xii.
6 Wellhausen, *Arab Kingdom*, xi.
7 Wellhausen, *Arab Kingdom*, xii.

describing him as a scholarly historian principally concerned with events in al-Baṣrah and Khurāsān from whose reports on these regions most subsequent accounts are taken.[8]

Yet, the work of these early historians is more nuanced than such classifications would imply.[9] Where the geographical location of these historians may prove more relevant is in the information they had access to: the fact that so many of the historians were resident in the Ḥijāz or Iraq might help explain why so much of the material on the early period focuses on Iraq, rather than Syria, and why details on leadership of the *ḥajj*, a ritual based in the Ḥijāz, were recorded every year.

The main sources used here to provide information on the *ḥajj* are Ibn Khayyāṭ's *Ta'rīkh*, al-Ya'qūbī's *Ta'rīkh al-Islām*, al-Ṭabarī's *Ta'rīkh al-rusul wa'l-mulūk* and al-Mas'ūdī's *Murūj al-Dhahab*. The motivation for relying on these particular sources is because all of them, unlike many other sources, record who led the *ḥajj* every year.

Ibn Khayyāṭ,[10] d. 240/854, an Iraqi writing during the 'Abbāsid period, offered an annalistic presentation of history and was arguably the first historian to do so.[11] Although his narratives are rather brief[12] and he did not always cite his sources, his *Ta'rīkh* is nevertheless a mine of information on certain administrative details, particularly leadership of the *ḥajj*: he noted who led the ritual at the end of each year, citing alternatives if necessary. He also gave a summary at the end of each caliphate of provincial governors, office holders and leaders of the *ṣā'ifah* and *ḥajj*.

Al-Ya'qūbī,[13] d. c. 284/897, another Iraqi, was employed at the court of the Ṭāhirids and authored the earliest surviving universal history in the Muslim tradition.[14] Said to have Shī'ī sympathies,[15] he was truly unique amongst Muslim historians in several ways: his use of Jewish and Christian sources for the early part of his history and his use of astrology to give two sets of dates, the non-Islamic as well as the Islamic.[16] He also presented his history in a less conventional way by omitting *isnāds*.[17] When al-Ya'qūbī reached the Islamic period in his *Ta'rīkh*, he organized the material caliphate by caliphate and gave administrative details, such as gubernatorial appointments and leadership of the *ḥajj* and *ṣā'ifah*, at the end of each reign. He did not, however, cite his sources for these lists. His history continued to the caliphate of the 'Abbāsid al-Mu'tamid, r. 256-279/870-892, but he stopped supplying details of leadership of the *ḥajj* after the caliphate of al-Amīn, r. 193-198/809-813.

Al-Ṭabarī,[18] d. 310/923, another historian writing in Iraq but one who travelled extensively in pursuit of knowledge, was arguably the greatest of all the Muslim historians. He was so influential that many later historians, including Ibn al-Athīr

8 Wellhausen, *Arab Kingdom*, xv.
9 Hawting, *First Dynasty*, 17-18.
10 *EI* 2nd edition, s.v. Ibn Khayyāṭ.
11 Robinson, *Islamic Historiography*, 77.
12 Blankinship, *Jihad*, 262.
13 *EI* 2nd edition, s.v. Ya'ḳūbī.
14 Khalidi, *Arabic historical thought*, 2 & 115; Robinson, *Islamic Historiography*, 136.
15 Robinson, *Islamic Historiography*, 137.
16 Khalid, *Arabic historical thought*, 120; Robinson, *Islamic Historiography*, 136.
17 Robinson, *Islamic Historiography*, 36 & 136.
18 *EI* 2nd edition, s.v. Ṭabarī.

(d. 630/1233), al-Dhahabī (d. 748/1348) and Ibn Kathīr (d. 774/1373), relied heavily on him a source of information. His history is impressive in its scale, beginning with creation and ending in 302/914-915. When he reached the Islamic period, he organized his material by year and, with few exceptions, he ended each year by recording who led the *ḥajj*, citing alternatives if necessary.

An expert on *tafsīr*, al-Ṭabarī at one point had a legal school, a *madhhab*, named after him.[19] His combined interests in religion and history have been neatly summed up by Khalidi's description of him as "the *Imām* of *Hadīth* Historiography".[20] As such, it is perhaps not surprising that al-Ṭabarī used every *isnād* he could when writing his history,[21] with the result that we have a very clear idea who his sources were: Abū Mikhnaf (d. 157/774); 'Awāna b. al-Ḥakam (d. 147/764); Sayf b. 'Umar (d. 180/796); al-Haytham b. 'Adī (d. 207/822); al-Wāqidī (d. 207/823); Abū 'Ubayda (d. 210/825); Hishām b. Muḥammad al-Kalbī (d. 204 or 206/819 or 821); and al-Madā'inī (d. 225/839). In contrast to other historians, the information he provided on his sources for leadership of the *ḥajj* is particularly detailed. The *ḥajj* of 42/663, for example, is typical of the chain of transmission he provided:

> 'Anbasah b. Abī Sufyān (the caliph's brother) led the people in the pilgrimage this year. I was told this by Aḥmad b. Thābit – someone – Isḥāq b. 'Īsā – Abū Ma'shar.[22]

While the gap in the *isnād* – the elusive "someone" – cannot be filled, some of the details of the other transmitters can be established. Aḥmad b. Thābit and Isḥāq b. 'Īsā were both traditionists: the former alive around the middle of the third/eighth century, whereas the latter died earlier, between 214/829 and 216/831[23]. Abū Ma'shar[24] was a former slave from Yemen who lived in Medina until 160/776-777 when he moved to Baghdad. He died there in 170/787. He too was a traditionist and the author of a work on the Prophet's campaigns, *maghāzī*. He was a useful source of information for, according to Wellhausen, his mind seemed to be full of dates.[25] It may have been this, as well as Abū Ma'shar's connection to Medina, which made him such a well of information on the *ḥajj*: many of the pilgrimages during this period were led by the governor of that city and Abū Ma'shar, as someone who had lived in the city, would have been familiar with such details.

Al-Mas'ūdī,[26] d. 345/956, also wrote a major work of history, *Murūj al-Dhahab*, a universal history which covered the pre-Islamic era through to the 'Abbāsid caliphate. He too provided a detailed list of *ḥajj* leaders at the end of his work, from the first *ḥajj* after the *Fatḥ* to the *ḥajj* of 335 AH. But the similarities with al-Ṭabarī

19 Khalidi, *Arabic historical thought*, 73.
20 Khalidi, *Arabic historical thought*, 73.
21 Robinson, *Islamic Historiography*, 98.
22 Al-Ṭabarī, *Ta'rīkh*, II 27; tr. Morony, *Between Civil Wars*, 31. He did also, on occasion, use the more general *isnād* "it was said".
23 Howard, tr. *Yazīd*, 90.
24 *EI* 2nd edition, s.v. Abū Ma'shar.
25 Wellhausen, *Arab Kingdom*, xii.
26 *EI* 2nd edition, s.v. Mas'ūdī.

end there. The two works may both be classed as *Ta'rīkh* but even a casual glance through them shows how differently they read. Al-Mas'ūdī did not use *isnāds*[27] and, perhaps influenced by his Mu'tazilī and philosophical interests, he was less than enthusiastic about traditionists and preferred to adopt a theoretical approach to his work. The result is a work of wide-ranging interests.[28]

Other contemporary sources – such as al-Dīnawarī (d. 282/895), al-Balādhurī (d. 279/892) and Ibn A'tham al-Kūfī (wr. 254/868?) – are less expansive on the details of the *ḥajj*, often referring to it only if the caliph led it or if something out of the ordinary happened during it. They are, however, invaluable for providing details on the broader political context of the period.

Al-Dīnawarī, also from Iraq, wrote a general history in his *Akhbār al-Ṭiwāl*, the Islamic sections of which are organized by caliphate. He did not use *isnāds*, preferring instead an authorial narrative voice,[29] and had an interest in Iranian matters.[30]

Also writing in Iraq at this time was al-Balādhurī,[31] whose two works *Kitāb al-Futūḥ* and *Ansāb al-Ashrāf* are of major importance. From Baghdad, al-Balādhurī was close to the centre of 'Abbāsid power: he worked in the 'Abbāsid bureaucracy,[32] knew several of the 'Abbāsid caliphs personally and even tutored one of their sons.[33] His administrative background comes through clearly in his *Kitāb al-Futūḥ*. Detailed yet concise, the *Kitāb* is primarily about the conquests[34] but also includes information on political conditions throughout the provinces of the Islamic empire and relies on local people to provide the data for some of these reports.[35] The sections on the Ḥijāz are useful here, especially the details about weather conditions such as flash floods and droughts, the detrimental effects of which – especially on pilgrims – help explain why caliphs gave such emphasis to the patronage of water wells and the like in the Holy City.[36]

Al-Balādhurī's other work, *Ansāb al-Ashrāf*, is even more impressive in its scale and is a major source of information on the Umayyads.[37] Its name suggests a work of genealogy but *Ansāb* is much more than that. According to Khalidi, it is "more like a comprehensive history loosely arranged around prominent families than a work of strict genealogy".[38] On the use of *isnāds*, al-Balādhurī occupies a position between al-Ṭabarī and al-Mas'ūdī: on occasion, he gave even more detailed *isnāds* than al-Ṭabarī but on others he used the collective *isnād* "they said". His sources include al-Zubayr, al-Zuhrī, Ibn Isḥāq, al-Madā'inī, and al-Wāqidī.[39]

27 Robinson, *Islamic Historiography*, 36 & 75.
28 Khalidi, *Arabic historical thought*, 131 & 136. He was considered Shī'ī: Khalidi, 198. Kennedy, *Prophet*, 363; Robinson, *Islamic Historiography*, 137.
29 Robinson, *Islamic Historiography*, 36.
30 Kennedy, *Prophet*, 361.
31 *EI* 2nd edition, s.v. Balādhurī.
32 Goitein, *Introduction, Ansāb*, Vol. 5, 15-16; Khalidi, *Arabic historical thought*, 59.
33 Hitti, *Origins*, 6.
34 Hitti, *Origins*, 5.
35 Khalidi, *Arabic historical thought*, 67.
36 Khalidi, *Arabic historical thought*, 67.
37 Goitein, *Introduction, Ansāb*, Vol. 5, 12; Kennedy, *Prophet*, 362; Khalidi, *Arabic historical thought*, 58.
38 Khalidi, *Arabic historical thought*, 58. See also Goitein, *Introduction, Ansāb*, Vol. 5, 14.
39 Goitein, *Introduction, Ansāb*, Vol. 5, 15; 19-20; Hitti, *Origins*, 8-9.

Another inhabitant of Iraq, Ibn A'tham al-Kūfī, wrote a work of history with the same name as al-Balādhurī's: *Kitāb al-Futūḥ*. In spite of the similarity in the name, the two works are very different. Ibn A'tham's is more of a political history, providing useful information on the Umayyads from the Kūfan point of view, than a work on the conquest of territory by Islam. It is organized chronologically (but does not provide annual details of the *ḥajj*) and makes use of *isnāds*.[40]

Stepping outside the *Ta'rīkh* genre, Muṣ'ab al-Zubayrī's (d. 236/851) *Nasab Quraysh* has been useful in this study. As Blankinship points out, the importance of this work stems from the fact that social status and tribal identity were inextricably linked during the Umayyad era and al-Zubayrī is almost unique in the degree of detail he provides about Umayyad women and their marriages.[41] The genealogy of Umayyad women was politically relevant during this time because the dynasty initially adhered to the belief that only the son of a free-born Arab woman was eligible to be caliph.

Later sources such as Ibn al-Athīr (d. 630/1233), al-Dhahabī (d. 748/1348), and Ibn Kathīr (d. 774/1373) offer a substantial amount of information on both the Umayyads and the *ḥajj*. Ibn al-Athīr is especially helpful in this regard because he adopts a broader geographical approach than the Iraq-centred context of al-Dhahabī, Ibn Kathīr and many of the earlier sources.[42] Ibn al-Athīr and Ibn Kathīr both present annalistic histories, citing the leader of the *ḥajj* at the end of every year, whereas al-Dhahabī presents his material in a mixture of yearly and biographical entries. The problem, however, with these sources as regards the information they provide on leadership of the *ḥajj* is the same as the problem presented by the information in another late source, the *Akhbār Makkah* of al-Azraqī, al-Fāsī, *et al*: these sources draw so heavily from al-Ṭabarī's *Ta'rīkh* that they cannot be viewed as independent sources. In most cases, they cite al-Ṭabarī directly as their source for the leader of the *ḥajj*. They are, however, still worth examining for the rare instance when they cite an alternative leader.

The sources cited here as most useful for this study are works of *Ta'rīkh*.[43] This is a study of the pilgrimage from the political perspective and as Hitti has pointed out, the primary interest of the Muslim historians was political history.[44] And it is the works of *Ta'rīkh* which provide the most information on leaders of the *ḥajj*. Furthermore, the *Ta'rīkh* genre is itself remarkably diverse[45] with the heterogeneity of its sources often cited as one of its strengths.[46] Al-Ṭabarī is an annalist like Ibn Khayyāṭ, yet their works are radically different in tone (not to mention size).

Al-Mas'ūdī, like al-Ya'qūbī before him, was said to have Shī'ī sympathies. And like al-Ya'qūbī, al-Mas'ūdī also wrote a caliphal history and preferred to leave out *isnāds*. Yet, in spite of these structural similarities, their works are very different.

In addition, the material presented in the sources shows noticeable differences and

40 Kennedy, *Prophet*, 362-363.
41 Blankinship, *Jihad*, 264-265.
42 Blankinship, *Jihad*, 262.
43 *EI* 1st edition, Supplement, s. v. *Ta'rīkh*.
44 Hitti, *Origins*, 8.
45 Landau-Tasseron, tr. *Biographies*, xxv.
46 Blankinship, *Jihad*, 253 & 255; Khalidi, *Arabic historical thought*, 81-82; Robinson, *Islamic Historiography*, 78.

it is this very heterogeneity which allows us to cross-reference the various historical accounts and therefore acquire a fuller picture of events at the time.[47] If, for example, we examine al-Ṭabarī's treatment of al-Ḥasan b. 'Alī's decision to give up politics after his father's assassination, we see that al-Ṭabarī, usually so exhaustive in his treatment of every subject, fails to mention that one of al-Ḥasan's conditions for doing so was that Mu'āwiyah agree to choose his successor by means of a *shūrā*.[48] Ibn A'tham, by contrast, furnishes al-Ḥasan's requests in great detail.[49] The omission of al-Ḥasan's requests from al-Ṭabarī's account has a significant impact on how Mu'āwiyah's subsequent attempts to insert his son into the succession may be interpreted. If Ibn A'tham's account is correct and the caliph did indeed agree to al-Ḥasan's request for a *shūrā*, then Mu'āwiyah's nomination of Yazīd as his heir apparent did not, as al-Ṭabarī's account seems to suggest, take place in a political vacuum but was in fact a calculated act of political aggression against the family of the fourth caliph.

The issue of a call for a *shūrā* – or its absence from al-Ṭabarī's account – featured at another time of political crisis: the beginning of Ibn al-Zubayr's revolt against Yazīd I. Al-Ṭabarī claims that Ibn al-Zubayr rebelled on his own behalf. Al-Balādhurī, by contrast, claims that he called for a *shūrā* to be held to decide upon a new caliph. The pursuit of power by Ibn al-Zubayr may have been the same in both cases – he may, for example, have believed that a *shūrā* would elect him – but the emphasis in the two accounts is vastly different.[50]

Al-Ṭabarī makes another significant political omission at the end of the Umayyad dynasty when he omits all mention of the murder of the surviving members of the family by the new elite. We have to go to other historians, al-Ya'qūbī[51] and Ibn al-Athīr[52] amongst others, to furnish details of these events. This is particularly interesting in the case of Ibn al-Athīr who, writing an annalistic history similar to al-Ṭabarī's in structure and drawing heavily upon him as a source, chooses to include information his main source omits.

Whether these three examples of omission occurred in al-Ṭabarī's account because of the material available, individual preference, selective omission or a combination of all three is difficult to say. What they do show is how the sources differ in the material they offer and how they do not try to impose a universal view of history.[53]

This, in turn, leads into the question of whether the historians allowed their personal viewpoints to seep through into their work.

Al-Balādhurī, for example, worked for the 'Abbāsid administration. As such, it is to legitimate to ask if he showed favouritism to the regime which paid his salary. Al-Ya'qūbī was said to be pro-Shī'ī. In his case, it is legitimate to ask if he discriminated against the Umayyads. And as for al-Ṭabarī, the "*Imām* of historiography", did he bring the weight of his immense religious learning to bear on his *Ta'rīkh*? Was that the reason he made such an effort to record who led the *ḥajj*, one of the

47 Blankinship, *Jihad*, 253.
48 Al-Ṭabarī, *Ta'rīkh*, II 3-7.
49 Ibn A'tham, *Futūḥ*, IV 151, 152-153, 157, 158-161.
50 Howard, *Yazīd*, xv.
51 Al-Ya'qūbī, *Ta'rīkh*, II 290-291.
52 Ibn al-Athīr, *al-Kāmil*, V 329-330.
53 Robinson, *Islamic Historiography*, 149.

foremost religious events in the Islamic calendar, each year for three centuries?[54]

In all of these cases, it would seem the historians did not prejudge the material they handled. Al-Balādhurī seems more the professional purveyor of information than the mouthpiece of the ruling regime.[55]

Al-Ya'qūbī's "bias" may be apparent in his references to the Umayyads as kings: he uses the verb *malaka* to denote their accession, a verb he does not use for the 'Abbāsids,[56] and in the fact that he comes closer than any other historian to describing Ibn al-Zubayr as caliph.[57] But such references do not mean that his *Ta'rīkh* could be described as a polemical work.[58] He did, after all, record the 'Abbāsid slaughter of the Umayyads. As for al-Ṭabarī, while his religious learning may have inclined him towards the use of a tool like the *isnād*, when it came to recording leadership of the *ḥajj*, he was not alone in doing so. Nor was he the first: Ibn Khayyāṭ and al-Ya'qūbī had done so before him and neither of them shared al-Ṭabarī's religious training.

The sources, in general, do not treat the Umayyads as negatively as might first be assumed.[59] There are numerous instances of the Umayyad caliphs' good works, particularly towards the pilgrims and the residents of the Ḥijāz. From Mu'āwiyah to 'Abd al-Malik to al-Walid II, there seems little attempt to suppress evidence of their commitment to the *ḥajj* and the patronage they gave to the residents of the Holy Cities and the travelling pilgrims. Even a historian like Ibn A'tham, with his Kūfan background, mentions Yazīd's generosity to the people of the Holy Cities during his *ḥajj* as heir apparent.[60] The beneficence of Hishām's son, Maslamah, on his *ḥajj* as heir apparent is likewise documented.[61]

The historians' apparent willingness to allow the Umayyad caliphs to be seen in a positive light may have been due to the profound sense of continuity in the Islamic community.[62] The sources make clear that leadership of the *ḥajj* was a practice which began with the Prophet. It was then adopted, with varying degrees of commitment, by the *Rāshidūn*, Umayyad and 'Abbāsid caliphs, thus making it serve as a tangible link between the past and the present. The Muslim sources, for all the challenges they present, would not have wished to suppress that.

THE CHALLENGES OF THE SOURCES

As may be seen from the survey above, one of the most pressing challenges the sources pose is one of timing: the history of the formative period was documented years after it happened by historians who based their work on sources which no

54 Robinson, *Islamic Historiography*, 138.
55 Goitein, *Introduction*, *Ansāb*, Vol. 5, 15-16.
56 Al-Ya'qūbī, *Ta'rīkh*, II 122, 154, 169, 187, 204, 21, 236, 243, 261, 265, 267, 268, 282, 299, 333, 348, 352, 373, 396, 430, 440, 446, 457, 458, 465, 471, 473.
57 Al-Ya'qūbī, *Ta'rīkh*, II 170; Robinson, *'Abd al-Malik*, 34.
58 Kennedy, *Prophet*, 361.
59 Goitein, *Introduction*, *Ansāb*, Vol. 5, 16; Hawting, *First Dynasty*, 14-15.
60 Ibn A'tham *Futūḥ*, IV 224-225.
61 Al-Ṭabarī, *Ta'rīkh*, II 1742.
62 Hawting, *First Dynasty*, 18; Khalidi, *Arabic historical thought*, 96; Robinson, *Islamic Historiography*, 133.

longer exist in written form and which cannot, therefore, be corroborated. This has led Hawting, amongst others, to question how much they should be relied upon as primary sources.[63]

To complicate the issue further, some of these lost early sources can hardly be described as contemporary with the events they recorded: al-Wāqidī, for example, died in 207/823 and al-Madā'inī even later, in 225/839.

Recording the events of the life of the Prophet Muḥammad nearly two centuries after he died, as Ibn Hishām does, or observing the political fortunes of the Umayyad caliphs nearly 150 years after their dynasty was overthrown, as al-Balādhurī, al-Dīnawarī, al-Ya'qūbī *et al* do, is the chronological equivalent of recording the life and reign of the English king Henry VIII during the time of Oliver Cromwell's rebellion or waiting until the end of the twenty-first century to record the definitive account of the Battle of Stalingrad.

Such a lengthy delay between the occurrence of events and their documentation into history has the potential to impact on the historians and the material they handled. For the historians, the issue is one of perspective and objectivity; for the material, it is one of reliability and accuracy.

The Muslim historians of the formative period of Islam wrote their history from the vantage point of a world that was vastly different from the one which they researched. The Prophet was long dead and the era of the *Rāshidūn* caliphs had passed into history. Their successors, the Umayyads, had likewise come and gone. And the current ruling elite, the 'Abbāsid dynasty, had experienced the upheaval of more than one civil war. Against the backdrop of so much change over such a long period of time, the question has to be asked whether we are seeing the events of the seventh and eighth centuries as they happened or if we are, in fact, witnessing them filtered through the *Weltanschauung* of the ninth and tenth centuries, the time when they were recorded.[64] By then, the *Sunnah* of the Prophet was recognized as a model of behaviour to be followed and rituals such as the *ḥajj* had been formalized. But questions have been raised as to whether this was indeed the case during the formative period.[65]

The degree to which a historian can separate himself from his prevailing cultural environment is not a dilemma unique to the Muslim historians of this period.[66] In their case, however, the considerable length of time which separates them from the events they record throws the issue into sharper relief. Crone, for one, was left in no doubt of the negative consequences of history being written so long after the events concerned had taken place.[67]

One area where the impact of this delay may be seen is in the Iraq-centred approach many historians took to their work.[68] Al-Ṭabarī, for one, wrote much of his history of the caliphate as if Iraq were the centre of the Muslim world. While it certainly was at the time he was writing his *Ta'rīkh*, the same could not be said for the

63 Hawting, *First Dynasty*, 121.

64 Crone, *Slaves on Horses*, 4, 6 & 13; Hawting, *First Dynasty*, 5 & 7.

65 Crone, *Slaves on Horses*, 4; Hawting, *First Dynasty*, 1, 5 & 7; Robinson, *Islamic Historiography*, 50-54.

66 Robinson, *Islamic Historiography*, 13.

67 Crone, *Slaves on Horses*, 12.

68 Blankinship, *Jihad*, 258-259. Robinson, *Islamic Historiography*, 124, makes the point that the sources are also unevenly focused on urban rather than rural events.

first 130 years of the Islamic era. Even so, al-Ṭabarī's emphasis falls on Iraq during the years when Syria was the political centre of the caliphate. This may have been due to the information he was able to gather from his sources or to the interests and preferences of his readership (or a combination of both). It is, nevertheless, a factor which has to be borne in mind when dealing with his account and with other sources.

As for the material itself, how well did it weather the journey from eye-witness accounts, often remembered orally through a chain of transmitters handed down through the years, to compilation into a written record, centuries later? According to Robinson, the orality of much of the early Islamic collective memory lent it a potential elasticity.[69] The counterweight to this was, of course, the *isnād* and the historians' commitment to checking it. Together, these were intended to act as the equivalent of a firewall to thwart false information from finding its way into the Islamic tradition. But this method of presenting historical material brought challenges of its own: the use of the *isnād* led to an episodic approach to history with the result that the narrative was often disjointed, making it difficult to piece events together and thus evaluate their impact on each other.[70]

It is, however, the potential malleability of the oral accounts, along with the loss of the corroborating early written reports from the likes of Abū Mikhnaf, al-Madā'inī, and al-Wāqidī, which has posed the greatest challenge to modern historians and which has given rise to scepticism in some quarters about the reliability of the sources for the formative period as a whole, leading Crone, amongst others,[71] to view Islamic historiography as the scattered remains of a past that has been wiped out.[72]

Others, however, have responded to this assessment of the usefulness of the sources with a completely different point of view.[73] Khalidi, for example, has challenged the view that the first century of Islam was oral, stating that the tradition was, on the contrary, a mixture of written *and* oral.[74] Such a tradition would by definition be less malleable and therefore less susceptible to potential corruption.

And Bulliet eloquently makes the point that it would have taken a conspiracy of quite staggering proportions to create a history of early Islam that was not grounded in reality; a conspiracy made even less likely by the fact that early Muslims disagreed – and often fought – over less important matters.[75]

---

69 Robinson, *Islamic Historiography*, 10.

70 Blankinship, *Jihad*, 270; Robinson, *Islamic Historiography*, 93.

71 These others include: Noth, A., *Quellenkritische Studien zu Themen, Formen und Tendenzen fruhislamischer Geschichtsuberlieferung*, Bonn 1973; Noth & Conrad, L.I., *The Early Arabic Historical Tradition: A Source Critical Study*, tr. M. Bohles, Princeton 1994; Crone P., and Cook, M., *Hagarism: The Making of the Islamic World*, Cambridge 1977; Wansbrough, J., *The Sectarian Milieu: Content and Composition of Islamic Salvation History*, Oxford 1978; Cook, M., *Muhammad*, Oxford, 1983. It should, however, be pointed out that each of these scholars take their own position vis-à-vis the sources and do not necessarily share or endorse Crone's scepticism to the same degree. Crone herself acknowledges a slight shift in her position regarding the use of the sources from *Hagarism* to *Slaves on Horses*: *Slaves on Horses*, 3.

72 Crone, *Slaves on Horses*, 10.

73 Decobert, *Le mendiant et le combatant*; Khalidi, *Arabic historical thought;* Bulliet, R.W., *Islam: the View from the Edge*, New York 1994.

74 Khalidi, *Arabic historical thought*, 26-27.

75 Bulliet, *View from the Edge*, 23-24.

So critical is the debate about the reliability of the early sources that much scholarship has been devoted to it in recent years.[76] Yet, for all the complexities involved in dealing with the sources for the formative period of Islam, there is no question of leaving them to one side. They still provide the best accounts we have for this period.[77] In working with the early sources, therefore, it is perhaps best to proceed mindful of the challenges they pose and the various points of view which have been put forward in response to them.[78]

76 Robinson, *Islamic Historiography*, 50, notes that the lack of consensus about how to reconstruct the period has meant that very little seventh- and eighth-century history has been written in the last 25 years, the academic focus falling instead on historiography. The following list is by no means exhaustive but includes some of the main contributions to the debate: Rosenthal, F., *A History of Muslim Historiography*, Leiden 1968; Duri, A.A., *The Rise of Historical Writing Among the Arabs*, tr. L.I. Conrad, Princeton 1983; Humphreys, R.S., *Islamic History: A Framework for Inquiry*, Princeton 1991; Hoyland, R.G., *Seeing Islam As Others Saw It: A Survey and Evaluation of Christian, Jewish, and Zoroastrian Writings on Early Islam*, Princeton 1997; Donner, F.M., *Narratives of Islamic Origins: The Beginnings of Islamic Historical Writing*, Princeton 1998.

77 Crone, *Slaves on Horses*, 3; Hawting, *First Dynasty*, 18; Kennedy, *Prophet*, 357-358; Blankinship, *Jihad*, 255; Robinson, *Islamic Historiography*, 53.

78 Hawting, *First Dynasty*, 24.

APPENDIX B

Further Reading on the *Ḥajj* and the Umayyads

A considerable body of scholarship exists on the *ḥajj*. As a starting point, the *Encyclopaedia of Islam* article on the ritual provides a comprehensive overview.[1] Within the Muslim tradition, there is an entire genre of pilgrim literature: guidebooks are published each year setting out the correct procedures to be followed on the *ḥajj*[2] and many pilgrims, both past and present, have recorded their experiences on the *ḥajj* for posterity.

Perhaps one of the most famous of these is from the medieval period: Ibn Jubayr's *Riḥlah*.[3] The pilgrim from Granada's descriptions of his experiences en route to Mecca and of the time he spent in the Holy City serve as an important historical document in themselves – his detailed reports on the architecture of Mecca, for example, are invaluable to anyone trying to understand and reconstruct the architecture of the period. It is, however, Ibn Jubayr's personal experiences as a pilgrim which bring the *ḥajj* most vividly to life and which show how the ritual acted as a centralizing force, inspiring Muslims from all parts of the Islamic world to return to the place where their religion began.

A modern parallel to Ibn Jubayr's account is that of the Moroccan anthropologist, Abdellah Hammoudi. In his *A Season in Mecca: Narrative of a Pilgrimage*,[4] Hammoudi tries to understand the rituals of the pilgrimage through his religious background as a Muslim and his academic training as an anthropologist. He sets out the rituals in great detail and, like Ibn Jubayr, shows the power of the *ḥajj* as a unifying element within Islam.

Pilgrims' tales were so successful in inspiring their own literary genre that they did not remain confined to Muslims: many an intrepid Victorian traveller headed off to the Ḥijāz, often disguised as a pious Muslim, and survived to write the tale.

1 *EI* 2nd edition, s.v. *ḥadjdj*. The articles on the Holy Cities are also useful.

2 Mohamed, M.N., *Hajj and 'Umrah from A to Z*, 1996; Davids, A.M.I., *Getting the Best out of Hajj*, Hounslow 2000; Kamal A.A., *Every Man's Guide to Hajj and Umrah*, Delhi n.d. I am grateful to Ms Safa Mabgar of al-Saqi Books, 26 Westbourne Grove, London, for her help in recommending and finding these books. All errors are mine.

3 Ibn Jubayr, *Riḥlah Ibn Jubayr*, Beirut 1981; tr. R.J.C. Broadhurst, *The Travels of Ibn Jubayr*, London 1952. There are many others in this genre of travel/*ḥajj* literature, most famously *Ibn Battuta: The Travels of Ibn Battuta A.D. 1325-1354*, translated with revisions and notes by H.A.R. Gibb, Vol. 1 Cambridge 1958. See Eickelman, D.F., and Piscatori, J., eds. *Muslim Travellers: Pilgrimage, migration and the religious imagination*, London and New York 1990; Netton, I.R., ed. *Golden Roads: Migration, Pilgrimage and Travel in Mediaeval and Modern Islam*, London 1993; Wolfe, M., *One Thousand Roads to Mecca: Ten Centuries of Travelers Writing about the Muslim Pilgrimage*, New York 1997.

4 Hammoudi, A., *A Season in Mecca: Narrative of a Pilgrimage*, New York 2006.

Some of these have more literary (or entertainment value) than academic merit,[5] but some – Burckhardt,[6] Burton[7] and Snouck Hurgronje[8] to name three – have contributed significantly to our understanding of the *ḥajj*.

Modern scholarship has approached the study of the *ḥajj* from various perspectives: the pre-Islamic origins of the sanctuary and the pilgrimage;[9] the *ḥajj* as a religious ritual, its development as such and details of its rites;[10] the history of the pilgrimage;[11] the *ḥajj* in the modern era (such studies often fall within the scope of works on the modern Kingdom of Saudi Arabia, especially in the wake of events at the *ḥajj* in 1979);[12] and articles focusing on the ritual from a particular perspective, for example gender-related issues.[13]

5 Blunt, Lady Anne, *A Pilgrimage to Nejd, the Cradle of the Arab Race*, London 1881; reprinted London 1985; Keane, J.F., *Six Months in Meccah: An Account of the Muhammedan Pilgrimage to Meccah*, London 1881; Doughty, C., *Travels in Arabia Deserta*, Cambridge 1888; Palgrave, W.G., *Personal Narrative of a Year's Journey Through Central and Eastern Arabia*, London 1865; reprinted London 1969.

6 Burckhardt, John Lewis, *Travels in Nubia*, London 1819; *Travels in Syria and the Holy Land*, London 1822; reprinted New York 1983; *Travels in Arabia*, London 1829; reprinted New York 1968.

7 Burton, R.F., *A Personal Narrative of a Pilgrimage to al-Madina and Mecca*, New York 1964.

8 Hurgronje, C. Snouck, *Mekka, Vol. 1: Die Stadt und Ihre Herren*, The Hague 1888; *Mekka in the Latter Part of the Nineteenth Century*, Leiden and London 1931.

9 See Kister. M.J., "Some aspects concerning Mecca from Jahiliyya to Islam" *JESHO* 15 (1972), 61-93; Hawting, G.R., "The Origins of the Islamic Sanctuary at Mecca", in Juynboll, G.H.A., ed. *Studies on the First Century of Islam*, Carbondale 1982, 25-47; "Al-Hudaybiyya and the Conquest of Mecca: A Reconsideration of Tradition about the Muslim Takeover of the Sanctuary" *JSAI* 8 (1986), 1-23, & "The 'Sacred Offices' of Mecca from Jahiliyya to Islam" *JSAI* 13 (1990), 62-84; Rubin, U., "The Ka'ba: Aspects of its ritual functions and position in pre-Islamic and early Islamic times" *JSAI* 8 (1986), 97-131, & "Hanafiyya and Ka'ba: An Inquiry into the Arabian Pre-Islamic Background of the *din Ibrahim*" *JSAI* 13 (1990), 85-112.

10 Gaudefroy-Demombynes, M., *Le pèlerinage à la Mekke*, Paris 1923; Lammens, H., *Islam: Beliefs and Institutions*, London 1929; Wensinck, A.J., *The Muslim Creed*, Cambridge 1932; von Grunebaum, G., *Muhammadan Festivals*, London and New York 1958; Kister, M.J., "'You Shall Only Set Out for Three Mosques': A Study of an Early Tradition" *Le Muséon* 82 (1969), 173-196, & "*Labbayka, Allahumma, Labbayka*...On a Monotheist Aspect of a Jahiliyya Practice" *JSAI* 2 (1980), 33-57; Hawting, G.R., "'We were not ordered with entering it but only with circumambulating it: Hadith and Fiqh on Entering the Ka'ba" *BSOAS* 47 (1984), 228-242, & ed. *The Development of Islamic Ritual*, Ashgate 2006; Roff, W.R., "Pilgrimage and the History of Religions: Theoretical Approaches to the Hajj" in R.C. Martin, ed., *Approaches to Islam in Religious Studies*, Tucson 1985.

11 Al-Rashid, S.A., *Darb Zubaydah: The Pilgrim Road from Kufa to Mecca*, Riyad 1980; Peters, F.E., *The Hajj: The Muslim Pilgrimage to Mecca and the Holy Places*, Princeton 1994, and *Mecca: A Literary History of the Muslim Holy Land*, Princeton 1994; al-Quʿaiṭī, S. G., *The Holy Cities, The Pilgrimage and the World of Islam*, Louisville 2007. Both Peters' works are impressive in their chronological scope, running from the *Jāhilīyah* to the 20th century, and the range of issues examined.

12 Sardar, Z., and Zaki Badawai, M.A., eds. *Hajj Studies*, Volume 1, London 1978; Long, D.E., *The Hajj Today: A Survey of the Contemporary Makkah Pilgrimage*, Albany 1979; Bianchi, R.R., *Guests of God: Pilgrimage and Politics in the Islamic World*, Oxford 2004, combines his personal experiences of performing the pilgrimage along with a series of case studies of how travel to the *ḥajj* is handled by the political administrations in a number of Muslim countries. See also Hiro, D., *Islamic Fundamentalism*, London 1988, 128-131; Ruthven, M., *Islam in the World*, London, 1991, (first chapter); Vassiliev, A., *The History of Saudi Arabia*, London 2000, 395-397; al-Rasheed. M., *A History of Saudi Arabia*, Cambridge 2002, 144-146.

13 Beelaert, A.L.F.A. "The Ka'ba as a Woman: A Topos in Classical Persian Literature" *Persica* 13 107-123; Young, W.C., "The Ka'ba, Gender, and the Rites of Pilgrimage" *IJMES* 25 (1993), 285-300; Tolmacheva, M., "Female Piety and Patronage in the Medieval *ḥajj*" in Hambly, G.R.G., ed. *Women*

A number of scholars have also given consideration to leadership of the *ḥajj*: Ahmad Dahlan's nineteenth-century work, *Khulāṣat al-kalām fī bayān umarā' al-balad al-ḥarām* begins with a list of governors of Mecca from the time of the city's conquest to the beginning of the 'Abbāsid era and includes dates and comments about leadership of the *ḥajj*.[14] Zambaur's *Manuel de Généalogie et de Chronologie pour L'Histoire de l'Islam*[15] provides lists of the governors of Mecca and Medina but does not include details of who led the *ḥajj*.

More recent scholarship has touched on the politics of pilgrimage during the formative period: Dixon, for example, notes the competition for leadership of the *ḥajj* in 68/688 at the height of the second civil war;[16] Hawting highlights the role of the *ḥajj* in that civil war;[17] Blankinship comments on the caliph Hishām's leadership of the *ḥajj* in 106/725;[18] and Robinson draws attention to the importance of leading the *ḥajj* as a prerequisite for being considered the legitimate caliph. He pays particular attention to Ibn al-Zubayr's control of the Holy Cities during the second civil war and suggests that he, rather than the Umayyads Marwān or 'Abd al-Malik, could claim to be the rightful caliph during those years.[19]

In a broader context, there are also a number of studies which analyze pilgrimage and its potential role in politics.[20] These tend, however, to focus on Christian pilgrimage and often allude to the *ḥajj* only in passing. They are, nevertheless, useful because the faith-based dynamics of pilgrimage are the same, regardless of religion; as are the uses to which those in political power wish to make of them.

As is the case with the *ḥajj*, a considerable amount of scholarship already exists on the Umayyads.[21] The *Encyclopaedia of Islam* articles on the dynasty and on individual caliphs are useful in providing a broad overview of the main personalities and events of the period. General overviews also appear in Hitti's *History of the Arabs*,[22] Kennedy's *The Prophet and the Age of the Caliphates*[23] and in political

in the Medieval Islamic World, New York 1999, 161-179.

14 I am grateful to Professor G.R. Hawting for drawing this work to my attention.

15 Zambaur, E. de, *Manuel de Généalogie et de Chronologie pour L'Histore de l'Islam*, Hanover 1927.

16 Dixon, 'A. 'A., *The Umayyad Caliphate 65-86/684-705: A Political Study*, London 1971, 172. See also Goitein, S., "The Sanctity of Jerusalem and Palestine in early Islam" in *Studies in Islamic History and Institutions*, Leiden 1966, 135-148.

17 Hawting, G.R., "The Hajj in the Second Civil War" in Netton, I.R., ed. *Golden Roads: Migration, Pilgrimage and Travel in Mediaeval and Modern Islam*, London 1993, 31-42. See also *The First Dynasty of Islam: The Umayyad Caliphate AD 661-750*, London and Sydney 1986, 49.

18 Blankinship, K.Y., *The End of the Jihad State: The Reign of Hishām Ibn 'Abd al-Malik and the Collapse of the Umayyads*, Albany 1994, 96.

19 Robinson, C.F., *Makers of the Muslim World: 'Abd al-Malik*, Oxford 2005, 31-48, particularly 34.

20 Turner, V., and Turner, E., *Image and Pilgrimage in Christian Culture: Anthropological Perspectives*, Oxford 1978; Kertzer, D.I., *Ritual, Politics, and Power*, New Haven and London 1988; Johnston, D., and Sampson, C., eds. *Religion: The Missing Dimension of Statecraft*, New York 1994; Coleman, S., and Elsner, J., *Pilgrimage: Past and Present in World Religions*, Cambridge MA 1995.

21 The list of works cited in the footnotes which follow does not seek to be exhaustive but refers to work useful for this study.

22 Hitti, P.K., *History of the Arabs*, London 2002, 189-287.

23 Kennedy, H.N., *The Prophet and the Age of the Caliphates: The Islamic Near East from the sixth to the eleventh century*, London and New York 1986, 82-123. See also Caetani, L., *Annali dell'Islam*, Milan 1905-1926; Hourani, A., *A History of the Arab Peoples*, London 1991.

histories such as Crone's *Medieval Islamic Political Thought*.[24] More specifically, the poetics of Umayyad political legitimacy – and 'Abd al-Malik's victory in the *fitnah* in particular – have been analyzed by Stetkevych,[25] and Crone and Hinds' *God's Caliph* provides an insight into the nature of religious authority during the Umayyad era.[26]

In all of these works, the Umayyad time in power is treated as one era amongst others. For a specific history of the Umayyad caliphate, Wellhausen's *The Arab Kingdom and Its Fall* and Hawting's *The First Dynasty of Islam: The Umayyad Caliphate AD 661-750* remain the best introductions to the Umayyad era as a whole.[27]

In addition to these, there are a number of works which focus on a particular caliph's time in power: Beg[28] and Lammens[29] on Mu'āwiyah I; Lammens[30] on Yazīd I; Hammarneh[31] on Marwān I; Robinson[32] on 'Abd al-Malik; Gibb[33] and Barthold[34] on 'Umar II; Gabrieli,[35] Khleifat[36] and Blankinship[37] on Hishām; Hamilton[38] on al-Walīd II; and Dennett[39] on Marwān II. 'Abd al-Malik's caliphate is often treated along with the events of the second civil war: see, for example, Dixon[40] and Rotter.[41]

Many aspects of Umayyad political culture have been studied in depth: Crone, for example, covers a great deal of ground in *Slaves on Horses*, where issues from the Umayyads' gubernatorial appointments to patterns of clientage and tribal allegiances are examined. Like Crone's *Slaves on Horses*, several works on Umayyad political administration also lead into the early 'Abbāsid period, as is the case with Biddle[42] and Bligh-Abramski.[43]

---

24 Crone, P., *Medieval Islamic Political Thought*, Edinburgh 2004, 33-47.

25 Stetkevych, S.P., *The Poetics of Islamic Legitimacy: Myth, Gender, and Ceremony in the Classical Arabic Ode*, Bloomington 2002, 80-143.

26 Crone, P., & Hinds, M., *God's Caliph: Religious Authority in the First Centuries of Islam*, Cambridge 1986.

27 See also Lammens, H., *Études sur le siècle des Omayyades*, Beirut 1930.

28 Beg, A.J., "The reign of Mu'āwiya: a critical survey" *Islamic Culture* 51, 1977, 83-107.

29 Lammens, H., *Études sur le règne du calife omaiyade Mo'awia 1er*, Paris 1908.

30 Lammens, H., *Le califat de Yazid 1er*, Beirut 1910-21.

31 Hammarneh, S.K., "Marwan b. al-Hakam and the Caliphate", *Der Islam* 65 (1988), 200-225.

32 Robinson, *'Abd al-Malik*.

33 Gibb, H.A.R., ""The Fiscal Rescript of 'Umar II", *Arabica* 2 (1955), 1-16.

34 Bartold, W.W., "The Caliph 'Umar II and the Conflicting Reports on his Personality", *Islamic Quarterly* 15, 1971, 69-95.

35 Gabrieli, F., *Il califfato di Hishām*, Alexandria 1935.

36 Khleifat, Awad Mohammad, *The Caliphate of Hishām b. 'Abd al-Malik (105-124/724-743), with Special Reference to Internal Problems*, PhD thesis, University of London 1973.

37 Blankinship, *Jihad*. See also Conrad, L.I., "Notes on al-Ṭabarī's History on the Caliphate of Hishām ibn 'Abd al-Malik", *JRAS* III, 1993, 1-31.

38 Hamilton, *Walid and His Friends: An Umayyad Tragedy, Oxford Studies in Islamic Art VI*, Oxford 1988.

39 Dennett, D., *Marwān b. Muḥammad: the passing of the Umayyad caliphate*, PhD thesis, Harvard University 1939.

40 Dixon, *Umayyad Caliphate*.

41 Rotter, G., *Die Umayyaden und der zweite Burgerkrieg (688-692)*, Wiesbaden 1982.

42 Biddle, D.W., *The Development of the Bureaucracy of the Islamic Empire during the Late Umayyad and Early 'Abbasid Period*, PhD dissertation, The University of Texas at Austin 1972.

43 Bligh-Abramski, I.I., *From Damascus to Baghdad: The 'Abbasid Administrative System as a Product of the Umayyad Heritage (41/661 – 320/932)*, PhD dissertation, Princeton University 1982; "Evolution

There are also studies which concentrate on a particular aspect of the Umayyad era: Yazīd I's political difficulties in the Ḥijāz;[44] 'Abd al-Malik's coinage reforms;[45] the succession dispute between Sulaymān and his brothers;[46] and the development of the 'Abbāsid revolutionary movement which overthrew the Umayyad dynasty.[47]

Some of the Umayyad caliphs were great patrons of architecture: 'Abd al-Malik had the Dome of the Rock built;[48] his son al-Walīd I ordered that renovations be made to the Prophet's Mosque in Medina, the Great Mosque in Damascus and al-Aqṣā in Jerusalem;[49] and other caliphs had palaces built in the desert.[50] As a result, the Umayyads have received a great deal of attention from scholars of Islamic art and architecture, much of which is useful in providing the political context for the patronage behind these great works.

---

versus Revolution: Umayyad elements in the 'Abbasid regime 133/750 – 320/932", *Der Islam* 65 (1988), 226-243. Robinson's *Empires and Elites after the Muslim Conquest: The Transformation of Northern Mesopotamia*, Cambridge 2000, also falls into this category. See Nicol, N.D., *Early 'Abbasid Administration in the Central and Eastern Provinces, 132-218 AH/750-833 AD*, PhD dissertation, University of Washington 1979, who begins at the last years of the Umayyad period.

44 Kister, M.J., "Battle of the Harra" in ed. M. Rosen-Ayalon, *Studies in memory of Gaston Wiet*, Jerusalem 1977.

45 Grierson, P., "The Monetary Reforms of 'Abd al-Malik", *JESHO* 3 (1960), 241-264.

46 Bosworth, C.E., "Raja' Ibn Haywa al-Kindi and the Umayyad Caliphs", *IQ* 16 (1972), 36-80.

47 Sharon, M., *Black banners from the east*, Leiden 1983; Blankinship, K.Y., "The Tribal Factor in the 'Abbasid Revolution", *JAOS* 108 (1988), 589-603.

48 The following are some of the main contributions to the debate: Grabar, O., "The Umayyad Dome of the Rock in Jerusalem", *Ars Orientalis* 3, 1959, 33-62, & "The Meaning of the Dome of the Rock in Jerusalem" in Hopwood, D., ed. *Studies in Islamic History*, 1990, 151-163; Kessler, C., "'Abd al-Malik's Inscription in the Dome of the Rock: A Reconsideration", *JRAS* (1970), 2-14; Rabbat, N., "The Meaning of the Umayyad Dome of the Rock", *Muqarnas* 6 (1989), 12-21; Elad, A. "Why did 'Abd al-Malik build the Dome of the Rock? A Re-examination of the Muslim Sources", in Raby J.A.J., and Johns, J., eds. *Bayt al-Maqdis: 'Abd al-Malik's Jerusalem*, Oxford Studies in Islamic Art, 9, part 1, 1992, 33-58. See also chapter 5 above.

49 For al-Walīd's patronage of these mosques, see Sauvaget, J., *La mosquée de Médine, études sur les origines architecturales de la mosquée*, Paris 1947; Bisheh, G.I., *The Mosque of the Prophet at Madīnah throughout the first century A.H., with special emphasis on the Umayyad Mosque*, PhD thesis, University of Michigan 1979; Brisch, K., "Observations on the Iconography of the Mosaics in the Great Mosque at Damascus" in Soucek, P.P., ed. *Content and Context of Visual Arts in the Islamic World: Papers from a Colloquium in Memory of Richard Ettinghausen, Institute of Fine Arts, New York University 2-4 April 1980*, University Park/London 1988, 13-20; Grafman, R., & Rosen-Ayalon, M., "The Two Great Syrian Umayyad Mosques: Jerusalem and Damascus", *Muqarnas* 16, 1999, 1-15; Flood, F.B., *The Great Mosque of Damascus: Studies on the Makings of an Umayyad Visual Culture*, Leiden 2000; Johns, J., ed. *Bayt al-Maqdis Part Two: Jerusalem and Early Islam*, Oxford Studies in Islamic Art 9, part 2, 2000.

50 Hillenbrand, R., "La *dolce vita* in Early Islamic Syria: the Evidence of Late Umayyad Palaces", *Art History* 5/1, 1982, 1-35; Conrad, L.I., "The *Qusur* of Medieval Islam: Some Implications for the Social History of the Near East", *Al-Abhath* 29 (1983), 7-23; King, G.R.D., "The Umayyad Qusur and Related Settlements in Jordan", *IVth International Conference on Bilad al-Sham*, Amman, University of Jordan 1989, 71-80, & "Settlement Patterns in Islamic Jordan: The Umayyads and Their Use of the Land" in *Studies in the History and Archaeology of Jordan* 4 (1993), 369-375; Bacharach, J.L., "Marwanid Umayyad Building Activities: Speculations on Patronage", *Muqarnas* 13 (1996), 27-44; Kennedy, D.L., and Petersen, A., "Guardians of the Pilgrim Wells: Damascus to Aqaba", *Saudi Aramco World*, Vol. 55 No.1, 2004, 12-19.

Bibliography

Afsaruddin, A.: *Excellence and Precedence: Medieval Islamic Discourse on Legitimate Leadership*, Leiden 2002

Ahsan, M.M.: *Social Life Under the 'Abbasids*, London and New York 1979

'Alī, 'Abdullāh Yūsuf, ed: *The Meaning of the Holy Qur'ān*, Maryland 1992

Amabe, F.: *The Emergence of the 'Abbasid Autocracy: The 'Abbasid Army, Khurasan and Adharbayjan*, Kyoto 1995

Asad, M.: *The Road to Mecca*, Louisville 2000

Ayalon, A.: *Language and Change in the Arab Middle East*, Oxford 1987

Al-Azmeh, A.: *Muslim Kingship: Power and the Sacred in Muslim, Christian and Pagan Polities*, London 1997

Al-Azraqī, Abū al-Walīd Muḥammad b. 'Abd Allāh: *Kitāb Akhbār Makkah*, ed. F. Wustenfeld in *Akhbār Makkah* (in volume 1), 4 volumes, Beirut 1964

Bacharach, J.L.: "Marwanid Umayyad Building Activities: Speculations on Patronage", *Muqarnas* 13 (1996), 27-44

Al-Balādhurī, Aḥmad b. Yaḥyā: *Ansāb al-Ashrāf*, vol. I, ed. Muḥammad Hamīd Allāh, Cairo 1959; vol. II A, ed. Muḥammad Bāqir al-Maḥmūdī, Beirut 1974; vol. II B, ed. Muḥammad Bāqir al-Maḥmūdī, Beirut 1977; vol. III, ed. 'Abd al-'Azīz al-Dūrī, Beirut and Wiesbaden 1978; vol. IV A, ed. M. Schloessinger and M.J. Kister, Jerusalem 1971; vol. IV B, ed. M. Schloessinger, Jerusalem 1938; vol. V, ed. S.D.F. Goitein, Jerusalem 1936; vol. VI, ed. Khalīl 'Athāminah, Jerusalem 1993; vol. XI, ed. W. Ahlwardt, Greifswald 1883 as *Anonyme arabische Chronik Kitāb Futūḥ al-Buldān*, ed. Ṣāliḥ al-Dīn Munajjid, Cairo 1956

Barthold, W.W.: "The Caliph 'Umar II and the Conflicting Reports on his Personality", *Islamic Quarterly* 15, 1971, 69-95.

Bashear, S.: *Arabs and Others in Early Islam*, Princeton 1997

Beelaert, A.L.F.A.: "The Ka'ba as Woman: A Topos in Classical Persian Literature" *Persica* 13, 107-123

Beg, A.J.: "The reign of Mu'āwiya: a critical survey", *Islamic Culture* 51, 1977, 83-107

Berkey, J.P.: *Popular Preaching & Religious Authority in the Medieval Islamic Near East*, Seattle and London 2001

—*The Formation of Islam: Religion and Society in the Near East 600-1800*, Cambridge 2003

Bianchi, R.R.: *Guests of God: Pilgrimage and Politics in the Islamic World*, Oxford 2004

Biddle, D.W.: *The Development of the Bureaucracy of the Islamic Empire during the Late Umayyad and Early 'Abbasid Period*, PhD dissertation, The University of Texas at Austin 1972

Bisheh, G.I.: *The Mosque of the Prophet at Madīnah throughout the first century A.H. with special emphasis on the Umayyad Mosque*, PhD thesis, University of Michigan 1979

Black, A.: *The History of Islamic Political Thought: From the Prophet to the Present*, Edinburgh 2001

Blankinship, K.Y.: "The Tribal Factor in the 'Abbasid Revolution", *Journal of the American Oriental Society* 108 (1988), 589-603

—tr. *The History of al-Ṭabarī, Volume XXV: The End of Expansion*, Albany 1989

—tr. *The History of al-Ṭabarī, Volume XI: The Challenge to the Empires*, Albany 1993

—*The End of the Jihad State: The Reign of Hishām Ibn 'Abd al-Malik and the Collapse of the Umayyads*, Albany 1994

Bligh-Abramski, I.I.: *From Damascus to Baghdad: The 'Abbasid Administrative System as a Product*

of the Umayyad Heritage (41/661 – 320/932), PhD dissertation, Princeton University 1982
—"Evolution versus Revolution: Umayyad elements in the 'Abbasid regime 133/750 – 320/932", *Der Islam* 65 (1988), 226-243
Blunt, Lady Anne: *A Pilgrimage to Nejd, the Cradle of the Arab Race,* London 1881, reprinted London 1985
Bosworth, C.E.: "Raja' Ibn Haywa al-Kindi and the Umayyad Caliphs", *The Islamic Quarterly* 16 (1972), 36-80
Brisch, K.: "Observations on the Iconography of the Mosaics in the Great Mosque at Damascus" in *Content and Context of Visual Arts in the Islamic World: Papers from a Colloquium in Memory of Richard Ettinghausen, Institute of Fine Arts, New York University 2-4 April 1980*, ed. P.P. Soucek, University Park/London 1988, 13-20
Broadhurst, R.J.C., tr: *The Travels of Ibn Jubayr*, London 1952
Brockett, A., tr: *The History of al-Ṭabarī, Volume XVI: The Community Divided: The Caliphate of 'Alī*, Albany 1997
Bulliet, R.W.: *The Camel and the Wheel*, New York 1990
—*Islam: The View from the Edge*, New York 1994
—*The Case for Islamo-Christian Civilization*, New York 2004
Burckhardt, J.L.: *Travels in Nubia*, London 1819
—*Travels in Syria and the Holy Land*, London 1822, reprinted New York 1983
—*Travels in Arabia*, London 1829, reprinted New York 1968
Burton, R.F.: *A Personal Narrative of a Pilgrimage to al-Madina and Mecca,* New York 1964
Caetani, L.: *Annali dell'Islam,* Milan 1905-1926
Chejne, A.G.: *Succession to the Rule in Islam: With Special Reference to the Early 'Abbasid Period*, PhD dissertation, University of Pennsylvania 1954
Coleman, S., and Elsner, J.: *Pilgrimage: Past and Present in World Religions*, Cambridge MA 1995
Conrad, L.I.: "The *Qusur* of Medieval Islam: Some Implications for the Social History of the Near East", *Al-Abhath* 29 (1983), 7-23
—"Notes on al-Ṭabarī's History on the Caliphate of Hishām ibn 'Abd al-Malik", *Journal of the Royal Asiatic Society* 3, 1993, 1-31
Cook, M.A.: *Muhammad*, Oxford 1983
—*Forbidding Wrong in Islam*, Cambridge 2003
Crone, P.: *Slaves on Horses: The Evolution of the Islamic Polity*, Cambridge 1980
—*Meccan Trade and the Rise of Islam,* Princeton 1987
—"The Significance of Wooden Weapons in al-Mukhtār's Revolt and the 'Abbāsid Revolution" in *Studies in Honour of Clifford Edmund Bosworth,* vol. I, ed. I.R. Netton, Leiden 2000, 174-187
—*Medieval Islamic Political Thought*, Edinburgh 2004
Crone, P. & Cook, M.A., *Hagarism: The Making of the Islamic World*, Cambridge 1977
Crone, P. & Hinds, M., *God's Caliph: Religious Authority in the First Centuries of Islam*, Cambridge 1986
Davids, A.M.I.: *Getting the Best out of Hajj*, Hounslow 2000
Decobert, C.: *Le mendiant et le combatant*, Paris 1991
Dennett, D.: *Marwān b. Muḥammad: the passing of the Umayyad caliphate*, PhD thesis, Harvard University 1939
Al-Dhahabī, Shams al-Dīn Muḥammad: *Ta'rīkh al-Islām wa Ṭabaqāt al-Mashāhīr wa'l-A'lām*, 6 volumes, Cairo 1948-1949
Al-Dīnawarī, Abū Ḥanīfah b. Dāwūd: *Kitāb al-Akhbār al-Ṭiwāl*, ed. Ḥ. al-Zayn, Beirut 1988
Dixon, 'A. 'A.: *The Umayyad Caliphate 65-86/684-705: A Political Study*, London 1971
Donner, F.M.: "Mecca's Food Supplies and Muhammad's Boycott", *Journal of the Economic and Social History of the Orient* 20 (1977), 249-266

—"The Formation of the Islamic State", *Journal of the American Oriental Society* 106 (1986), 283-296

—*Narratives of Islamic Origins: The Beginnings of Islamic Historical Writing*, Princeton 1998

Doughty, C.: *Travels in Arabia Deserta*, Cambridge 1888

Duri, A.A.: *The Rise of Historical Writing Among the Arabs*, tr. L.I. Conrad, Princeton 1983

Eickelman, D.F., & Piscatori, J., eds: *Muslim Travellers: Pilgrimage, migration and the religious imagination*, London and New York 1990

Elad, A.: "Why did 'Abd al-Malik build the Dome of the Rock? A Re-examination of the Muslim sources", in ed. J.A.J. Raby and J. Johns, *Bayt al-Maqdis: 'Abd al-Malik's Jerusalem*, Oxford Studies in Islamic Art, 9, part 1, 1992, 33-58

—*Medieval Jerusalem and Islamic Worship: Holy Places, Ceremonies, Pilgrimage*, Leiden 1995

—"Aspects of the Transition from the Umayyad to the 'Abbasid Caliphate", *Jerusalem Studies in Arabic and Islam* 19 (1995) 89-132

El-Hibri, T.: "Harun al-Rashid and the Mecca Protocol of 802: A Plan for Division or Succession?" *International Journal of Middle East Studies* 24 (1992), 461-480

—*Reinterpreting Islamic Historiography*, Cambridge 1999

Encyclopaedia of Islam, 1st and 2nd editions

Endress, G.: *Islam: An Historical Introduction*, Edinburgh 2002

Ettinghausen, R., & Grabar, O.: *The Art and Architecture of Islam 650-1250*, New Haven and London 1994

Al-Fākihī, Abū 'Abd Allāh Muḥammad b. Isḥāq: *Ta'rīkh Makkah*, ed. F. Wustenfeld in *Akhbār Makkah* (in volume 2), 4 volumes, Beirut 1964

Al-Fāsī, Muḥammad b. Aḥmad: *Shafā' al-Gharām bi Akhbār al-Balad al-Ḥarām*, ed. F. Wustenfeld in *Akhbār Makkah* (in volume 2), 4 volumes, Beirut 1964

Firestone, R.: *Jihad: The Origins of Holy War in Islam*, Oxford 1999

Fishbein, M., tr: *The History of al-Ṭabarī, Volume XXI: The Victory of the Marwānids*, Albany 1990

Flood, F.B.: *The Great Mosque of Damascus: Studies on the Makings of an Umayyad Visual Culture*, Leiden 2000

Forand, P.G.: "The Relation of the Slave and the Client to the Master or Patron in Medieval Islam", *International Journal of Middle East Studies* 2 (1971), 59-66

Freeman-Grenville, G.S.P.: *The Muslim and Christian Calendars*, New York and Toronto 1963

Friedman, Y., tr: *The History of al-Ṭabarī, Volume XII: The Battle of al-Qādisiyyah and the Conquest of Syria and Palestine*, Albany 1992

Frye, R.N.: "The Role of Abu Muslim in the 'Abbasid Revolt", *The Muslim World* 37 (1937), 28-38

Gabrieli, F.: *Il califfato di Hisham*, Alexandria 1935

Gaudefroy-Demombynes, M.: *Le pèlerinage à la Mekke*, Paris 1923

Gibb, H.A.R.: "The Fiscal Rescript of 'Umar II", *Arabica* 2 (1955), 1-16

—tr. *Ibn Battuta: The Travels of Ibn Battuta, A.D 1325-1354, Volume 1*, Cambridge 1958

Goitein, S.D.: "Historical Background to the Erection of the Dome of the Rock", *Journal of the American Oriental Society*, 70, 1950, 104-108

—*Studies in Islamic History and Institutions*, Leiden 1966

Grabar, O.: "The Umayyad Dome of the Rock in Jerusalem", *Ars Orientalis* 3 1959, 33-62

—"The Meaning of the Dome of the Rock in Jerusalem" in ed. D. Hopwood, *Studies in Islamic History*, 1990, 151-163

Grafman, R., & Rosen-Ayalon, M.: "The Two Great Syrian Umayyad Mosques: Jerusalem and Damascus", *Muqarnas* 16, 1999, 115

Grierson, P.: "The Monetary Reforms of 'Abd al-Malik", *Journal of the Economic and Social History of the Orient* 3 (1960), 241-264

Grunebaum, G.E. von: *Medieval Islam*, Chicago and London, 1953

—*Muhammadan Festivals*, London and New York, 1958

Guillaume, A.: *The Life of Muḥammad: A Translation of Ibn Isḥāq's Sīrat Rasūl Allāh*, Oxford 2003
Hamilton, R.: *Walid and His Friends: An Umayyad Tragedy, Oxford Studies in Islamic Art VI*, Oxford 1988
Hammarneh, S.K.: "Marwan b. al-Hakam and the Caliphate", *Der Islam* 65 (1988), 200-225
Hammoudi, A.: *A Season in Mecca: Narrative of a Pilgrimage*, New York 2006
Hawting, G.R.: "The disappearance and rediscovery of Zamzam and the 'well of the Ka'ba'", *Bulletin of the School of Oriental and African Studies* 43 (1980), 44-54
—"The Origins of the Islamic Sanctuary at Mecca" in ed. G.H.A. Juynboll, *Studies on the First Century of Islam*, Carbondale 1982, 25-47
—"'We were not ordered with entering it but only with circumambulating it': *Hadith* and *fiqh* on entering the Ka'ba", *Bulletin of the School of Oriental and African Studies* 47 (1984), 228-242
—*The First Dynasty of Islam: The Umayyad Caliphate AD 661-750*, London and Sydney 1986
—"Al-Hudaybiyya and the conquest of Mecca: a reconsideration of the tradition about the Muslim takeover of the sanctuary", *Jerusalem Studies in Arabic and Islam* 8 (1986), 1-23
—tr. *The History of al-Ṭabarī, Volume XX: The Collapse of Sufyānid Authority and the Coming of the Marwānids*, Albany 1989
—"The 'Sacred Offices' of Mecca from Jahiliyya to Islam", *Jerusalem Studies in Arabic and Islam* 13 (1990), 62-84
—"The Hajj in the Second Civil War" in ed. I.R. Netton, *Golden Roads: Migration, Pilgrimage and Travel in Mediaeval and Modern Islam*, London 1993
—tr. *The History of al-Ṭabarī, Volume XVII: The First Civil War*, Albany 1996
—ed. *The Development of Islamic Ritual*, Ashgate 2006
Heilman, E.G., *Popular Protest in Medieval Baghdad, 295-334 A.H./908-46 A.D.*, PhD. dissertation, Princeton University, 1978
Hillenbrand, C., tr: *The History of al-Ṭabarī, Volume XXVI: The Waning of the Umayyad Caliphate*, Albany 1989
Hillenbrand, R.: "La dolce vita in Early Islamic Syria: the Evidence of Late Umayyad Palaces", *Art History* 5/1, 1982, 1-35
Hinds, M.: "Kufan Political Alignments and Their Background in the Mid-Seventh Century A.D.", *International Journal of Middle East Studies* 2 (1971), 346-367
—"The Siffin Arbitration Agreement", *Journal of Semitic Studies* 17 (1972), 93-129
—"The Murder of the Caliph 'Uthman", *International Journal of Middle East Studies* 3 (1972), 450-469
—tr. *The History of al-Ṭabarī, Volume XXIII: The Zenith of the Marwānid House*, Albany 1990
Hiro, D.: *Islamic Fundamentalism*, London 1988
Hitti, P.K.: *Capital Cities of Arab Islam*, Minneapolis 1973
—*History of the Arabs*, London 2002
—tr. *Al-Balādhurī: The Origins of the Islamic State (Kitāb Futūḥ al-Buldān)*, New Jersey 2002
Hodgson, M.G.S.: "How did the Early Shi'a become Sectarian?" *Journal of the American Oriental Society* 75 (1955), 1-13
—*The Venture of Islam: Conscience and History in a World Civilization*, 3 volumes, Chicago 1974
Hourani, A.H.: *A History of the Arab Peoples*, London 1991
Hourani, A.H. & Stern, S.M., eds. *The Islamic City*, Oxford 1970
Howard, I.K.A, tr: *The History of al-Ṭabarī, Volume XIX: The Caliphate of Yazīd b. Mu'āwiyah*, Albany 1990

Hoyland, R.G.: *Seeing Islam as Others Saw It; A Survey and Evaluation of Christian, Jewish, and Zoroastrian Writings on Early Islam*, Princeton 1997

—*Arabia and the Arabs*, London 2001

Hurgronje, C. Snouck: *Mekka, Vol. 1: Die Stadt and Ihre Herren*, The Hague 1888

—*Mekka in the Latter Part of the Nineteenth Century*, Leiden and London 1931

Humphreys, R. S.: tr. *The History of al-Ṭabarī, Volume XV: The Crisis of the Early Caliphate: The Reign of 'Uthmān*, Albany 1990

—*Islamic History: A Framework for Inquiry*, Princeton 1991

Ibn 'Asākir, 'Alī al-Ḥasan: *Ta'rīkh Madīnat Dimashq*, ed. 'Umar al-'Amrawī, 70 volumes, Cairo 1415-1419/1995-1999

Ibn A'tham, Abū Muḥammad Aḥmad al-Kūfī: *Kitāb al-Futūḥ*, ed. M.A. Khan, 8 volumes, Hyderabad 1971-1975

Ibn al-Athīr, 'Izz al-Dīn: *al-Kāmil fi'l-Ta'rīkh*, ed. C.J. Tornberg, 13 volumes, Leiden 1851-1876

Ibn Bakkār, Zubair: *Jamharat Nasab Quraish*, ed. M.M. Shākir, volume 1, Cairo 1961

Ibn Hishām: *al-Sīrah al-Nabawiyah*, eds. I. al-Abyārī, M. al-Saqqā, & 'A. Shiblī, 2 volumes, Cairo 1955

Ibn Jubayr, Abū al-Ḥasan Muḥammad b. Aḥmad: *Riḥlah Ibn al-Jubayr*, Beirut 1981

Ibn Kathīr, Abū al-Fidā': *al-Bidāyah wa'l-Nihāyah*, 14 volumes, Beirut and Riyad 1966

Ibn Khaldūn, 'Abd al-Raḥmān: *Muqaddimah*, Volume 1, Egypt, not dated

Ibn Khayyāṭ, Khalīfah: *al-Ta'rīkh*, ed. A. D. al-'Umarī, 2 volumes, Najaf 1967

Al-Jahshiyārī, Abū 'Abd Allāh Muḥammad: *Kitāb al-wuzarā' wa'l-kuttāb*, eds. I. al-Abyārī, M. al-Saqqā & 'A. Shiblī, Cairo 1938

Johns, J.: ed. *Bayt al-Maqdis Part Two: Jerusalem and Early Islam*, Oxford Studies in Islamic Art, 9, part 2, 2000

—"Archaeology and the History of Early Islam: The First Seventy Years", *Journal of the Economic and Social History of the Orient* 46 (2003), 411-436

Johnston, D. & Sampson, C., eds: *Religion: The Missing Dimension of Statecraft*, New York 1994

Juynboll, G.H.A.: ed. *Studies on the First Century of Islam*, Carbondale 1982

—tr. *The History of al-Ṭabarī, Volume XIII: The Conquest of Southwestern Persia and Egypt*, Albany 1989

Kamal, A.A.: *Every Man's Guide to Hajj and Umrah*, Delhi, not dated

Keane, J.F.: *Six Months in Meccah: An Account of the Muhammedan Pilgrimage to Meccah*, London 1881

Kennedy, D.L. & Petersen, A.: "Guardians of the Pilgrim Wells: Damascus to Aqaba", *Saudi Aramco World*, Volume 55, No.1 2004, 12-19

Kennedy, H.N.: *The Prophet and the Age of the Caliphates: The Islamic Near East from the sixth to the eleventh century*, London and New York 1986

—*The Armies of the Caliphs: Military and Society in the Early Islamic State*, London 2001

Kertzer, D.I.: *Ritual, Politics, and Power*, New Haven and London 1988

Kessler, C.: "'Abd al-Malik's Inscription in the Dome of the Rock: A Reconsideration", *Journal of the Royal Asiatic Society* (1970), 2-14

Khalidi, T.: *Arabic historical thought in the classical period*, Cambridge 1994

Khleifat, A.M.: *The Caliphate of Hishām b. 'Abd al-Malik (105-124/724-743), with Special Reference to Internal Problems*, PhD thesis, University of London 1973

Kimber, R.A.: *Harun al-Rashid and the 'Abbasid Succession*, PhD. dissertation, University of Cambridge 1989

King, G.R.D.: "The Umayyad Qusur and Related Settlements in Jordan", *IVth International Conference on Bilad al-Sham*, Amman, University of Jordan 1989, 71-80

—"Settlement Patterns in Islamic Jordan: The Umayyad and Their Use of the Land", in *Studies in the History and Archaeology of Jordan* 4 (1993), 369-375

—"Settlement in Western and Central Arabia and the Gulf in the Sixth-Eighth Centuries A.D.", in *The Byzantine and Early Islamic Near East: Land Use and Settlement Patterns*, eds. G.R.D. King & A. Cameron, Princeton 1994, 181-212

Kister, M.J.: "Mecca and Tamim: Aspects of their relations", *Journal of the Economic and Social History of the Orient* 8 (1965), 113-163

—"'You Shall Only Set Out for Three Mosques': A Study of an Early Tradition" *Le Muséon* 82 (1969), 173-196

—"Some aspects concerning Mecca from Jahiliyya to Islam", *Journal of the Economic and Social History of the Orient* 15 (1972), 61-93

—"Battle of the Harra" in ed. M. Rosen-Ayalon, *Studies in memory of Gaston Wiet*, Jerusalem 1977

—"*Labbayka, Allahumma, Labbayka*...On a Monotheist Aspect of a Jahiliyya Practice", *Jerusalem Studies in Arabic and Islam* 2 (1980), 33-57

Lammens, H.: *Études sur le règne du calife omaiyade Mo'awia 1er*, Paris 1908

—*Le califat de Yazid 1er*, Beirut 1910-21

—*Islam: Beliefs and Institutions*, London 1929

—*Études sur le siècle des Omayyades*, Beirut 1930

Landau-Tasseron, E., tr: *The History of al-Ṭabarī, Volume XXXIX: Biographies of the Prophet's Companions and Their Successors*, Albany 1998

Lane, E.W.: *English-Arabic Lexicon*, 2 volumes, London 1984

Lapidus, I.M.: ed. *Middle Eastern Cities*, Berkeley and Los Angeles 1969

—"The Separation of State and Religion in the Development of Early Islamic Society", *International Journal of Middle East Studies* 6 (1975), 363-385

—*A History of Islamic Societies*, Cambridge 2002

Lassner, J.: *Islamic Revolution and Historical Memory: An Inquiry into the Art of 'Abbasid Apologetics*, New Haven 1986

Lecker, M.: "Muhammad at Medina – a geographical approach", *Jerusalem Studies in Arabic and Islam* 6 (1985), 29-62

Levy, R.: *The Social Structure of Islam*, Cambridge 1957

Lewis, B.: *The Political Language of Islam*, Chicago 1988

Long, D.E.: *The Hajj Today: A Survey of the Contemporary Makkah Pilgrimage*, Albany 1979

Lunde, P. & Stone, C., ed. & tr: *The Meadows of Gold: The 'Abbāsids by al-Mas'ūdī*, London and New York 1989

McAuliffe, J.D., tr: *The History of al-Ṭabarī, Volume XXVIII: 'Abbāsid Authority Affirmed*, Albany 1995

Madelung, W.: *The Succession to Muhammad: a study of the early Caliphate*, Cambridge 1997

Marlow, L.: *Hierarchy and egalitarianism in Islamic thought*, Cambridge 2002

Martin, R.C., ed: *Approaches to Islam in Religious Studies*, Tucson 1985

Al-Mas'ūdī, Abū al-Ḥasan 'Alī: *Murūj al-Dhahab*, ed. C. Barbier de Maynard & P. de Courteille, revised C. Pellat, 7 volumes, Beirut 1970

Al-Māwardī, Abū al-Ḥasan 'Alī b. Muḥammad: *al-Aḥkām al-Sulṭāniyyah wa'l-Wilāyah al-Dīniyyah*, Cairo 1960

Mez. A.: *Renaissance of Islam*, tr. S. Khuda Baksh & D.S. Margoliouth, Patna 1937

Mohamed, M.N.: *Hajj & 'Umrah from A to Z*, 1996 (no place of publication cited)

Morony, M.G.: *Iraq after the Muslim Conquest*, Princeton 1984

—tr. *The History of al-Ṭabarī, Volume XVIII: Between Civil Wars: The Caliphate of Mu'āwiyah*, Albany 1987

Mottahedeh, R.: *Loyalty and Leadership in an Early Islamic Society*, London 2001

Al-Muqaddasī: *Aḥsan al-taqāsīm fī ma'rifat al-aqālīm*, ed. M.J. de Goeje, Leiden 1906

Al-Nahrawālī, al-Shaykh Quṭb al-Dīn: *Kitāb al-A'lām bi A'lām Bayt Allāh al-Ḥarām*, ed. F.

Wustenfeld in *Akhbār Makkah* (in volume 3), 4 volumes, Beirut 1964
Netton, I.R., ed: *Golden Roads: Migration, Pilgrimage and Travel in Mediaeval and Modern Islam,* London 1993
Nicol, N.D.: *Early 'Abbasid Administration in the Central and Eastern Provinces, 132-218 AH/750-833 AD*, PhD. dissertation, University of Washington 1979
Northedge, A.: "Archaeology and New Urban Settlement in Early Islamic Syria and Iraq" in *The Byzantine and Early Islamic Near East*, 231-265
Noth, A.: *Quellenkritische Studien zu Themen, Formen und Tendenzen fruhislamischer Geschichtsuberlieferung*, Bonn 1973
Noth, A. & Conrad, L.I., *The Early Arabic Historical Tradition: A Source Critical Study,* tr. M. Bohles, Princeton 1994
Omar, F.: *The 'Abbasid Caliphate 132/750 – 170/786*, Baghdad 1969
Palgrave, W.G.: *Personal Narrative of a Year's Journey Through Central and Eastern Arabia*, London 1865, reprinted London 1969
Peters, F.E.: "The Quest for the Historical Muhammad", *International Journal of Middle East Studies* 23 (1991), 291-315
—*Mecca: A Literary History of the Muslim Holy Land*, Princeton 1994
—*The Hajj: The Muslim Pilgrimage to Mecca and the Holy Places*, Princeton 1996
Powers, D.S., tr: *The History of al-Ṭabarī, Volume XXIV: The Empire in Transition*, Albany 1989
Al-Qu'āitī, S.G.: *The Holy Cities, The Pilgrimage and the World of Islam: A History from the Earliest Traditions till 1925 (1344 AH)*, Louisville 2007
Rabbat, N.: "The Meaning of the Umayyad Dome of the Rock", *Muqarnas* 6 (1989), 12-21
Raby, J.A.J. & Johns, J., eds: *Bayt al-Maqdis: 'Abd al-Malik's Jerusalem,* Oxford Studies in Islamic Art, 9, part 1, 1992
Al-Rasheed, M.: *A History of Saudi Arabia*, Cambridge 2002
Al-Rashid, S.A.: *Darb Zubaydah: The Pilgrim Road from Kufa to Mecca*, Riyad 1980
Robinson, A.E.: "The Mahmal of the Moslem Pilgrimage", *Journal of the Royal Asiatic Society* 31 (1931), 117-127
Robinson, C.F.: *Empires and Elites after the Muslim Conquest: The Transformation of Northern Mesopotamia*, Cambridge 2000
—*Islamic Historiography*, Cambridge 2003
—*Makers of the Muslim World: 'Abd al-Malik*, Oxford 2005
Rodinson, M.: *Mohammed*, London 1973
Rodwell, J.M., intr. A. Jones: *The Koran*, London 1995
Roff, W.R.: "Pilgrimage and the History of Religions: Theoretical Approaches to the *Hajj*" in ed. R.C. Martin, *Approaches to Islam in Religious Studies*, Tucson 1985, 78-86
Rosen-Ayalon, M., ed: *Studies in Memory of Gaston Wiet,* Jerusalem 1977
Rosenthal, E.I.J.: *Political Thought in Medieval Islam: An Introductory Outline*, Cambridge 1958
Rosenthal, F.: *A History of Muslim Historiography,* Leiden 1968
—tr. *A History of al-Ṭabarī, Volume XXXVIII: The Return of the Caliphate to Baghdād*, Albany 1985
—tr. & ed. with N.J. Dawood, *Ibn Khaldūn: The Muqaddimah – An Introduction to History*, Princeton and Oxford 2005
Rotter, G.: *Die Umayyaden und der zweite Burgerkrieg (688-692)*, Wiesbaden 1982
Rowson, E.K., tr: *The History of al-Ṭabarī, Volume XXII: The Marwānid Restoration*, Albany 1989
Rubin, U.: "The Ka'ba: Aspects of its ritual functions and position in pre-Islamic and early Islamic times", *Jerusalem Studies in Arabic and Islam* 8 (1986), 97-131
—"Hanafiyya and Ka'ba: An Inquiry into the Arabian Pre-Islamic Background of the *din Ibrahim*", *Jersualem Studies in Arabic and Islam* 13 (1990), 85-112
Ruthven, M.: *Islam in the World*, London 1991

Sanders, P.: *Ritual, Politics, and the City in Fatimid Cairo*, Albany 1994
Sardar, Z. & Zaki Badawi, M.A., eds: *Hajj Studies Volume 1*, London 1978
Sauvaget, J.: *La mosquée de Médine, études sur les origins architecturales de la mosquée*, Paris 1947
Schacht, J.: *An Introduction to Islamic Law*, Oxford 1982
Serjeant, R.B., ed: *The Islamic City*, UNESCO Paris 1980
Shaban, M.A.: *The ʿAbbasid Revolution*, Cambridge 1970
—*Islamic history: a new interpretation*, 2 volumes, Cambridge 1971 & 1976
Shacklady, H.: "The ʿAbbasid Movement in Khurasan", University of St Andrews, School of ʿAbbasid Studies, Occasional Papers 1 (1986), 98-112
Sharon, M.: *Black Banners from the east*, Leiden 1983
—"The development of the debate around the legitimacy of authority in early Islam", *Jerusalem Studies in Arabic and Islam* 5 (1984), 121-141
—"Ahl al-Bayt – People of the House", *Jerusalem Studies in Arabic and Islam* 8 (1986), 169-184
—*Revolt: The Social and Military Aspects of the ʿAbbasid Revolution*, Jerusalem 1990
Smith, G. R., tr: *The History of al-Ṭabarī, Volume XIV: The Conquest of Irān*, Albany 1994
Sourdel, D.: *Medieval Islam*, tr. J. Montgomery Watt, London and New York 1985
Stetkevych, S.P.: *The Poetics of Islamic Legitimacy: Myth, Gender, and Ceremony in the Classical Arabic Ode*, Bloomington 2002
Al-Ṭabarī, Abū Jaʿfar Muḥammad b. Jarīr: *Taʾrīkh al-Rusul waʾl-Mulūk*, ed. M.J. de Goeje & others, 3 volumes, Leiden 1879-1901
Tolmacheva, M.: "Female Piety and Patronage in the Medieval Hajj", in *Women in the Medieval Islamic World*, ed. G.R.G. Hambly, New York 1999, 161-179
Tschanz, D.W.: "Journeys of Faith, Roads of Civilization," *Saudi Aramco World*, Volume 55, No.1 2004, 2-11
Turner, V. & Turner, E.: *Image and Pilgrimage in Christian Culture: Anthropological Perspectives*, Oxford 1978
Vaglieri, L.V.: "The Patriarchal and Umayyad Caliphates" in *The Cambridge History of Islam*, Volume 1, 57-103
Vassiliev, A.: *The History of Saudi Arabia*, London 2000
Wahba, W.H., tr: *Al-Māwardī: The Ordinances of Government*, Reading 1996
Wansbrough, J.: *The Sectarian Milieu: Content and Composition of Islamic Salvation History*, Oxford 1978
Watt, W.M.: *Muhammad: Prophet and Statesman*, Oxford 1961
Wellhausen, J.: *The Arab Kingdom and its Fall*, tr. M.G. Weir, Calcutta 1927
Wensinck, A.J.: *The Muslim Creed*, Cambridge 1932
Williams, J.A., tr: *The History of al-Ṭabarī, Volume XXVII: The ʿAbbāsid Revolution*, Albany 1985
Al-Ṭabarī: *The Early ʿAbbāsī Empire*, 2 volumes, Cambridge 1988 & 1989
Wolfe, M.: *One Thousand Roads to Mecca: Ten Centuries of Travelers Writing about the Muslim Pilgrimage*, New York 1997
Al-Yaʿqūbī, Aḥmad: *al-Taʾrīkh*, 2 volumes, Beirut 1993
Young, W.C.: "The Kaʿba, Gender, and the Rites of Pilgrimage," *International Journal of Middle East Studies* 25 (1993), 285-300
Zaman, M.Q.: *Religion and Politics under the Early ʿAbbasids: The Emergence of the Proto-Sunni Elite*, Leiden 1997
Zambaur, E. de: *Manuel de Généalogie et de Chronologie pour L'Histoire de l'Islam*, Hannover 1927
Al-Zubayrī, Muṣʿab b. ʿAbd Allāh: *Kitāb Nasab Quraish*, ed. E. Levi-Provencal, Cairo 1953

Index